D0421751

MICHELLE MEDLOCK ADAMS
and GENA MASELLI

Fabulous & Focused

365

Daily Devotions for Working Women

WORTHY®
Inspired

Published by Worthy Inspired, an imprint of Worthy Publishing Group, a division of Worthy Media, Inc., One Franklin Park, 6100 Tower Circle, Suite 210, Franklin, TN 37067.

WORTHY is a registered trademark of Worthy Media, Inc.

HELPING PEOPLE EXPERIENCE THE HEART OF GOD.

Library of Congress Cataloging-in-Publication Data

Names: Adams, Michelle Medlock, author.
Title: Fabulous & focused : 365 daily devotions for working women / by
  Michelle Medlock Adams and Gena Maselli.
Other titles: Fabulous and focused
Description: Franklin, TN : Worthy Publishing, 2018.
Identifiers: LCCN 2018022247 | ISBN 9781683972624 (hardcover)
Subjects: LCSH: Businesswomen--Prayers and devotions. | Devotional calendars.
Classification: LCC BV4596.B8 A33 2018 | DDC 242/.643--dc23
LC record available at https://lccn.loc.gov/2018022247

For foreign and subsidiary rights, contact rights@worthypublishing.com.

Published in association with Cyle Young of the Hartline Literary Agency, LLC.

ISBN: 978-1-68397-262-4

Cover Art: Shutterstock
Cover Design by Bruce Gore | GoreStudio.com
Page Layout by Bart Dawson

Printed in the United States of America
18 19 20 21 22 LBM 8 7 6 5 4 3 2 1

Introduction

· ·

Welcome to the *Fabulous & Focused* family. We're so glad you've joined us on this journey. Whether it's your first, second, or tenth time through, we hope you find it rewarding, inspiring, and encouraging.

As you begin this *Fabulous and Focused* journey, take a moment to consider how you can make this time the most rewarding for yourself. Could you set this devotion by your bed so that it is either the first thing you read in the morning or the last thing you read at night? Could you place it on your desk or in your purse so it's with you during lunch? Could you journal about each day—what you learn, how the Lord speaks to your heart, what you want to pray about, or what actions you need to take?

This is your time...and you're worth taking it. As you read these devotions, be mindful that you serve an amazing God who loves you and has called you by name. And if you let Him, He will use you in every area of life—at home, at work, at church, and in your community.

So whether you have yet to make a decision for Christ, are a new Christian eager to learn how to live a godly life at work, want to pursue God more faithfully by making time for a daily devotion, or have served Him for years, thank you for taking this journey with us. We are all in this together, and as sisters in Christ and working women, we are strong, called, and equipped.

We are excited about this season, and we hope you are, too! We pray this devotional helps you become even more fabulous and focused.

Your sisters in Christ,
Michelle & Gena

DAY
1

New Beginnings

We can make our plans, but the LORD determines our steps.
Proverbs 16:9 NLT

I love new beginnings—the beginning of a new year, the beginning of a new adventure, the beginning of a new project, whatever. There's something about all that newness and possibility that speaks to me.

And I've learned that the best way to tackle any new year, adventure, project, or dream is to plan. I open my planner (yes, I still use a paper one) and write out all the goals, steps, and resources I'll need to get the desired results.

I pray for God's blessing and perspective as I do this. Thankfully, He never disappoints. So often He brings steps, resources, and ideas to my mind for how to begin my new whatever.

So right now, take a moment and pray about your new whatever. Ask the Lord to help you plan by directing your steps and giving you creative ideas for accomplishing your goals. He's so faithful. He wants to be involved in your life. You can trust that He will "determine your steps." —*MMA*

. . . .

*Heavenly Father, I ask for Your perspective and direction
on my day today. I want to hear from You, and I ask
that You would help me know the best way to accomplish
all that I plan to do. Amen.*

Pardon Me,
May I Use You as a Rung?

Love...is not self-seeking.
1 Corinthians 13:4–5

*L*ove is not self-seeking. Well, that's a tough one to practice in today's workplace, isn't it? I mean, if you don't look out for Number One, nobody else will, right? The world would have you think that you must push and claw your way to the top—even at the expense of others. But that's not God's way of doing things. God wants to promote you in His way—in His time.

You don't have to play the game to climb the corporate ladder. You don't have to step on others to get ahead. You can rest in God, knowing that He has a good plan for your life.

Maybe you've been hurt by a coworker. Maybe someone you trusted at work betrayed you to gain placement in the company. It happens, but don't let that situation derail you. Continue to walk in love and allow God to open doors for you. He will!

See, God is looking out for you. He wants you to succeed, and He knows the best path for you to follow. If you follow Him and let love be your guide, you'll receive every promotion and success He intends for you to have. —*MMA*

. . . .

Lord, I trust You with my career. I know that You
will cause me to succeed. I love You. Amen.

Nurturing the Blooms

Lazy hands make for poverty, but diligent hands bring wealth.
Proverbs 10:4

One of my favorite hobbies is gardening. I could spend whole afternoons in my garden. I imagine how I want it look in one or two years. I plan the flower beds, choose the right plants, and get them settled into the ground. Then, once I've done the initial work, I nurture the plants so they can thrive. I must be diligent if I want to enjoy the benefits of my work. It's relaxing yet challenging.

I think about my job and relationships while I'm gardening. There are a lot of similarities between them. This is a fast-food world, where results are expected quickly and diligence is sorely underdeveloped. But often, just like in gardening, it takes diligence to see the fruit of your labor. It takes time and effort to excel. A smart employer won't hand over important responsibilities to someone who hasn't proven herself to be a hard-working employee. He wants someone he can trust.

There are some qualities with which people are born, but others—like flowers in a garden—must be nurtured. Decide to develop the quality of diligence in your life. In the end, you'll enjoy the colorful, lush benefits of your hard work. —*GM*

. . . .

*Lord, thank You for all that You've given me in my life.
I'm thankful for it, and I will be diligent in everything I do—
my family, my work, and my relationship with You. Amen.*

Guess What I Learned at the Water Cooler

*Do not let any unwholesome talk come out of your mouths,
but only what is helpful for building others up according
to their needs, that it may benefit those who listen.*

Ephesians 4:29

He is such a moron," your coworker whispers over lunch. "No kidding. How did he get to be boss?" your other friend chimes in. "He's so incompetent. And what's with the polyester suits? Does he not own a mirror?"

Ahh...lunchtime chatter. It's all harmless, right? Well, not exactly. According to Ephesians 4:29, we aren't supposed to let *any* unwholesome talk come out of our mouths.

Take your mother's advice: If you can't say something nice, don't say anything at all. Remember, your words are powerful. They can be building blocks or wrecking balls, so use them wisely. Don't bad-mouth your boss with your coworkers. You are giving ammunition to those same coworkers to talk about you next time. Instead, find positive comments and observations to make. Be the positive force in your office.

This will take practice. You may have to severely bite your tongue to keep from participating in the next boss-bashing session, but God will help you. Ask the Holy Spirit to keep a watch over your words. He will. And soon, your words will create a better work environment. —*MMA*

. . . .

*Lord, help me to speak only words that build up
and none that tear down. Amen.*

Out of Balance

By the seventh day God had finished the work he had been doing;
so on the seventh day he rested from all his work.

Genesis 2:2

When Friday night rolls around, are you exhausted? Have you given so much at work during the week that you have nothing left to give to your family and friends? If you answered yes to either question, you might be a workaholic.

While you should give your company 110 percent while you're on the job, if you take mounds of work home or are constantly on your cell phone after hours, fielding questions from clients, you've probably crossed over into the land of workaholics.

It's a tough call. You want to be the go-to gal when your boss is looking for someone to promote. If that means taking work home, you're willing to do it, but at what expense? If your job is stealing time away from your family, your friends, and your God, then your life is out of balance. And you know what happens when we're out of balance? We fall on our hind ends.

So take time today to ask God to help you get your life in balance. He will! He is the great prioritizer. Follow His example. He worked hard for six days and rested on the seventh. We should do the same. —*MMA*

. . . .

Lord, I'm asking You to put my life in balance.
I love You and trust You. Amen.

No-Man's-Land

I trust in the LORD for protection.
So why do you say to me,
"Fly like a bird to the mountains for safety!"
Psalm 11:1 NLT

I once worked with two managers who feuded constantly. I don't know what started the feuding, but I do know that it made for a *challenging* work environment. The office was a no-man's-land, a place where no one won and even the simplest task became a major battle.

Unfortunately, this isn't unusual. Even in the Bible, Jonathan lived in a no-man's-land between his father, Saul, and best friend, David. His father sought to kill David, while David raced around the countryside trying to understand why (1 Samuel 20). Fortunately, God's plan won out—David remained safe because Jonathan warned him of the danger.

In the same way, God has a plan for you. It doesn't mean that you won't face uncomfortable situations, but it does mean God can give you the grace to handle them. He may lead you to another position or show you how to endure the tension professionally and peacefully. Regardless, don't get dragged into office battles. Instead, focus on your work and pray—for wisdom and for peace. Trust your heavenly Father to give you exactly what you need to stand strong in the midst of the difficulty. —GM

. . . .

Lord, You know the situation far better than I do.
Show me how to pray for the people involved.
Help me be an example of peace and professionalism
today and every day. Amen.

My Size 12 versus Your Size 4

Not that we dare to classify or compare ourselves with some
of those who are commending themselves. But when they measure
themselves by one another and compare themselves
with one another, they are without understanding.

2 Corinthians 10:12 ESV

She was everything I wanted to be. I looked across the news-room at her, and I wondered how she was able to write award-winning stories, parent such wonderful children, and still remain a size 4. I admired her, and yes, at times I was jealous of her—especially when I started playing the comparison game.

Ever played that game?

At first, it seems harmless. You simply admire a coworker. But if you take it further, you'll be sorry. That's when you start wondering, "Why can't I do my job as well as she does hers? How does she afford such wonderful suits?" From there, it's a down-ward spiral. By the time you hit the bottom, you dislike your coworker and you can't stand yourself.

I've got three words for you—*don't go there*! The next time the devil whispers in your ear, "See Carol over there? She earns ten thousand dollars more a year than you do, and she's two sizes smaller!" tell him to back off. Begin praising God for who you are through Him and thank Him for the plans He has for your life. They are awesome—just as awesome as Carol's. I promise! —*MMA*

. . . .

Lord, help me to stop comparing myself to others.
Help me be happy with who I am in You. Amen.

Pencil In Your Divine Appointment

The LORD directs the steps of the godly.
He delights in every detail of their lives.
Psalm 37:23 NLT

Did you know God sets up divine appointments for us? It's true!

My business partner recently took her laptop to a nearby coffee shop to do some writing. As she settled in, the owner approached and asked if he could post a photo on the shop's Instagram account of her working there. He explained they were trying to attract more professionals. She agreed, and as they chatted, she quickly realized this was a divine appointment.

When she told the owner she was a writer, he told her he was writing a children's book and asked if she might have any advice. She answered, "My business partner is flying in tomorrow, and she's a children's author. She even teaches children's writing at conferences. Our agent will be here, too."

We all met at the coffee shop the next day, and before the weekend was over, my partner and I signed him as a client, and our agent took him on as well. We believe his book will be successful. It was a divine appointment for all of us.

Ask God each morning to order your steps. Watch for divine appointments and thank Him for the opportunities He brings your way. Wake up each day expectant! —*MMA*

. . . .

Thank You, Lord, for divine appointments.
Help me follow Your leading every day. Amen.

There Ain't Enough Room for the Two of Us

God is not a God of disorder but of peace.
1 Corinthians 14:33

Have you ever been in a situation where you felt strongly that you were right, yet you were unable to voice your opinion because of your lack of authority? It's tough, isn't it?

Difficult as it sometimes is, we must honor those in authority over us. That doesn't mean we have to agree with our bosses all the time, but we do have to show them respect. See, God is a God of order—not of confusion. To come against those in authority over us would never be God's way.

Need more convincing? Read Numbers 12. Miriam and Aaron didn't like it when Moses, their leader, married a Cushite woman, and they talked badly about him. Well, the Lord heard them, and verse 9 says, "The anger of the LORD burned against them." And there were some serious consequences.

So if you're feeling badly toward your boss, ask God to forgive you. If you truly feel the leaders in your company are going in the wrong direction, pray for God to change their hearts—or start looking for another position. But don't come against them. Trust God to direct the situation and walk away in peace. —*MMA*

. . . .

*Lord, help me to honor those who are in authority over me,
even when I disagree. Amen.*

If You Need Me, I'll Be under My Desk with Bonbons

"Don't be afraid," the prophet answered. "Those who are with us are more than those who are with them."

2 Kings 6:16

Have you ever gone up against a much bigger competitor to win a contract? Or handled a huge project for your company with very little manpower and a crazy tight deadline? It can feel overwhelming at times—so much so that you might want to hide under your desk and eat a big box of chocolates.

But isn't it comforting to know you're not alone? God's got your back. Even though you can't see Him, He's right there.

Need more convincing? Read about Elisha in 2 Kings 6. The king of Aram was angry with Elisha and went after him. Elisha and his servant awoke one morning to find the enemy's army surrounding the city with their horses and chariots. Frightened, the servant asked, "What shall we do?" Elisha assured him, "Those who are with us are more than those who are with them." Then Elisha prayed for the servant's eyes to be opened so he could see the real situation—the hills full of horses and chariots of fire all around them. God had the situation well under control.

When you feel alone or overwhelmed, trust that God is in control. Ask Him to show you the situation as He sees it. Ask Him to send help or to give you favor with your employer. Whatever you need, ask. God can make it happen. Now come out from under your desk and trust in Him. —*MMA*

- -

Thank You, Lord, for showing me Your presence in my situation.
I know I can trust You, no matter what. Amen.

Does This Cubicle Come in a Bigger Size?

I am not saying this because I am in need, for I have learned to be content whatever the circumstances.

Philippians 4:11

Recently, I heard a preacher say you should enjoy the journey on the way to where you're going. I wish I'd known that truth when I first started my career as a reporter for a daily newspaper. My first writing gig? I was hired as a police-beat reporter. I had to work long weekday hours and most Friday nights. I desperately wanted to work in a different area of the newspaper—anything but the police beat. But I spent so much time dreaming about a new assignment that I didn't enjoy the one I had. I took for granted that I was able to hang out with the cool sports guys on Friday nights. I took for granted that working on Friday nights allowed me to work side by side with the managing editor. I took many things for granted.

Looking back, I realize those days were critical to my development as a writer. God placed me in that job for a season. No, it wasn't my dream job—but I wasn't ready for that one yet. I had some stuff to learn before it could manifest. Maybe you're in that learning place today. If so, hang in there. You're on the way. Be content where you are and enjoy the journey. —*MMA*

. . . .

Lord, help me to enjoy the journey. Amen.

In One Day, Out the Next

*If I have found favor in your eyes, my lord,
do not pass your servant by.*

Genesis 18:3

"Michelle Adams to the marketing conference room, please." As I heard the page over the company PA system, I wondered, *What have I done?*

I stopped outside the conference room, took a deep breath, and pushed open the door. My boss, my director, and a dozen of my coworkers stood and began applauding as I entered the room.

"I just wanted to congratulate you in front of your peers for a job well done," my director said. "That is the best annual report I've ever read."

It was official—I was the golden child of the moment.

The adulation lasted about two days. Then, for reasons unknown to me, I couldn't even write my name accurately in my supervisor's eyes. What changed? I was the same writer who had written "the best annual report ever" just days before!

My golden child status had departed as quickly as it had arrived.

You can easily fall out of favor with people, but you can't fall out of favor with God. That's why you shouldn't base your worth on people's accolades or the lack thereof. Instead, know that your value is in Him. Even if you're not the golden child at your company, you are one with your heavenly Father, and that's worth celebrating. —*MMA*

. . . .

Thank You, Lord, for loving me unconditionally. Amen.

Big Changes

*Be strong and courageous...for the LORD your God
goes with you; he will never leave you nor forsake you.*

Deuteronomy 31:6

I had received a tremendous offer for a magazine writing job in Fort Worth, Texas, and I was so excited. And then I wasn't. After all, my high-school-sweetheart husband and I were quite happy in our hometown. It was our comfort zone. We both had nice, cushy jobs and lifelong friends nearby. My parents even lived next door. It was the perfect setup. But this job...it was amazing.

Unsure of what to do, we turned to God for direction. After much prayer, we knew He was calling us west. So I accepted the offer, and we began the big move.

Talk about changes! As I watched the moving truck pull away, fear shot through my body. Waves of questions followed: *Are we doing the right thing? How will we survive in a big city? Is this fair to our children? What if I don't like my new job?*

It would have been easy to give in to the fear, but you know what? God was with us every step of the way, reassuring us. He was with us as we celebrated new adventures, and He was there when homesickness overwhelmed us. Best of all, He was with me as I greeted my new coworkers and took on a new position.

No matter what change you're facing today—even a job transfer or a cross-country move—you don't have to go it alone. God is right by your side. —*MMA*

. . . .

*Lord, I am afraid of change. Help me to face what's coming
with joy and strength. I love You. Amen.*

The Golden Rule of Getting Ahead

As you wish that others would do to you, do so to them.
Luke 6:31 ESV

I worked my way through college as a clerk in a large department store. It wasn't a glamorous job, but it paid my rent and allowed me to buy designer clothes at a discount. That was good.

I worked on commission there, and we were expected to meet our sales quotas regardless of what it cost our coworkers. This created a sometimes not-so-friendly competition among the employees.

We didn't use the "it's-your-turn" method. Nope, this store's philosophy was to move in before your coworker and make the sale. So that's what I did. I soon learned that, while I made my quota, I didn't make any friends. I was ruthless. But I knew I wasn't doing unto others as I wanted them to do to me, and it began to bother me. So I stopped pushing and simply allowed God to open sales opportunities for me. And He did.

There is nothing wrong with being ambitious and working to succeed, but that doesn't mean you do it at someone else's expense. Trust God to help you achieve your goals, and you won't have to step on anyone else to get ahead. —*MMA*

. . . .

Lord, help me to be sensitive to others as I move up the corporate ladder. Amen.

Consultant Enigma

Now go; I will help you speak and will teach you what to say.
Exodus 4:12

Not long ago, my company hired consultants to review our work procedures and recommend ways we could improve them. In frustration, I listened as they made the same suggestions that employees had been making for years, yet management reacted as if it were all new. "Yes, that's exactly what we need to do!" they cheered, nodding like bobblehead dolls in a car window.

Of course, businesses aren't the only ones who miss when important things are said. God deals with this all the time. He continually speaks to us, showing us how we can work and minister better. But too often, we aren't listening.

If it's been a while since you've heard God's voice, then take the time to listen to Him. If you're having trouble getting started, put on some praise music. Close your eyes and focus on the lyrics. Then, begin praying—give thanks, make your requests, and then sit quietly in His presence as you listen to those suggestions and impressions that He speaks into your heart. As you make this a habit, you'll find that you are more peaceful, productive, and in tune with Him than ever. —*GM*

- -

Dear Lord, I want to hear Your voice and follow Your will.
Help me to develop my prayer time
so that I can hear You clearly. Amen.

Help! I'm Surrounded by Yes-Men

God is with you in everything you do.
Genesis 21:22

Are you surrounded by yes-men at work? You know the type. The boss says, "I think it would be a good idea if we all dye our hair green—the color of money." And suddenly every person in the room agrees. "Absolutely. I've always wanted green hair. Green is my favorite color! Green hair rules! Why didn't I think of that?"

Ahh! It makes you want to run out of the conference room screaming, doesn't it?

Every time it happens, the rebel spirit in me wants to stand up and say the exact opposite—even if I actually agree with the popular consensus. But it's more upsetting when I know in my heart of hearts that the yes-men are enthusiastically backing a wrong decision.

Working with brownnosers and yes-men is never easy. It's hard to stand up for what you believe, especially if you're the only one willing to have a different opinion than the boss. But don't despair. You don't have to go it alone. God will be your ally. You can voice your position respectfully, even if the consensus goes against you. You will be known for your integrity. —*MMA*

. . . .

*Lord, help me to have the courage to speak my mind,
but help me do so with respect and tact. Amen.*

There's Not Enough of Me to Go Around

I can do all this through him who gives me strength.
Philippians 4:13

I loved gymnastics when I was growing up, but I was never very good on the balance beam. I'd topple off to one side or the other quite often. You know what's ironic? I'm still having trouble with that whole balancing concept. Only now, the trouble is balancing my personal and professional life.

How about you? Maybe you're an employee, a wife, a mom, a friend, a daughter, a sister, an aunt, a church volunteer (and probably more)—and you're just not sure how to be all those things at once. Well, welcome to the sisterhood of "There's Not Enough of Me to Go Around."

There are days when I wonder how I am supposed to accomplish everything that is on my plate. But you know what? *I'm* not! God never intended me to do all this by myself, and He never intended for you to do it alone, either. The Word tells us that we can do all things through Christ who gives us strength. *All* means *all*, right? So no matter how many roles you're fulfilling today, don't sweat it! God will help you. —*MMA*

. . . .

Thank You, Lord, for giving me the strength and wisdom
to stay centered on the balance beam of life.
I know I can do all things through You. Amen.

You Can't Win 'em All

*I tell you, love your enemies and pray
for those who persecute you.*
Matthew 5:44

I was a senior in college, working my way through school in the misses designer clothing section of a large department store. I was young and full of enthusiasm, high ideals, and big dreams—all of which thoroughly irritated my thirtysomething boss. Just when I thought I'd won her over, I found out differently. I was in a stall in the ladies' room when my boss and another department head came in to fix their lipstick.

"I have to figure a way to get rid of Michelle," my boss whispered. "She drives me crazy. She's just so bright-eyed and bushy-tailed. Maybe I can transfer her to men's accessories."

I was the only Michelle in her department. I was crushed. I stayed in the stall until they left, had a good cry, and took my post back at the cash register. I learned a hard lesson that day: not everyone in the workforce is going to like you—no matter how hard you try.

If you're dealing with persecution at work, hang in there. First, take a good hard look at yourself. If the criticism has merit, make adjustments. If you're being persecuted for petty, jealous-hearted reasons, ask God to show you how to handle the situation. He may have a way out...possibly even a job change. Just remember this: You are loved by the King of kings. He thinks you're amazing, and His opinion trumps those of your critics. —*MMA*

. . . .

*Lord, I pray for those workers who are being mean to me right now.
And I thank You for vindication and favor. Amen.*

Lighten Up

God hath not given us the spirit of fear;
but of power, and of love, and of a sound mind.
2 Timothy 1:7 KJV

Are you too hard on yourself? If you are, you're not alone. As working women, we expect a lot of ourselves. We have to if we want to stay in the game, right? But many times, we put such unrealistic expectations on ourselves that we're in a constant state of panic—afraid of failure.

That's no way to live, sister. The Bible says that we have not been given a spirit of fear but of power, love, and a sound mind. Yet we go around biting our freshly manicured fingernails and worrying about a missed opportunity or a less-than-stellar job review. Take a deep breath and stop worrying. Don't beat yourself up. You're human—you're going to drop the ball once in a while. When you do, accept your mistakes, learn from them, and move on.

Don't waste your time worrying (that's just a sneaky form of fear) about what could've, should've, or might've been. God wants you to live free from fear. And remember, 2 Corinthians 12:9–10 tells us that Christ's strength is made perfect in our weakness. It's when we know we're weak that He can be the strongest in us.

That means we can trust Him to make things right, even in our failures. Don't worry—God's got your back! —*MMA*

. . . .

Lord, I give all my fears to You today.
Help me to stop setting unrealistic goals.
I only want what You want for me. Amen.

Ouch!

*Whoever disregards discipline comes to poverty and shame,
but whoever heeds correction is honored.*

Proverbs 13:18

We've come to a subject that no one likes to address: correction. It's up there with submission and gluttony on the list of Christian principles we'd like to ignore.

I know, I know. None of us likes to admit we're wrong. We like to believe that either we're right or, at the least, that we made the best decision possible with the information we had available.

Translation: it wasn't our fault.

Why is it so hard to admit when we're wrong? Is it pride? Maybe. Conviction? Sometimes.

In our spiritual lives, we know that we're never beyond hope; there's always forgiveness. As a former pastor loved to say, "Nothing is fatal or final in Jesus."

In our work lives, we must learn to accept correction gracefully if we want to advance. Even when we don't totally agree, we must accept leadership's decisions respectfully. Not only will that make our work lives easier, but, as Proverbs 13:18 reminds us, "whoever heeds correction is honored." Isn't that a good thing? —*GM*

. . . .

*Lord, help me to remain humble and to respectfully
accept correction. Amen.*

Solitaire

Agree with each other, love each other, be deep-spirited friends.
Philippians 2:2 MSG

Solitary games are everywhere—on our computers, our tablets, and our smartphones. Zoning out on a game can be entertaining as we block out everything and everyone around us. But if we approach life and our work like one of those games, we can quickly find ourselves in isolation.

When we prefer to accomplish goals and tasks alone, we interact with others only when it's necessary. We avoid group work, and if we're put on a team, we feel like we're wasting our time because group work slows us down. We could do things so much better on our own—or so we believe.

But we aren't meant to live in solitude. God intends for us to have relationships with other Christians. Together, we can accomplish more for Him than we would alone. And aside from Christians, God calls us to be a light for Him. We can't do that if we never venture outside our tiny circle of like-minded friends and family.

No, effectively working with others and in groups doesn't always come easily. It's a practiced art, but it can allow us to accomplish more than we would on our own. The next time you cringe when asked to join a group, take time to appreciate all you can do together. As you work toward a common goal, you'll see the benefits in the outcome. —*GM*

. . . .

Lord, thank You for the coworkers You've placed around me.
Help me to be a positive team player with them. Amen.

Nobody Likes Me

*You made them a little lower than the angels
and crowned them with glory and honor.*

Psalm 8:5

Whenever I used to have a feel-sorry-for-myself day, my mother would sing this silly little song: "Nobody likes me. Everybody hates me. Guess I'll go eat worms."

How about you? Have you felt like eating a big, fat, juicy worm lately? Are you feeling sorry for yourself? Do you feel as though you'll never succeed in your job? If you answered yes to any of those questions, you need to give your insecurities to God and ask Him to replace them with confidence and supernatural favor.

Here's what the Bible says about you in Deuteronomy 28:13: "The Lord will make you the head, not the tail." I like being the head. How about you? And John 12:26 says, "My Father will honor the one who serves me." Did you get that? God will honor you! So stop feeling bad about yourself.

Start thinking, feeling, believing, and saying what God says about you. When you do, others will think more highly of you, too. It's true, but you have to walk in it every day. C'mon, now. Put down that big, juicy worm and start walking in God's divine favor. It's the only way to walk! —*MMA*

. . . .

Lord, replace my insecurities with Your kind of confidence. Amen.

Passed Over

*The LORD is a refuge for the oppressed, a stronghold in times
of trouble. Those who know your name trust in you,
for you, LORD, have never forsaken those who seek you.*

Psalm 9:9–10

When I graduated college, I interviewed for five different
positions in one company, and yet I kept losing those positions to other people, some of whom were less qualified. During
that three-month period, I worked in a temporary position, waiting for something—anything—to open up. Then, right before
my temporary commitment ended, an opportunity opened in a
great area, and I got the job. I went from feeling like a wallflower
to feeling very blessed.

I confess that I questioned God during that time when
I interviewed and interviewed to no avail, but looking back, I
see how faithful He was. The temporary work He had provided
allowed me to learn about the organization—its mission and its
processes—and trained me for my ultimate position. God was
working even when I didn't see it.

If you've been passed over for a job, don't be discouraged or
doubt your worth. You *are* valuable, and God *is* working on your
behalf. He hasn't forgotten you. You may not be able to see it yet,
but He has your best interest at heart. Don't give up on Him; He
certainly hasn't given up on you. —*GM*

. . . .

*Lord, Your Word says that You will never forsake those who
seek You, and that's just what I'm doing. You are my refuge
during this difficult time, and I trust You. Amen.*

The Power of Positive Speaking

Truly I tell you, if anyone says to this mountain,
"Go throw yourself into the sea," and does not doubt
in their heart but believes that what they say will happen,
it will be done for them.

Mark 11:23

Have you ever justified your negative workplace commentary with "Well, I just tell it like it is"? I have, unfortunately. If you've spent your whole life "telling it like it is," stop! We shouldn't use our mouths to comment on the negative state of our workplaces or our difficult bosses. Proverbs 18:21 clearly reminds us that the words we use can bring life to a situation—but they can also destroy. Instead of using our mouths to report the sorry state of things, we should use them to "speak faith" over our situations.

What exactly does that mean? It means we can declare things about our situation that agree with the Word of God—not our negative circumstances.

No matter how ugly your boss treated you yesterday, claim that you have favor in her eyes today. No matter how many people have been laid off in your division, claim that your job is secure. No matter how many of your ideas have been shot down in the past, claim that your ideas rise to the top. Use your mouth to speak good things until they become the norm. Stop telling it like it is and start telling it like it's going to be! *—MMA*

. . . .

Lord, help me to speak only those words that line up
with Your Word. Amen.

New Kids on the Block

The end of a matter is better than its beginning,
and patience is better than pride.

Ecclesiastes 7:8

God bless new bosses and coworkers. They're in a tough place. They've walked into new positions, not knowing the office history or procedures. They come with their own experiences and expertise. Many times, they've been hired to bring about change and improve productivity or sales.

For those who work with them, it can be challenging. You've done your job to the best of your ability within the boundaries of the current organization. You've carved out your own niche, only to have a newcomer decide to change everything. Your instincts tell you to resist the person and her ideas because, well, everything's been working just fine up until now, right?

Of course, not all changes are bad. When Jesus came into your life, He made *big* changes. He's completely changed the way you think about life. The ideas in His Word might have seemed foreign, but they worked—even better than you could have imagined.

So when that newcomer shows up at your office, be patient. You never know...her ideas might improve things, too. —*GM*

. . . .

Heavenly Father, please give me patience and insight
as I work with the new people who come into my office.
Help me to listen to and discuss their ideas
clearly and sensibly. Amen.

Jesus's Leadership Style

You've observed how godless rulers throw their weight around,
how quickly a little power goes to their heads.
It's not going to be that way with you.
Whoever wants to be great must become a servant.

Matthew 20:25–26 MSG

Some people expect that when they attain the power of a leadership position, they'll also automatically get the respect they think they deserve or they'll be able to make the changes they want.

But leadership and respect aren't one and the same. We've all known bosses who didn't have the respect of their subordinates because they had not worked to earn that respect. Given the opportunity, their employees would sell them down the river for a smile and a wink because, instead of building up their team, these bosses lead by intimidation.

In Matthew 20:25–26, Jesus responded to a mother's request that her two sons hold powerful positions in heaven by saying, "Whoever wants to be great must become a servant." Regardless of what position you hold, develop an attitude of servanthood. Don't think of yourself more highly than others or look for chances to intimidate people. As you develop Jesus's leadership style, you'll become a leader others will respect and want to follow. —GM

. . . .

Lord, help me to become a godly leader who has an attitude
of serving others. Whatever position I hold,
I want to honor You. Amen.

I Want My Old Job Back

*Am I now trying to win the approval of human beings, or of God?
Or am I trying to please people? If I were still trying to please
people, I would not be a servant of Christ.*

Galatians 1:10

I was standing in the grocery checkout line when my thoughts were interrupted by a conversation behind me.

"I don't know why that Michelle Adams person has to write all of that garbage in the newspaper," the woman said. "We don't need to know that stuff."

As the two women continued bashing me, I tried not to hyperventilate. I paid for my groceries and quickly escaped, wondering why I was being persecuted for simply doing my job—reporting on the school system's scandal.

I had recently been promoted from city government reporter to education reporter, and this was my first big story on that beat. Unfortunately, it wasn't a very flattering story for the community, and I wasn't gaining any popularity points. I suddenly longed for my boring city government beat. It was much safer there.

Even a promotion can be a difficult change, especially when it comes with critics. Criticism is never easy to digest, especially when it's not the constructive kind we can grow from. During seasons of change or when you're on the criticism hot seat, let God love on you. People are fickle. Their perceptions of you can change on a whim, but God's love for you is unending and never changing. You've already got His approval. —*MMA*

. . . .

*Lord, help me to trust You no matter what, and help me to handle
seasons of change and criticism with grace and love. Amen.*

Surviving the Boys' Club

Refrain from anger and turn from wrath;
do not fret—it leads only to evil.
Psalm 37:8

Have you ever heard the saying: "A woman has to be twice as good as a man to receive half as much credit"? I wouldn't say this is true in all situations, but I do believe that there is still a stigma against women in some offices. A woman can say the same thing a man says, but the man's opinion carries more weight.

Slowly but surely, the tide is changing. Not all male coworkers and bosses subscribe to the good old boys' club mentality. Yes, it may still exist, but you can stand your ground and be respectful even while demanding the same respect they would give a male colleague.

Learn from the successful women in your organization or industry. Trust God to show you how to be effective and then rest in the knowledge that you're doing all that He's told you to do. Pray for opportunities to change the hearts of those who still see women as the lesser gender. With perseverance and faith, you can change the culture and the future for the women who follow you. —*GM*

. . . .

Lord, help me to be the best employee I can possibly be.
I want to be successful in the position that You've given me,
and I trust that You'll show me the steps
to take to do that. Amen.

Open

*God is able to bless you abundantly, so that in all things at all times,
having all that you need, you will abound in every good work.*

2 Corinthians 9:8

I'd been invited to speak at a professional conference, and I couldn't wait! I planned to give my talk then spend the rest of the time relaxing and attending lectures. That didn't happen.

An hour before my scheduled talk, the conference coordinator asked me to fill in for another speaker. I ended up speaking back to back, first in the new lecture and then in the one I'd prepared. Then, several attendees requested meetings with me. I was busy! I ended up attending only a handful of the lectures I had looked forward to. My plans and expectations had changed, but I stayed flexible and still had a great time. Yes, I was disappointed that I had missed the other lectures, but I knew I could listen to the recordings later. My flexibility was rewarded when I received an invitation to return the next year.

We all have expectations. We expect a meeting to flow seamlessly. We expect to pull off a project without hiccups. We expect employees to get along with each other. We expect employers to follow the plans they've already approved. And yet...plans change and we must adjust.

Don't be surprised when great plans have to change. Commit to remain flexible, no matter what happens. Trust your heavenly Father to help you adjust and remain positive. With the right mindset, you might just end up having a great time, too. —*GM*

. . . .

*Dear God, teach me to be flexible and open to change
so I can do what I need to do. Amen.*

Out for Blood

Love your enemies, do good to those who hate you,
bless those who curse you, pray for those who mistreat you.
Luke 6:27–28

Janet was very unhappy in her job, and I had to work with her. She disagreed with management and thought she knew how both the office and the organization should be run. Though she was angry at management, she decided to take her hostility out on me.

Wherever I turned, her accusations followed. She questioned my motives and my integrity. What's worse, if I tried to defend myself, people looked at me as though *I* were guilty. When she finally left the company, I learned I wasn't her only victim. Whole departments had refused to work with her. What a horrible situation!

Wouldn't it be wonderful if everyone played by fair and decent rules? Unfortunately, some people are out for blood. Maybe you stand between them and a promotion. Maybe you have favor with management. Or maybe you're simply the nearest victim.

If you have a coworker who is out for blood, pray for her. Be wise in your dealings with her and follow God's advice to bless her. Eventually the truth will rise to the surface. —*GM*

. . . .

Lord, You know the truth about this situation.
I am determined to bless this person and ask
for Your wisdom as I deal with her. Amen.

Bring Your Own Paper Clips

Cast your cares on the LORD and he will sustain you.
Psalm 55:22

Ever felt persecuted at work? Ever felt like everyone else was treated better than you?

Once when I was working for a magazine, I requested a box of paper clips on the office order sheet. I didn't ask for a display phone like every other writer had (even though mine was so old, no longer rang—it just moaned). No, all I requested was a box of paper clips. I never dreamed my request would be denied.

That afternoon, my supervisor poked her head into my office and said, "You'll need to bring paper clips from home. We're only purchasing absolutely necessary items." I could not believe it! I thought, *Do you mean I work my guts out for this company, and I'm not even worth a two-dollar box of paper clips?*

Then I started noticing other office items my cowriters had that I did not have. The more mental notes I made about my have-not situation, the worse I felt and the worse I acted. I'm not saying I wasn't justified in feeling hurt or insulted, but dwelling on those daily injustices couldn't help me, nor could it change my toxic environment.

If you're getting the short end of the stick in your workplace, too, don't dwell on it. Give your situation to God. Ask Him to change your work environment or show you how to make the best of the situation. God cares about everything that affects you—even a paper clip shortage! *—MMA*

. . . .

*Lord, help me to keep my heart right in the midst
of this mistreatment. Amen.*

Smile!

A cheerful heart is good medicine,
but a crushed spirit dries up the bones.
Proverbs 17:22

For those wanting to change their image in the workplace, here's some advice: Smile. Sounds simple, doesn't it? But walk through your office and see how many people consistently look bored or irritated. Then consider which coworkers you would trust with a new assignment or turn to in a pinch—probably those with a good attitude.

I've known people who desperately wanted a promotion, but they went through their days looking like they hated their jobs and sucked a lemon to prove it. They never smiled, and if you dared to inconvenience them in the slightest way, well, forget about it. You'd worry that they might slash your tires in the parking lot. The sad thing was that most of them just didn't know how to express themselves in a positive way. Maybe if they had smiled and taken a more positive approach to their jobs, they might have been trusted with more.

The Word says, "A cheerful heart is good medicine." Happiness is a choice. If you're looking for a way to improve your standing in your office and to better enjoy your life in general, then take this one simple step: smile! —*GM*

. . . .

Lord, thank You for giving me my job.
Help me have a good attitude as I do it. Amen.

Kill Her with Kindness

Love is kind.

1 Corinthians 13:4

Happy birthday!" Three of my closest coworkers had decorated my office and sprinkled it with fun-sized chocolate candy bars. They knew I needed an extra lift that day. After all, it was my thirtieth birthday. I had been dreading it for weeks. Leaving behind my twenties was a tough one. I feared that crow's-feet were just around the corner. My buddies were there to cheer me up—but "Claire" wasn't.

As I headed downstairs for my morning break, she stopped me in the hallway. "So how old are you today?"

"I'm thirty."

"Really?" Claire said, raising her eyebrows. "I thought you were *way* older than that."

She was great at spewing hurtful comments; she did it every day. Oh, how I longed to toss some zingers of my own back at her. I crafted them carefully in my mind, just waiting for the right time to unleash them. But somehow, every time an opportunity arose, I couldn't do it. I'd be just about to really zing her, and then I'd remember what my dad always said: "Walk in love, honey. Err on the side of love."

Maybe there's a "Claire" in your office that you'd like to throttle. Well, don't. Instead, kill her with kindness. Walk in love. Yes, it's difficult, but you don't have to walk it alone. God will help you. —*MMA*

. . . .

Father, help me walk in Your love. Amen.

Just Say No

Pride goes before destruction, a haughty spirit before a fall.
Proverbs 16:18

Do you have trouble saying no to your superiors? I have a classic case of "Sure, I can do that," even though I know I'm saying yes when I should be saying no.

I learned this lesson the hard way. One summer, I signed two book contracts, both with September 1 deadlines. When the publishers asked if I needed more time, I proudly said, "No, I can totally meet that deadline." I didn't want to admit I needed more time. They might see it as a sign of weakness and lose confidence in me. So I practically killed myself to meet those deadlines. Ugh.

Looking back, I know that fear and pride kept me from being honest with myself and my publishers. I was afraid of disappointing anyone, and I was too proud to admit that I'd be struggling to accomplish what they were asking me to do.

Maybe you're on that same merry-go-round. If so, jump off! Ask God to help you say no when that's the needed answer. And ask Him to help you swallow your pride and admit when you need help. There's no shame in being human. —*MMA*

. . . .

Lord, help me to walk free from fear and pride. Amen.

DAY
35

Dreams and Callings

If you believe, you will receive whatever you ask for in prayer.
Matthew 21:22

I have a friend whose actual job is to go into people's homes and organize them from top to bottom. I can't even imagine doing that. I mean, I have so many junk drawers in my house, it takes me a good thirty minutes to locate the scissors each time I need them. Obviously, organization is not one of my gifts.

I have another friend who teaches twenty-five kindergarteners for a living. And yes, she is a wonderful teacher. While I adore children, it took only a brief stint of substitute teaching to know I wasn't called to be a teacher. Who knew 8:00 a.m. to 3:00 p.m. could last so long?

But you know what's cool? Both of my friends absolutely love what they do, and they are awesome at their individual callings. They are walking in their professional dreams.

That's one of the many things I love about our heavenly Father. He gives each of us unique dreams, then He equips us to accomplish those dreams if we'll only believe. It gives Him great joy to see us pursuing the ambitions He's placed within us. Don't give up on your dreams. God can't wait to see you walking in them. —*MMA*

. . . .

Lord, thank You for placing unique dreams
in my heart. Amen.

Putting the Golden Rule to Work

So in everything, do to others what
you would have them do to you.
Matthew 7:12

Bosses have a tough time of it. Yes, there are those who ignore serious issues or get a thrill out of flexing their authoritative muscles, but most bosses try to do a respectable job. They walk a fine line between being too lenient and too harsh. They need to be sure the job gets done even while they're preventing their natives from becoming too restless—and they're held accountable for the work of every person under them.

We've all criticized our bosses at one time or another. It's kind of funny—and unfair—how employees often demand perfection from their bosses yet expect mercy regarding their own work. It's a double standard, to be sure.

Scripture instructs us to "do to others what you would have them do to you." Remember this as you go through your week—even with your boss. If you don't want him to expect perfection from you, then you shouldn't expect perfection from him either. He's in a tough place, and in addition to your good work, he needs your support and understanding. —*GM*

. . . .

Lord, I want to be a support to my boss this week
and show favor toward him.
Show me how to do that. Amen.

Changes

*You will keep in perfect peace those whose minds are
steadfast, because they trust in you.*

Isaiah 26:3

I wish I could say that I lived for change, that I'm one of those remarkable people who thrive on learning new procedures, or that my idea of a fun Saturday afternoon includes rearranging the living room furniture. Unfortunately, that gift passed me by.

Of course, I don't absolutely *hate* it. Sometimes I change the pillows on my sofa. Does that count?

Change can be uncomfortable, especially in the workplace. When change comes, take a deep breath. God's still in control. Step back and objectively ask yourself if the change is good. Has it been carefully thought out? Is the goal to help the office function more smoothly? Are your managers supporting it 100 percent? If the answer to any of these questions is yes, then it's time to jump on board. If you have concerns, voice them appropriately. Once the decision has been made, however, become a team player and make the most of the situation. Your submission and positive attitude will be appreciated by management, your coworkers, and most importantly, by God. —*GM*

. . . .

*Lord, You know change is difficult for me.
Please help me to be a team player and a positive influence
when changes come. Amen.*

Run Your Own Race

*Let us throw off everything that hinders and the sin that
so easily entangles. And let us run with perseverance
the race marked out for us.*

Hebrews 12:1

Have you ever looked across the conference table, stared your supervisor in the eyes, and wondered, *Just how, may I ask, did you ever advance to that position?* C'mon, be honest.

It can be tough to be respectful when the person you call boss knows less than you do. It's even more difficult if your boss rose to that position through office politics, nepotism, or some other unfair avenue.

But hey, that's not your concern.

Don't waste time dwelling on such things. Instead, keep your eyes on God. Run your own race—don't worry about anyone else. Keep your heart right. Pray for your boss. Then just do your best at your position. Remember—God can cause bosses to move; He can cause eyes to be opened; and He can cause you to have supernatural favor with the powers that be. I'm not saying your current situation will change overnight, but it could. It's better to remain hopeful and faithful as you do your job to the best of your ability. Let God have room to work on your behalf.

Be encouraged. God can open doors that no man can open. Your job is to keep running your race so you'll be able to sprint right through that next open door. —*MMA*

. . . .

*Thank You, Father, for my job. Keep my heart right, Lord,
in the midst of nepotism and office politics.
Help me to run my race with excellence. Amen.*

Livin' for the Bell

*Our citizenship is in heaven. And we eagerly await
a Savior from there, the Lord Jesus Christ.*

Philippians 3:20

There are days when even the most dedicated employees are "livin' for the bell." We can't wait until the end of the day or the end of the shift. We're not really clock watchers, but on those difficult days or when we have something important to do after work...yes, we pack up five minutes early and bolt when the time comes.

As Christians, there's another bell we should eagerly be awaiting—the return of our Lord Jesus Christ. The apostle Paul understood a great truth: his real home was in heaven. And with all that he did, he still wrote that he eagerly awaited Jesus's return. It can be difficult to imagine Jesus's return in today's world, but it isn't any less of a reality, and we should be just as eager for it as Paul was.

As you go about your business, don't forget to eagerly await the Lord's return. Remember that, as important as anything you do here on earth may be, heaven—your true home—awaits. —*GM*

. . . .

*Lord, help me to remember You in everything I do.
I recognize Your Lordship in my life and in this world
and realize that this earth is not my true home. Amen.*

Painful Punctuality

*Whatever you do or say,
do it as a representative of the Lord Jesus.*
Colossians 3:17 NLT

*P*unctuality. Just writing the word is painful to me. I've never been very good at being on time. It's not that I don't give myself ample time to get ready. It's just that I try to do too much before I leave the house. For instance, I'll get ready and head for the door, and then I'll remember that I need to switch the laundry. Next thing I know, I'm off to another late start.

I once worked in an optometry office for a very kind doctor. He never yelled about my five- or ten-minute-late arrivals, but one day he did pull me aside. "Listen," he said. "I don't care if you're a little late. But some of the other employees are upset about it. So, just try to be on time, okay?"

I left his office feeling just awful. I realized that my tardiness was creating stress for my wonderful boss, and it was ruining my Christian witness. I asked God to help me change that very day, and I did a lot better. Of course, I'm still a work in progress.

If you're challenged with punctuality, ask God to help you. He wants to be involved in every part of your life. Go ahead and talk to Him. He's got the time. —*MMA*

. . . .

*Lord, help me to be on time.
I want to be a good witness for You. Amen.*

Readjusting the Compass

*The steps of a good man are ordered by the LORD:
and he delighteth in his way.*

Psalm 37:23 KJV

My friends sometimes ask me, "Are you still working as much, or are you taking time off to relax?" I usually laugh and shrug because, to me, it's just life as usual. I'm like most women; I work, play, socialize, and worship—sometimes all at the same time.

But every so often, I have to readjust my schedule. It's as though the needle on my internal compass has to be reset to point north again. I take a deep breath, put aside some time for myself, and get before the Lord for a heart-to-heart. This isn't a quick five-minute appointment. It's a several-day journey where I reevaluate my priorities and ask God to nix anything that isn't necessary to help me refocus.

If you're feeling low on energy, overwhelmed, and overscheduled, make time to have a heart-to-heart with God. Ask Him to readjust your compass and show you where to focus your energies. With a renewed sense of purpose and direction, you'll have the energy to do what you really need to be doing. —*GM*

. . . .

*Lord, I am so busy that I can't even decipher which things
on my to-do list are truly necessary. Help me to reprioritize
and focus on what You want me to do. Amen.*

You Are Enough

I traded their lives for yours because you are precious to me.
You are honored, and I love you.
Isaiah 43:4 NLT

I had just learned that, after serving faithfully on the faculty of a writers' conference for over a decade, I wasn't being asked back that year. I was devastated. Sure, I understood that it was probably time to switch out faculty members and give others a chance to teach, but it still hurt. After all, I'd never taught at that conference (or any conference for that matter) for the money or the prestige or the networking. Those were all added bonuses. I taught because I'd promised God that, if He could use me to encourage others in writing, I would be faithful to do so. I'd always felt it was a calling and a privilege to serve in that way.

The situation made me question my worth. Was I still relevant? Could God not use me anymore? I just didn't know. I ran to Big Lots that afternoon to pick up some batteries and discovered that God had a special message waiting there to recharge mine. There in front of me was an inspirational home décor sign that simply said, "You are enough." As I read it, the Lord spoke gently into my spirit.

"You are enough, and I'm not through with you yet."

It's easy to feel rejected in this world, and at times you're going to question your own worth, so remember this—you are enough. And God isn't through with you yet either. —*MMA*

. . . .

Lord, help me to find my worth in You.
Thanks for loving me like You do. Amen.

Looking Out for Number One

*At that time the disciples came to Jesus and asked,
"Who, then, is the greatest in the kingdom of heaven?"
He called a little child and placed the child among them.
And he said: "...whoever takes the lowly position
of this child is the greatest in the kingdom of heaven."*

Matthew 18:1–4

What an interesting passage. We often forget that the disciples were just normal people with the same feelings and ambitions we have. Here, we see they were sometimes more concerned about their positions in the kingdom of God than they were about the task at hand. I'm sure they weren't expecting the answer Jesus gave them, either. He gently picked up a child and set him among them as a standard of faith and humility. They were probably scratching their heads at that one.

If I had been standing there, I probably would have been tempted to ask, "Yeah, but what are the three steps to being number one?" I can be a bit hardheaded at times.

So, how can we be our best selves with God? Well, if we love and serve Him with childlike faith and humility, we already are. Take comfort in that and continue to be faithful to Him. Loving Him with your whole heart will bring you more satisfaction than any other position you'll ever hold. —*GM*

. . . .

*Lord, thank You for loving me and calling me to be Your child.
I commit to serving You with childlike faith and humility.
You are an awesome God, and I love You. Amen.*

Territorial Standoffs

A gentle answer turns away wrath,
but a harsh word stirs up anger.

Proverbs 15:1

Once as a new hire, I found myself facing off with a veteran coworker. At the time, I couldn't figure out what I had done to offend her, but whatever it was, she obviously did not like it or me. Eventually, I learned that management had shifted many of her responsibilities over to me. Apparently, there was a lot more going on with her than what I knew.

When you become the object of someone's scorn for no obvious reason, it may have nothing to do with you personally. You may simply be the catalyst. Anger is a difficult emotion to navigate, whether in the workplace, home, or even at the dry cleaner's. God's Word instructs us to have a kind word for those who are angry.

If you must deal with a perpetually angry person, pray for wisdom in the situation. Resolve not to match their actions. Instead, remain calm, kind, and objective. You may not see an immediate change in their demeanor by doing this, but you'll be a witness—possibly the only one—of kindness in their life. —*GM*

· ·

Dear Lord, thank You for helping me
to be kind to others, even when they're angry.
Help me to be a witness for You today. Amen.

One-Upmanship

For where you have envy and selfish ambition,
there you find disorder and every evil practice.

James 3:16

Ever worked with someone who always one-ups you? Uh-huh, you know the type. If you have an idea that could save the company hundreds of dollars, she comes up with a plan to save thousands. Irritating, isn't it?

Be honest. That old green-eyed monster occasionally rears its ugly head when she enters the room. Jealousy is a funny thing. It sneaks up on you when you least expect it. Unfortunately, it brings a few of its friends, like anger, frustration, and strife. Let's face it—that's no way to live.

Instead of focusing all your energy on the one-upper, turn your attention to God. Ask God to help you see her through *His* eyes. Ask Him to fill you up with so much love that there won't be room for jealousy, anger, frustration, or strife.

Be happy when your coworker succeeds. Rejoice with her, because until you can celebrate her accomplishments, you'll never fully experience success of your own. Remember, God is no respecter of persons. What He's done for her, He will also do for you—if you keep your heart right. —*MMA*

. . . .

Father, help me to celebrate—and not be jealous of—
those who are advancing in the company.
Change my heart, Lord. I love You. Amen.

The Great Unknown

Fearless now, I trust in God; what can mere mortals do to me?
Psalm 56:11 MSG

As much as the fear of failure can hinder us, the fear of success can hold us back, too. This is a difficult fear to overcome because the end results are unknown. You know what's expected in your current position, and the thought of moving on leaves you scared and nervous.

The only way to rid yourself of any fear is with the Word of God. By studying the Word of God and discovering what God says about you, your faith in Him will increase. You'll begin to view the obstacles in your career as small in comparison to Him.

So if you're struggling with the fear of success, take time to read and meditate on God's Word. Find Scriptures you can relate to, copy them down, and put them somewhere you will see them every day—your Bible, the home screen on your phone, your desk drawer, or your car. Don't read them like you're reading your grocery list; read them as what they are—personal words from your heavenly Father. Continue to pray and surround your-self with positive Christian friends who will encourage you. With all this, you're sure to succeed. —*GM*

. . . .

Lord, as I meditate on Your Word,
I trust You to fulfill Your plan in my life and to help me
follow that plan without fear. Amen.

The Choice

I have learned the secret of being content in any and every situation,
whether well fed or hungry, whether living in plenty or in want.
I can do all this through him who gives me strength.

Philippians 4:12–13

Paul is a great example of someone who chose to be content. Though he was imprisoned for preaching the gospel and his surroundings were filthy, he continued to teach other Christians through his letters. In fact, while he was in prison, he wrote, "I have learned the secret of being content in any and every situation." He knew that his personal comfort wasn't as important as his eternal calling. What a challenge for us!

Regardless of what position you hold, now or in the future, you are first called to be a child of God and a light to the world. It isn't wrong to pursue promotions, but you must know that true happiness and contentment don't come because of outward circumstances. Contentment is a choice you make every day.

As you work at your job—whether you love it or hate it—choose to be a light for Jesus. Through your attitude and work ethic, you could be more of an example and blessing to a coworker than you ever realized. —*GM*

. . . .

Lord, I choose to be content today. I know that,
more than anything else,
I'm called to be a light for You. Amen.

In His Shadow

*Whoever dwells in the shelter of the Most High will rest
in the shadow of the Almighty. I will say of the* LORD,
"He is my refuge and my fortress, my God, in whom I trust."

Psalm 91:1–2

I love Psalm 91. It has been such a comfort to me in those times in my life when things looked uncertain. Look again at the first verse: "He who dwells in the shelter of the Most High will rest in the shadow of the Almighty." Isn't that a beautiful picture? As a child of God, you dwell in God's shelter, and because you do, you can rest in His shadow.

When things look bleak or upsetting, you aren't forgotten. People often envision God either as a taskmaster who's ready to wallop them when they step out of line or as a distant, disinterested figure. Both views are incorrect. Psalm 91 is a great reminder of the protection that He offers to His children.

I challenge you to read Psalm 91 and consider your life through its lens. As you do, I pray you'll begin to see the depth of God's love and interest in you. You can be confident that He's available to help you through any situation, whether at home or at work. —*GM*

. . . .

*Lord, thank You for protecting me and allowing me to rest
in Your shadow. I trust You as my refuge and fortress. Amen.*

Fear Not

Such love has no fear, because perfect love expels all fear.
1 John 4:18 NLT

He smiled a big toothy grin, looking exactly like the Grinch as he plotted and planned against Whoville. He may have been my new team lead, but I considered him questionable. He had a reputation for shaking things up without regard for anyone's feelings, so I was prepared for a battle.

As he talked about the upcoming changes and how they would positively affect our department, I remained skeptical. I wanted to see where he was coming from before I offered any help or input. Bottom line? I was being a jerk—a jerk motivated by fear. I was so afraid he might be as bad as I'd heard, that I wasn't willing to give the guy a chance. But you know what? He ended up being a nice addition to our department.

We often face change with an unhealthy dose of fear. And fear causes us to act inappropriately. If you're in the midst of changes in your workplace and you're walking in fear—stop! Fear is not of God. Ask the Lord to replace that fear with His love. And if you get a new boss who seems highly suspicious, pray for him—don't eyeball him.

Besides, God is your ultimate boss, and you can always trust Him. —*MMA*

. . . .

Lord, keep my heart full of love, not fear.
I trust You during these uncertain times. Amen.

His Way

Get wisdom, get understanding;
do not forget my words or turn away from them.

Proverbs 4:5

I have always loved the *Legally Blonde* movies. In *Legally Blonde 2: Red, White, and Blonde*, Elle Woods goes to Washington, DC, to get some legislation passed that would outlaw animal testing. But this bubbly blonde runs into Washington politics at their worst. She tries to play the game, but nothing goes her way. Finally, after several failed attempts, Elle perkily says to her colleague, "You do it the Washington way...I'm going to do it the Elle Woods way." The "Elle Woods way" was a nice, upfront way, and it proved successful.

Doing things the right way—God's way—is always the best course of action. Sure, you might enjoy a degree of success doing it the world's way, but God's way is much better. You don't have to play underhanded games to get ahead when you know the Head. You can call on God for wisdom and counsel any time of the day or night. Proverbs 3:5–6 says that we should not lean on our own understanding, but in all our ways we should acknowledge Him, and He will direct our paths. Why not get God involved in your business today? *—MMA*

. . . .

Lord, help me to lean on Your understanding and not my own.
I want to make good decisions today. Amen.

Stars and Starfish

The battle is the LORD's.
1 Samuel 17:47

When I was in seventh grade, the teacher divided our biology class into pairs and instructed us to dissect a starfish. Yuck! I had a weak stomach, and I knew I'd hurl if I had to touch that stinky starfish. However, I was a fast note taker and a pretty good typist. So my partner and I agreed to work with our strengths—he did the gross stuff, and I did the rest. Our teamwork paid off! We received an A.

If only every task worked out so well in the real world.

Have you ever been paired up with someone in your company who wouldn't do any work? It's the worst! You want to rat out your lazy partner, but you're afraid to appear like less than a team player. It's a difficult yet common situation.

Maybe that's where you are today. If so, hang in there. Just remember, even if your boss never knows how much work you've done (and how little your partner has produced), God knows. Don't become bitter. Simply continue doing your best work. Eventually, God will cause those in authority to see your actions—and your partner's inaction. Soon you'll be a star, and your partner will be a stinky starfish. —*MMA*

. . . .

Lord, help me keep a right attitude even in bad situations. Amen.

Round and Round It Goes

The words of a gossip are like choice morsels;
they go down to the inmost parts.

Proverbs 26:22

A few years ago, my organization underwent a restructure. Several important people were reassigned or dismissed. It was a difficult time for everyone. But even worse than what happened was listening to the rumor mill churn. Every day, more and more theories were tossed around about who was leaving and how our jobs were going to be reorganized. Listening to the churning caused people to become anxious—whether the rumors were true or not.

I have a friend who is brilliant at avoiding the rumor mill. She changes the subject or quietly walks away from such conversations. I'll admit that I strive to be more like her 100 percent of the time. Unfortunately, sometimes I fail.

Imagine what would happen if everyone avoided the rumor mill, if we all decided to change the subject or walk away from hurtful conversations. Maybe the next hapless victim would be saved, and we'd all experience less anxiety in the workplace. You never know, it could just be the first step in winning your office for Jesus. —*GM*

* *

Lord, please help me stand strong against
the office rumor mill so that I don't hurt others.
Let me be a part of the rumor mill solution. Amen.

Not Just a Worker Bee

*From him the whole body, joined and held together
by every supporting ligament, grows and builds itself up in love,
as each part does its work.*

Ephesians 4:16

In a meeting that my husband attended, an executive referred to the attending staff as "worker bees." He said they were not to set the vision, only to carry out the project. They weren't to have any ownership in the result of their work; they were only drones. Of course this fell flat—way flat. On that day, my husband and I both determined that we were more than mere worker bees. And I hope that you make that same determination for yourself.

Your position may require you to carry out others' plans, but that doesn't make you a drone who mindlessly works without adding to or taking pride in your job. God has placed gifts and talents in you, some of which you don't even understand yet. He's using you to provide for your family, help others, and be His example. That's not mindless droning.

The next time you feel like a drone, remember: You are more than a worker bee. You are a chosen, called, and gifted child of God! —*GM*

. . . .

*Thank You, Father, for calling me by name and giving me
every gift and talent that I have. Help me to use them
diligently to bless You and others. Amen.*

Love Them Anyway

A new command I give you: Love one another.
As I have loved you, so you must love one another.
John 13:34

It was happening again. The company needed a scapegoat, and my friend was the chosen victim. While heating up my lunch in the company microwave, I overheard my boss's plan to fire my friend. As my boss discussed the particulars with another department head, I felt sick inside. I wanted to stand on top of the lunch table and say, "Liar, liar. Pants on fire." Everything they were saying about my friend was untrue. Still, she received a pink slip the next Friday.

After witnessing that fiasco, I had absolutely no respect left for my boss. I so wanted to talk about her with my coworkers. I wanted to tell them how she'd sold out to protect her own job. But she was still my boss, and I had to honor her until I could find another job. And because I was a Christian, I had to love her. Ugh! The Bible says we are to love our enemies, and she certainly felt like an enemy. That was a tough one.

Maybe you have a boss who is hard to respect. Maybe you're in a similar situation yourself, and you're struggling. Well, I have good news. Your situation is temporal. God can open a new job for you, or He might move your boss out of your department. Submit your situation to the Lord and trust Him to work it out. Meanwhile, you can be proactive and start updating your résumé so you'll be ready when that new door opens. —*MMA*

. . . .

Lord, I turn this situation over to You. Direct my steps
and keep my heart right, even through this difficult time. Amen.

Follow the Leader

Anyone who intends to come with me has to let me lead.
You're not in the driver's seat; I am.

Matthew 16:24 MSG

The workplace is an interesting and comical place to play follow-the-leader. I once had a beautiful, talented boss who was successful in many areas. She was a visionary at work and a wonder-woman wife and mother. Many wanted to be like her. If she changed her hairstyle, women changed theirs, too. If she wore certain brand-name clothes, others followed. People followed her diets, exercise regimens, and even changed to use her ob/gyn doctor. Because obviously hers was better, right?

There will always be talented people you admire. They'll teach you how to succeed, and it would be foolish not to learn from them. Ultimately, however, Jesus is the best role model you could ever have. His is the greatest example of love, compassion, leadership, hard work, and humility. His life is the one you want to emulate. So play follow-the-leader with Jesus, allowing His ways to become your ways. Put Him in the driver's seat of your life, realizing that He is your ultimate role model. As you do, you'll become more and more like Him. —GM

. . . .

Lord, thank You for being in the driver's seat in my life.
I follow You and pray that Your ways become my ways. Amen.

Bad Days

But David encouraged himself in the LORD his God.
1 Samuel 30:6 KJV

Stop for a minute and think about the very worst day you've ever spent on the job. Okay, do you have a visual? Did you just want to throw your hands into the air and quit? Did you feel like God had forsaken you? Did you want to head for a tropical island and never return? I think we've all been there. Even David had bad days on the job.

In 1 Samuel 30, David was doing exactly what God had told him to do, fighting battles for God. But he and his men had just returned from the war, only to find that their city had been burned and their wives and children had been taken captive. Talk about a bad day on the job! Then, to make matters worse, all David's men turned on him and plotted together to stone him.

Things looked pretty bleak, but David didn't crawl into a hole and curse God. Instead, the Bible says he "encouraged himself in the LORD." And you know what? It wasn't long before that entire situation turned around in David's favor.

No matter how bad it may get at work, follow David's example. Encourage yourself in the Lord and watch your situation turn around! —*MMA*

Thank You, Lord, for Your never-ending faithfulness! Amen.

Powerful Words

*The soothing tongue is a tree of life,
but a perverse tongue crushes the spirit.*

Proverbs 15:4

Have you ever considered how powerful words are? People have said things to me—both positive and negative—that still resonate in my mind. I've been called a creative problem solver, but I've also been told that I'm a pushover. The good is nice to hear, but the bad is hard to swallow. I have to consciously remind myself not to see myself that way.

Why? Because words are powerful. They can build up or tear down; it's that simple. When you think about it, it's amazing to realize that our words can have such power over other people. What we say can build them up or tear them down, affecting how they view themselves.

As an ambassador of Christ, you have the power and responsibility to build others up, to be a positive influence in their lives, and to never be a destructive force. Determine today to build up your coworkers—even those who grate on your nerves. Don't tear them down. You never know, your kind words may be the only ones they hear. —*GM*

. . . .

*Lord, as an ambassador for You, help me to bring healing
and encouragement to others today. Amen.*

Longest Boat Ride Ever!

*But God remembered Noah and all the wild animals
and the livestock that were with him in the ark,
and he sent a wind over the earth, and the waters receded.*

Genesis 8:1

Can you imagine being on a boat with a bunch of smelly animals for a year? Well, Noah and his family did just that. Some people think they were only on that boat for forty days and forty nights, but Bible says it *rained* for those forty days and nights. It then took 150 days for the water to go down enough for Noah to see the mountaintops around them. Several more months passed before God released them from the ark.

I'm sure there were days when Noah and his family wished they hadn't been chosen for the ark assignment. But Noah knew God, and he believed that God would deliver them—no matter how many days he looked outside and saw nothing but water. But the Lord was causing the wind to blow and push back the floodwaters. God was working behind the scenes the whole time.

Even if you know you are right where God called you to be, you can still be afraid and overwhelmed. You may not be able to see a change today, but keep trusting. God hasn't forgotten you. In fact, your miracle may blow in on the very next breeze. —*MMA*

. . . .

Lord, help me to trust You more. Amen.

Tending the Sheep

*From that day on, the Spirit of the LORD
came powerfully upon David.... But David went back
and forth from Saul to tend his father's sheep at Bethlehem.*
1 Samuel 16:13; 17:14–15

Everyone knows that David was a great leader, but he didn't look like one when he was out tending his father's sheep. He was the youngest of several brothers—probably picked on by the older ones and given the chores no one else wanted to do. In fact, that's where he was when God chose him to be king. God saw David's potential, even though David didn't ascend to the throne until long after Samuel anointed him. Instead, he worked as a professional musician and then as a military warrior. And even then, he tended sheep. He wasn't exactly on the fast track.

You might find that even though God has called you to do something, you'll need patience and perseverance for it to happen. You might know that you're going to have your own company or a higher position, but until then, allow God to equip and prepare you for that position. Through patience and perseverance, you can see your plans fulfilled. —*GM*

. . . .

*Lord, thank You for preparing me for Your plans.
I submit to You in all I do. Amen.*

Thankfulness Goes a Long Way

*So then, just as you received Christ Jesus as Lord,
continue to live your lives in him, rooted and built up
in him, strengthened in the faith as you were taught,
and overflowing with thankfulness.*

Colossians 2:6–7

Do you work around people who complain constantly? They don't like the boss's decisions or the company's policies or the receptionist's attitude. Everything's a problem; nothing's easy. Their complaints are like nails on a chalkboard. All they have to do is start talking, and everyone around them cringes. Needless to say, they won't win the Miss Congeniality award.

Every office has challenges, but a person who constantly points them out quickly becomes annoying. We'd all rather be around positive people who are thankful for their jobs and peers.

Thankfulness goes a long way toward developing a positive attitude. Through it, we acknowledge that God is in control and works through—and sometimes in spite of—the people around us.

Start working today to develop an attitude of thankfulness, realizing that it'll help you become a favorite among your peers and strengthen your relationship with the Lord. —*GM*

. . . .

*Lord, I thank You for Your provision. I thank You for the job
You've given me and the people You've placed around me.
I trust You in all I do. Amen.*

Change Is in the Air

He changes times and seasons;
he deposes kings and raises up others.
He gives wisdom to the wise
and knowledge to the discerning.
Daniel 2:21

Change is coming; you can sense it. Perhaps it's a job. A relationship. A volunteer ministry. Something. Anything. And that's exciting! It's as if a beautiful Christmas present has been placed under the tree with your name on it. You're just waiting for the perfect time to unwrap it and peek inside.

The best part about these waiting times is that you are once again reminded that God is working on your behalf. He thinks enough of you to direct you to another job or bring a new relationship into your life. It's one more reminder that you are special to Him.

Of course, until the day arrives when you know exactly what the change is, you must be patient, consistently doing what you know to do. Then pray for insight and watch as God directs you. You are not alone. The God of the universe, the Beginning and the End, is beside you, working in your life. Now, isn't that comforting? —*GM*

. . . .

Lord, I feel impressed that You're going to do something new
in my life. I thank You for it in advance—
and I'm ready to see what it is. Amen.

Not What I Asked for!

Yet not my will, but yours be done.
Luke 22:42

Have you ever heard the song "Unanswered Prayers" by Garth Brooks? In the song, he thanks God for not answering his youthful prayer of always loving his high school girlfriend, because he's so thankful for the wife God gave him later in life. It really is a beautiful reminder that God knows best.

There are times when it's better *not* to get what you pray for. Sometimes that promotion or assignment that looked so enticing ends up feeling like a death sentence. At the least, it can seem like you've jumped into an erupting volcano.

If you've prayed for something that didn't happen the way you expected it to happen, or if God didn't answer your prayer the way you wanted Him to answer it, don't be discouraged. He might have been saving you from a difficult situation or preparing you for something better in the future. Even when it seems that God has missed the deal for you, remember that He's always preparing and protecting you. You can trust Him; He has your best interest at heart. —*GM*

. . . .

Lord, let Your will be done in my life.
I know that You only want what's best for me,
so I'm choosing to trust You. Amen.

Press toward the Mark

*I press toward the mark for the prize
of the high calling of God in Christ Jesus.*
Philippians 3:14–15 KJV

The ability to motivate others is an amazing gift. I've worked for bosses and with other coworkers who were flat-out inspiring. They could rally any group to follow them. People wanted to help them and loved being around them. This generally made them much more productive than the taskmasters who used fear to motivate their people.

The apostle Paul was a motivator. The letters he wrote were for correction, but they also reminded the Christians of what they were really doing. He inspired them to "press toward the mark for the prize of the high calling of God in Christ Jesus." That's the example he lived, and he encouraged others to do it, too.

If you're looking for a way to be more productive or to have a more positive, inspiring influence on those around you, become a motivator. As you do, you'll share the joy that Jesus has placed in your life with those around you. —*GM*

. . . .

*Lord, I want to inspire others to press toward
the mark of Jesus, too. Please show me how to become
a motivator for You. Amen.*

Rubies, Gold, and Short Skirts

Charm is deceptive, and beauty is fleeting;
but a woman who fears the LORD is to be praised.
Proverbs 31:30

I watched a reality TV show recently, where several young professional women were competing for a promotion. They were trying to land accounts and increase sales. Sadly, they were relying on their sexuality to be successful by flirting with potential clients. They were trying to get ahead based on something other than their talents.

There is a difference between being charming and engaging and using sexuality in a manipulative and inappropriate way. Just as it is wrong for a man to use his power to sexually harass and intimidate his subordinates, it is equally wrong for a woman to use her attractiveness and behavior to get ahead. God gave us gifts and talents and the drive to succeed, but that success only comes through hard work and integrity.

As God's daughter, you don't have to rely on cheap tricks to get ahead. You can rest knowing that God has given you every talent and ability you need to succeed. You can keep His standard of holiness and be "a woman who fears the LORD." —*GM*

. . . .

Lord, thank You for loving me. Help me be a woman
who fears and loves You. Amen.

The Flu

*In peace I will lie down and sleep, for you alone,
Lord, make me dwell in safety.*
Psalm 4:8

It was the first day off that I'd had in two weeks, and I was lying on my couch, feeling like I'd been run over by a truck. I was so exhausted, I could barely move. I ached all over and didn't want to eat. I didn't have a fever or an upset stomach, but I felt sick. At the time, I didn't understand my symptoms, but later I found a newspaper article that enlightened me. It talked about a common illness found among Americans. The symptoms likened themselves to the flu but were caused by stress-induced fatigue. *Well, at least I'm not alone,* I consoled myself, secretly wondering how long I could keep up the pace.

You don't have to live a stressed-out life. You can have peace. Turn to God and allow Him to help you. He might lead you— like He did me—to leave your position. He might show you how to delegate or prioritize better, or maybe He'll give you peace to endure your job. Just know that you are not alone. God is ready to help you. —*GM*

. . . .

*Lord, thank You for Your peace, which surpasses all understanding.
I pray that it would continue to guard my heart and mind
as You show me how to live in it all the time. Amen.*

Zinged

Bless those who curse you, pray for those who mistreat you.
Luke 6:28

Let's be honest; we've all been zinged. You know, those comments that sound so sweet—until you walk away and realize you've just been insulted. Things like, "I *love* your hair; it looks like something from the 1940s." Um, yeah, I loved hearing that one...until the muffled snort that followed gave it away.

As an individual who is blessed to breathe air, you're sure to have received a zinger. And as a woman, you've probably been blessed with a long memory that allows you to relive those comments many times over.

When the zingers come—and they will—you have two choices. You can respond emotionally, leaving godly grace at the door, or you can respond in love, either by remaining silent or by gently responding to the comment. The choice is yours.

Of course, if you're listening to the Holy Spirit, you know He won't let you get away with launching your own verbal assault in response. No, it's much better to respond in love. After all, that person may be feeling insecure or harboring some past hurt herself.

The next time you see that office zingee, follow the advice from Luke 6:28 and pray for God's blessing in her life. As you do, God promises that "your reward will be great" (Luke 6:35). —*GM*

. . . .

*Lord, please help me to be an example of Your love
and grace in everything I do. Amen.*

Green-Eyed Monster

*Anger is cruel and fury overwhelming,
but who can stand before jealousy?*

Proverbs 27:4

Wouldn't it be great if adults could avoid jealousy; if they could celebrate each other regardless of looks, style, talent, money, or position? Well, that's not usually the case.

I had two friends—we'll call them Melissa and Kendra—who just did not get along. Melissa was a vivacious, beautiful, and talented woman. Kendra was also beautiful and talented, but whenever Melissa's name was mentioned, she tensed. I couldn't figure out the problem. Then one day in an angry fit, Kendra exploded over something I thought was small. "Who does she think she is!" Kendra yelled, and a light bulb went on for me. Kendra was jealous.

Everyone has weaknesses and strengths, but it's unfortunate when someone else's strengths feel threatening to you. Jealousy keeps you from appreciating the God-given gifts in others. It hinders you from doing your best work because your view is altered.

Don't let jealousy take hold of you. Pray for wisdom to see the truth in someone; take time to get to know her. Many times, if you can put your insecurities aside, you'll find something endearing about that person. Then you can celebrate the gifts that God has given to her, realizing that they're not better, they're just different from your own. —*GM*

. . . .

*Lord, help me to celebrate the gifts You've given to others
and to avoid jealousy. Amen.*

Messing Up

Neither height nor depth, nor anything else in all creation,
will be able to separate us from the love of God
that is in Christ Jesus our Lord.

Romans 8:39

Have you seen the boss yet?" my friend and coworker asked.
"No, why?"

"You had an error in your story. It's causing quite a stir in the newsroom."

I thought I would be sick. I had written an entire story, quoting the wrong man. I had lost my credibility with my source and my readers. I had lost my credibility with my boss and my coworkers. And I had totally humiliated myself. It was a very bad day. There was nothing to do but own up to my mistake and run a retraction the next day. I had let everyone down.

Everyone but God. Not once did I feel condemned when I brought the dilemma to Him. In fact, I felt nothing but love. You see, nothing can separate us from the love of God.

No matter how many times you mess up, no matter how many things you do wrong—even if your mistake is on the front page of the local newspaper!—God still adores you. He's right there with you, ready to help you pick yourself up and start again. So if you've made a gigantic mistake and you need some unconditional love, run to God. He wants to love on you today. —*MMA*

. . . .

Thank You, Lord, for loving me—
even when I make big mistakes. Amen.

Pick Your Battles

A gentle answer turns away wrath,
but a harsh word stirs up anger.

Proverbs 15:1

One of the greatest lessons I've learned in the workplace is to pick my battles wisely. In stressful environments with intense people, I've seen some people roll with the punches and others explode over every little frustration, causing coworkers to hide under their desks or, at the least, avoid working with them.

There are times when going to battle to correct a wrong is appropriate, but there are other times when peacefully working out a creative solution is more effective. Being proactive instead of reactive will help you instill trust and cooperation in your coworkers instead of fear and anger.

Just imagine if every time you approached God, He beat you over the head with your failure. Wouldn't you eventually stop approaching Him or live in constant fear of His reaction? Yes, He still corrects you and His Holy Spirit still convicts you for wrongdoing, but you can be peaceful in knowing that He only wants what's best for you. —*GM*

. . . .

Lord, thank You for Your correction and mercy in my life.
As I go to work today, please help me to pick my battles wisely—
to speak up when I need to speak up and to extend mercy
when I need to extend mercy. Amen.

Driven to Succeed

*Don't panic. I'm with you. There's no need to fear
for I'm your God. I'll give you strength. I'll help you.
I'll hold you steady, keep a firm grip on you.*
Isaiah 41:10 MSG

In a recent seminar, a successful female executive admitted that the catalyst that drove her to succeed was her fear of failure. She owned several businesses, including a consulting firm and two employment agencies. Personally, she had faced divorce, remarriage, stepparenting, and a substance abuse problem. I admired her success, but her talk left me wondering whether she had a relationship with the Lord to help her through those difficult times or if she had faced them alone. I hoped she had a relationship with the Lord, because I couldn't imagine facing all of that without Him.

As Christians, we are never alone.

When fear has gripped me in the past, it was often because my eyes were not focused on Jesus. Instead, I was trying to do everything in my own strength, a predicament that many women fall into. We try to accomplish so much, both personally and professionally, that it's easy to forget we don't have to manage the burden alone. But Jesus is there to help us carry the load and overcome our fears. We can trust Him to increase our faith and destroy every fear through His Word. —*GM*

. . . .

*Lord, I am struggling with a fear that's making it difficult for me
to make the decisions I need to make. I trust that through
Your Word, my faith and peace will increase. Amen.*

The Big Picture

*This vision is for a future time. It describes the end,
and it will be fulfilled. If it seems slow in coming, wait patiently,
for it will surely take place. It will not be delayed.*

Habakkuk 2:3 NLT

I've learned from some wonderful bosses how important it is to continually keep the vision of a project in front of a team. In fact, in the most successful projects I've ever been involved with, everyone knew the common goal *and* his/her place in bringing it to pass.

Having a vision is vital. I've met many women who struggle with knowing the vision God has for their lives. They jokingly say they want to know what they're going to be when they grow up—regardless of their age.

Though it might sound simple to some, discovering your life's goal can be challenging. It takes time for all the pieces to come together, but don't get discouraged while you wait. Be faithful to what He's put in front of you right now. Continue to pray, read His Word, and talk to your pastor or mentor. As the pieces come together, you'll understand more what God was preparing you for, even when you felt like you were just spinning your wheels. Never doubt that He has a vision for you! —*GM*

. . . .

*Lord, thank You for directing me in every area of my life.
Give me a clear vision of what I should do,
both now and in the future. Amen.*

An Open Line

Then Jesus told his disciples a parable to show them that they should always pray and not give up.

Luke 18:1

Recently I attended a meeting with a woman who, in the middle of our meeting, received a phone call on her landline. She took it, and a few minutes later, while she was still on that phone, her cell phone rang. She answered that one, too. Over the next five minutes, I marveled as she juggled both calls at once—a phone on each ear—never faltering in what she needed to do and communicate to those callers.

It's funny, but that memory makes me think of prayer. As Christians, we need to have two receivers open, too—one to those around us and the other to God. In Luke 18, Jesus told the disciples to "always pray." As eager as you might be to get that helpful phone call with just the right information at work, as a child of God, you should be just as eager to get direction and information from God. Some people assume that, if you're not in a certain place or praying in a certain way, it doesn't count. But God never hangs up the spiritual phone—He's always on the line, hoping that you'll have your receiver pressed against your ear.

As you go through your day, keep your prayer line open so you can be increasingly more in tune with Him. —*GM*

. . . .

Lord, I love You and trust You today. I am committing to keep communications open between us. Amen.

A Fresh Start

*At that time the Spirit of the LORD will come powerfully
upon you.... You will be changed into a different person.*

1 Samuel 10:6 NLT

There's never a better time to reevaluate your life, your goals, or your walk with the Lord than right now. If you're new in your relationship with the Lord, congratulations! You're on a wonderful journey that will change the rest of your life for the better. And if you already have a close relationship with the Lord and are committed to continuing and strengthening that relationship, you're an inspiration to others. Through your kindness and faithfulness, you can share Jesus's love both personally and professionally.

Wherever you are in your journey of faith, take time to examine your relationship with Him. What have you learned? In what areas do you want to grow? How is God calling you to serve Him? Prayerfully consider how these answers affect your work itself and the way you relate to others on the job. Allow the Lord to direct and answer you. He may call you to pray faithfully for your coworkers; He may direct you to mentor (or be mentored by) a fellow employee; or He may ask you to develop a new skill that in time He'll use.

Through this evaluation process, press into Him. Read your Bible, pray, and surround yourself with strong Christian friends. As you do, you'll find that your peace, joy, and faith will grow, allowing you to live a more rewarding life for Him! *—GM*

. . . .

*Lord, I love You. I know that You will give me
all I need to meet the challenges You bring my way.
Help me to glorify You in all I do. Amen.*

Hitting the Mark

*Whenever you failed to do one of these things
to someone who was being overlooked or ignored,
that was me—you failed to do it to me.*
Matthew 25:45 MSG

I had been freelancing full time for more than a year when I ran into a woman who used to work at the same company where I had been employed. She waved to me from across the room at a local restaurant. I walked over to her table, and we chatted for a few moments. Then she introduced me to her husband. "This is the writer I told you about, honey...the one who always took time to talk to me and the rest of the cleaning staff." I smiled and shook his hand. As I walked back to my table, my heart was smiling, too.

I miss the mark much of the time, but for once I had hit it. My taking the time to chat with her on the nights I worked late had really meant something to her. And I knew it had meant something to God, as well.

See, we should never let a person's title or position determine how we treat that person. Whether you run into the janitor or the vice president, you should be equally friendly. Love doesn't see titles—only people. —*MMA*

. . . .

*Father, help me to see others
the same way You see them. Amen.*

Achievement

*Ah, Sovereign LORD, you have made the heavens and the earth by
your great power and outstretched arm. Nothing is too hard for you.*
Jeremiah 32:17

I recently sold a children's book to a publishing house I've been
trying to break into since I started writing. I was so excited!
But as contract negotiations went back and forth, it became clear
I would have to accept a no-compete clause. The clause is pretty
standard these days, but this would mean I could no longer show a
series of children's books I'd cowritten with a long-time friend and
respected colleague to other publishers. She and I had crafted a
beautiful proposal for those books, but if I signed this contract, I'd
be forced to pull out of that partnership. My agent, my husband,
and other close friends assured me, "It's just business," but I knew
to my coauthor, it would feel personal...and it did.

I'll soon be celebrating the release of my book, but I'm sad-
dened by the way it went down. My former coauthor is no longer
chummy with me, and I don't know how to make the situation
right. But here's the thing—God does. So I've given it to Him.

Business isn't always easy. It isn't always fair. Sometimes
others get hurt along the way, despite our best intentions. I've
learned I have to give God the situations I can't fix. He can handle
them. My God is a God of turnaround and restoration. I know
I can trust Him, His ways, and His timing. He knows how this
story ends. —*MMA*

. . . .

*Father, please keep my heart right and help me
to be sensitive to all parties involved in my business decisions.
I pray for turnaround and restoration. Amen.*

DAY
76

The Balancing Act

Fight the good fight of the faith.
1 Timothy 6:12

Balancing commitment between faith and work can be difficult. At times, bosses or clients may question your commitment to your job, or they may honor your coworkers for success achieved through lowering their ethics or living for their jobs.

I've experienced this. I've struggled against the pull to be more like some peers. And though I was committed to my job, I've found I had to be more committed to my convictions and my family's time. Unfortunately, that trait isn't always honored in business. Sometimes others gained promotions or glory, but in the end, I appreciated the peace of mind that my faith gave me. For me, the trade-off was worth it.

If you're finding it difficult to balance your convictions and your job, don't get frustrated or doubt yourself. Follow the truth. Fight the good fight of faith and do what you know is right. Then rest in the peace of mind that only Jesus gives as you trust Him to promote you and give you favor. It might be in a completely different position with another company, but God will honor your faithfulness. —*GM*

. . . .

Lord, thank You for giving me this job. I commit to following
You with all my heart, regardless of the pressures others
try to place on me. Help me to stand strong in Your truth
and to see the value in the stand I take. Amen.

Temple Maintenance

Do you not know that your bodies are temples of the Holy Spirit,
who is in you, whom you have received from God?
You are not your own.

1 Corinthians 6:19

Do you ever just make time for yourself? When is the last time you took time out for a facial or a massage? Or spent an afternoon hiking or simply sitting in front of a fire, reading a good book? If Michael Jackson was topping the music charts the last time you spent a whole day taking care of you—it's time to take a personal day.

If you don't occasionally make time for you, you'll burn out faster than that dollar-bin relaxation candle you recently purchased. God wants you to take care of yourself. If you don't, you won't have the energy, enthusiasm, or will to take care of business or your family.

The Word says that our bodies are the temples of God, so we need to do occasional temple maintenance. And in between those special pampering days, we should start taking better care of ourselves. Drink more water. Get eight hours of sleep. Find time for fitness. Make time for Bible study and prayer. Take time to have fun with family and friends. In short, we should enjoy the journey—especially the rest stops! —*MMA*

· ·

Lord, help me to find time in my busy schedule
to take care of me. Help me to make good choices
for my spirit, body, and soul. Amen.

Give Them Your Due

The whole law can be summed up in this one command:
"Love your neighbor as yourself."
Galatians 5:14 NLT

Do you feel like you're always going the extra mile and being taken advantage of? I imagine Abraham felt the same way when Lot chose the best piece of land. Remember that story?

Abraham followed God's leading and gathered all his family, traveling for months before finally arriving at the new land. But after being there a short while, they discovered there wasn't enough land and water to support all the people and flocks. So Abraham told Lot, "We're going to have to separate. Choose whichever piece of land you want, and I'll take whatever is left over." Lot looked around and chose the beautiful, lush, green valley, leaving Abraham an old, dry field.

Don't you imagine that Abraham felt used and unappreciated? But that's not where the story ends. See, God told Abraham to climb the highest mountain and look in every direction. Then He said, "As far as you can see, I'll give it all to you." That's the kind of God we serve.

When you're good to people, God will make sure you come out on top. God sees you preferring other people. Nothing that you do goes unnoticed by Almighty God. Honor others, and God will honor you. —*MMA*

. . . .

Lord, help me to treat others as You would have me do. Amen.

DAY
79

Through His Eyes

People look at the outward appearance,
but the LORD looks at the heart.
1 Samuel 16:7

I remember when I first learned that "Gretta" had been promoted. I almost fainted. Gretta wasn't a very hard worker, and she was always causing strife within the ranks.

I discovered that my coworkers were also quite dumbfounded by Gretta's move up the ladder. We basically spent one entire lunch hour trashing Gretta. We criticized everything from her educational background to her lack of personality. It felt good at the time, but as I did my devotions that night, the Lord brought it back to my remembrance. Then He took me to this Scripture in 1 Samuel. Although He didn't speak audibly to me, I could hear that still, small voice saying, "You don't know Gretta's heart." He was right. I had judged her unfairly. Maybe she did deserve the promotion—but even if she didn't, I had no right to judge her.

It's not our job to judge any person's merit or worth. Only God knows that person's heart. All we can be responsible for is ourselves. If you tend to judge others too quickly, ask God to help you see your coworkers through His eyes. His vision is 20/20! —*MMA*

. . . .

Lord, remind me that I do not see all that You do.
Help me to treat others kindly and without prejudice. Amen.

Lily Life

Therefore I tell you, do not worry about your life, what you will eat or drink; or about your body, what you will wear.
Matthew 6:25

Every once in a while, I catch myself obsessing about something—a past conversation or a project's due date. When I realize I've started to worry, I stop and pray for God's help to let the worry go.

In this hustle-bustle world, it's important to remember that God is in control. He's masterfully created the universe and our place in it. Nothing illustrates this better than Matthew 6. In this chapter, Jesus reminded the people that God creates the lilies of the field. Nothing the flowers do helps them to grow. It's all God. As beautiful as those intricately designed flowers are, God cares for us even more. He ended by saying, "Do not worry about tomorrow, for tomorrow will worry about itself" (Matthew 6:34).

If you find that you worry about things, consider this verse. Then when something disturbing arises, let God's Word comfort you. As His Word becomes more real to you, you'll rest more easily, knowing that you are more precious and cared for than the lilies of the field. —*GM*

. . . .

Lord, You are greater than anything else.
I trust You with my life and ask You to help me not worry
about tomorrow or anything in my life. Amen.

The Best Kind of Thinking

As charcoal to embers and as wood to fire,
so is a quarrelsome person for kindling strife.
Proverbs 26:21

I once worked with a woman who was an exceptional team builder. She could rally a group of people to work harder and longer than ever before. When challenges came her way, she wasn't always happy about it, but she always gave people the benefit of the doubt. Through experience, she'd learned that workers sometimes face unusual challenges, and her example taught me a valuable lesson: to think the best of others.

Over the years, I've tried to keep this lesson at the forefront of my mind. There will, of course, be those few difficult, incompetent workers, but most people want to excel at their jobs. Now, while you may have to deal with a few bad apples, wouldn't you rather err on the side of thinking the best of someone who didn't deserve it than the other way around?

God wants you to be a peacemaker wherever you go. He wants you to stand out as someone who avoids strife and builds others up. As you do, the light you reflect—His light—will grow, and others will trust and follow. —*GM*

· ·

Lord, help me to see the best in others.
Help me to be a peacemaker who builds others up.
Help me to be a light for You in everything I do. Amen.

Speak Up

I am not ashamed of the gospel, because it is the power
of God that brings salvation to everyone who believes.

Romans 1:16

Have you ever been afraid to voice your opinion? Too often everyone else in the company feels free to say exactly what is on their minds, but you can't manage to utter a single syllable. I am usually capable of saying exactly what I think—sometimes too easily, I might add—but I remember a time when I couldn't open my mouth either.

I was in a brainstorming meeting with my peers; we were debating whether we should run a certain controversial comic strip in our ultraconservative newspaper. Politically correct comments rolled off everyone's tongues. My peers seemed to be in favor of running the comic. When the discussion came around to me, my heart beat fast and hard. I wanted to say something insightful and uplifting. I wanted to change the atmosphere of the room. But instead, I said nothing. I've relived that moment many times, wishing I wouldn't have been so afraid to say what I thought.

If you've ever stifled your comments for fear of upsetting someone or saying the wrong thing, you know how icky you feel afterward. Be wise in what you say, but don't live in regret. Don't let fear stop you from speaking your mind, or better yet, His mind. —*MMA*

. . . .

Lord, help me to always speak Your mind. Amen.

On Your Way to the Corner Office

A heart at peace gives life to the body, but envy rots the bones.
Proverbs 14:30

Staring at the walls of my green cubicle, I wondered if God even knew I existed. It seemed everyone around me was moving up in the company, but not me. No matter how hard I worked, no one seemed to notice or care. Ever been there?

It's an unpleasant place to be. A what-about-me mentality eventually leads to jealousy, envy, bitterness, and hopelessness. So if you're dwelling in what-about-me land, head for the border!

If you can't be happy when your coworker finally gets promoted, God won't be able to bless you with your dream job. If you can't celebrate when your boss is awarded a Caribbean cruise for a job well done, God won't be able to reward you with company perks.

When it seems everyone's dreams but yours are coming true, work to keep your heart right. Keep your eyes on God, and He will make your dreams come true, too. Don't worry when you see others getting blessed. He has more than enough blessings to go around. —*MMA*

. . . .

Lord, help me to be happy when my coworkers realize
their dreams because I know that, in Your time,
my dreams will also come true. Amen.

Favor for a Lifetime

Surely, LORD, you bless the righteous;
you surround them with your favor as with a shield.
Psalm 5:12

Finding favor with your coworkers and your superiors is a good thing. It certainly makes your work environment more pleasant, right? But if you achieve that favor by constantly trying to impress them, you'll have to keep working to maintain that place of favor.

In other words, if you are your director's favorite employee because you stay late and keep working after everyone else in your department has gone home, you'd better learn to love the late nights. Pretty soon you'll probably be expected to come in on Saturdays, too, in order to maintain that favored status. That's the funny thing about gaining favor through your own means—you always have to "work it" to maintain it.

That's not the kind of favor the Bible speaks of. Psalm 30:5 says the Lord's favor lasts a lifetime. Isn't that good to know? We can't fall out of favor with God because we haven't met our quota of good deeds or hours in a week. He is a God of mercy. He loves us. We don't have to earn His favor. We just enjoy it. —*MMA*

. . . .

Thank You, Lord, for crowning my head with Your favor.
Help me to walk in Your supernatural favor
with my coworkers and superiors. Amen.

Ward Off Worry

*Do not be afraid, little flock, for your Father
has been pleased to give you the kingdom.*

Luke 12:32

Layoffs. They happen. And when they do, it's scary. When my writing contract was up for renewal, believe me, I was sweating it. We get used to having those paychecks show up every two weeks, because they help us pay the bills that show up every month, right? It's only natural to be concerned when people all around you are cleaning out their desks. But you don't need to worry.

Worry never changed a thing. When I was waiting to hear whether I'd be rehired by my company, my husband said the most comforting thing to me. He said, "Honey, that company is not your source. God is your source." Such wisdom from such a cutie! He was right.

No matter what is going on around you—no matter how many people pack up their offices; no matter what state the economy is in; no matter how many pink slips have been distributed—God is your source. No matter what! Philippians 4:19 (NLT) says, "This same God who takes care of me will supply all your needs from his glorious riches, which have been given to us in Christ Jesus." So, don't worry. God is on the throne, and heaven's economy is just fine! *—MMA*

. . . .

*Lord, I trust You with my career and my finances.
I love You. Amen.*

A Cubicle by the Window

Do not think of yourself more highly than you ought,
but rather think of yourself with sober judgment,
in accordance with the faith God has distributed to...you.

Romans 12:3

Isn't it funny how small things can determine someone's perceived importance? Some revere those who are born to a certain family. Others honor those who have certain possessions. In office society, corner offices and those with windows are coveted. They're given to the chosen, the honored few.

Everyone wants to be respected. If you have made it to that position of respect and honor, don't forget that there was a time when you didn't have the corner office or window view. Once, you were the one desperately trying to prove yourself to the office veterans.

When it comes to respecting others, it's best to follow God's example. He never looks down on you because of what you do or don't have. Instead, He looks at your heart. And even when you were covered with ugly ungodliness, He sent His Son to die for you.

As you go through your day, don't forget to show compassion and kindness to those around you. Value everyone for the people that God made them to be. After all, that's what's truly important. *—GM*

. . . .

Thank You, Lord, for helping me to value others.
Show me how to be an example of Your compassion
and kindness to them. Amen.

Nagging Relaxation

*On the seventh day, God had finished his work of creation,
so he rested from all his work.*
Genesis 2:2 NLT

I admit it: I'm terrible at relaxing. A multitasker to the core, I try to fill my time—even my days off—with as many projects and chores as possible. At work, if I'm on the phone, I organize my desk at the same time. At home, if I stream a Netflix show, I simultaneously flip through the magazines that have curiously appeared on my desk. The worst part is that, if I don't keep up this frantic pace, I feel guilty, as though I'm not taking every opportunity to be productive.

I have to remind myself that relaxation was God's idea. He didn't tell us to take a day off because He wanted to torture us. He did it because He knew that we needed to rest. We need to refill our reserves and declutter our minds at least once a week. We need a weekly mental health day.

If you're like me and relaxation is a practiced art, start practicing this week. With a refreshed mind and spirit, you'll be able to tackle your job with more efficiency than ever before—minus the guilt. —*GM*

. . . .

*Heavenly Father, I know that You want me to take a day for rest.
Help me to do that so I'm more relaxed and productive. Amen.*

That Nasty Nepotism

You too, be patient and stand firm.
James 5:8

Okay, so he went from delivering the mail to being your manager in no time flat. Is he qualified for a managerial position? No. Is he knowledgeable about the area he now manages? No. Is he a relative of the big boss? Bingo!

As aggravating as it is when nepotism runs rampant, you must still honor your manager. It's not his fault that he was shown such favor. He probably knows he isn't qualified and might even be feeling a bit threatened right now. The worst thing you can do, professionally and spiritually, is challenge his authority. Instead, find ways to honor him. Look for ways to help him succeed. Don't give into your flesh that's whispering, "Let's undermine him and make him look really bad." Be an asset to him.

Even if you feel that position should've been yours, let it go. If you keep your heart right and walk in love, a promotion will be in your future, too. God honors those who honor Him, and by honoring your boss (even when you don't want to), you're honoring your heavenly Father. You may not be related to someone who can pull the strings for you in your company, but you are in good with the Creator of the universe. And that's a connection you just can't beat! *—MMA*

. . . .

Father, help me to always honor my superiors. Amen.

Somebody, Stop
This Merry-Go-Round!

*But seek first his kingdom and his righteousness,
and all these things will be given to you as well.*
Matthew 6:33

I worked full time at an inspirational magazine, my girls were little, and I was a crazy person. There were days when I felt like I was on a merry-go-round that was spinning about 100 mph. In addition to work responsibilities, I had to take my children to after-school endeavors, help them with their homework, pick up the dry cleaning, do some laundry and maybe a little light housework, and so on. Then, if I felt really ambitious, I'd work out and shower before my husband came traipsing in from his long workday. By bedtime, I was spent.

Yet that was the time I'd reserved for God. Many times, I found myself falling asleep before I'd even read an entire passage in the Bible. Or I'd manage to finish my Bible study but snooze all through prayer time.

This became a pattern, and the Lord began dealing with me about it. It finally dawned on me that I should be giving God the *best* minutes of my day, not the leftovers. So that's been my daily goal ever since. And you know what? I've discovered that God can multiply my time. When I put Him first, He gets involved in the rest of my day. So give God your best minutes today, and He will bless the rest of your day. That's just the kind of God He is! —*MMA*

. . . .

Lord, I give You my best minutes today. Amen.

Rain Down Fire

A person's wisdom yields patience;
it is to one's glory to overlook an offense.
Proverbs 19:11

Sometimes when working with difficult people, I've imagined that I could pull a big lever and make them disappear through the floor. Nice, huh? This most often crosses my mind when someone is giving me 1,001 excuses or playing devil's advocate.

When I came across Luke 9:52–56, I realized I wasn't the only one to have felt this way. In this passage, Jesus and His disciples had entered a Samaritan village but hadn't received a warm welcome. In response, the disciples asked if they should "call fire down from heaven to destroy them."

Can you feel their frustration? Surely there's been a time when you wanted to call down fire from heaven on someone who was making your life hard. Thankfully, Jesus wasn't as easily offended, because He corrected His disciples. He knew the Samaritans were acting out of ignorance and needed His patience. In the same way, we need to have patience with others. Far more than judgment, those who irritate us need our patience.

The next time you're tempted to grab that imaginary lever or call down fire from heaven, take a moment—and a deep breath—and pray for patience. You might be the first one to show that person mercy. —*GM*

. . . .

Lord, help me to have patience and overlook offenses. Amen.

Comparisons

Pay careful attention to your own work,
for then you will get the satisfaction a job well done,
and you won't need to compare yourself to anyone else.
Galatians 6:4 NLT

Okay, let's have a Dr. Phil moment. Step outside of yourself and take a good look. Are you really doing the very best you can every day on the job? Are you reaching the goals you set for yourself? Are you meeting and exceeding your job requirements? If you are, celebrate with me, sister! Maybe you don't have a corner office (or even a corner cubicle), but if you are giving it your all, you are more than all right!

So why do so many of us feel badly about ourselves? I'll tell you why—we fall into the comparison trap. And we fall short when we compare ourselves to others. The result? Feelings of inadequacy, despair, and insecurity follow, and none of those feelings are from God.

I once read a plaque that said, "God isn't interested in your ability—He is interested in your availability." You should always strive to do your best, then feel good about your efforts. God isn't comparing you to others, so you shouldn't do it, either. Your best is plenty good enough for God. —*MMA*

. . . .

Father, help me feel good about my good work...
and help me stop comparing myself with others, too. Amen.

Mount Everest

If you have faith and do not doubt...
you can say to this mountain,
"Go throw yourself into the sea," and it will be done.
Matthew 21:21

I recently read a bumper sticker that said, "Focusing on our problems blinds us to our blessings." Isn't it amazing how God uses little things to get our attention? I love that. It's so true, isn't it? If we look long enough at our problems, they'll seem to get bigger and bigger. What started as a molehill suddenly looks like a big old mountain—a mountain that blinds you to all the blessings in your life. Before you know it, you're facing the Mount Everest of problems!

Rather than dwelling on how big your problems are, think about how big your God is. Start counting all the blessings in your life!

If you have trouble meditating on God's goodness instead of on your problems, I have an assignment for you. Start keeping a little praise journal. Every day, find something to praise God for—the sunny day, your pay raise, your health, and so on. Thank Him for the little things, and soon your big problems won't seem so big anymore. —*MMA*

. . . .

Thank You, God, for the blessings You shower down
on me every day. I love You. Amen.

Mr. Grumpy

A cheerful look brings joy to the heart.
Proverbs 15:30 NLT

He was always grumpy. He hated his marriage, he hated his job, he hated everyone in the office.... From what I could tell, he hated his life. Call me crazy, but it became my mission to get a grin out of this guy. He didn't make it easy. He grouched and grumbled every day. Once, as I headed to the lunchroom, I offered to bring back a soft drink for him. "Are you trying to kill me?" he grumbled. "Do you know what's in that junk?"

This guy was a real piece of work. I didn't make much progress with that grumpy old guy, but I did manage to muster a smile or two out of him over the years. When I moved to take another job, he even gave me a hug at my going-away luncheon. The entire office gasped. I'll admit, I was pretty surprised, too.

You know, there are grumpy people at every workplace—people who'd rather scowl than smile. Don't let their grumpiness steal your joy. Instead, share your joy with them! Go out of your way to be nice to them. Just think...you might be the only Christian in their lives. —*MMA*

. . . .

*Lord, fill me with Your joy that I might
share it with others. Amen.*

No Limits

The Spirit itself beareth witness with our spirit,
that we are the children of God: and if children, then heirs;
heirs of God, and joint-heirs with Christ.
Romans 8:16–17 KJV

When you look in the mirror, what do you see? Do you see a woman who is smart and talented, or do you see a woman who never quite measures up? Often the limitations that we place on ourselves have nothing to do with who we really are, or the strengths God has given us. They're more about how we see ourselves. Even if the rest of the world sees us as confident, smart women, we limit ourselves by our own view.

If you're limiting your success and peace of mind because of how you see yourself, immerse yourself in God's Word. If necessary, talk to a pastor or counselor. God doesn't want you to live with the heaviness of thinking you're not good enough. As a child of God, you are His heir and a joint-heir with Jesus. Through the sacrifice of Jesus Christ, you *are* good enough—regardless of what others say or have said...and regardless of what you've ever done. If you don't believe me, just ask your heavenly Father. —*GM*

. . . .

Jesus, thank You for Your sacrifice. Help me to see myself
as God's heir and a joint-heir with You. Amen.

DAY 95

Straight from the Top

Your word is a lamp for my feet, a light on my path.
Psalm 119:105

"If you want to know God's will, you've got to study His Word," the minister said. He also said that if we really want to know someone, we've got to spend time listening to him, because a person's character can't be separated from his words. The two go hand in hand.

As simple as his message was, it resonated with me. Instead of discovering God's will through His Word, we sometimes haphazardly throw up a prayer and attach an "if it's Your will" to it. We treat God like an absent parent we barely know. Of course, God sees the big picture in our lives, and His ways are not always our ways (Isaiah 55:8), but that doesn't mean we can't more clearly grasp His character through His Word.

If you're struggling with a dilemma—a job change, an illness, an ethical question, or whatever—turn to God's Word to better understand His will in the situation. Don't treat Him like an absent parent. Get to know Him as your Father who loves you and cares about the things that concern you. —*GM*

. . . .

Lord, I trust You and pray that through Your Word,
I'll discover Your will. Amen.

Aim for Excellence

Whatever you do, work heartily, as for the Lord and not for men.
Colossians 3:23 ESV

Early in our marriage, I wanted to become a good cook, but I had very little experience in the kitchen other than pressing Start on the microwave. So I made copies of all the recipes my mama made on a regular basis and decided to begin there. One evening, as I was proudly making dinner for my cute hubby, I scanned the pantry for the two cans of cream of mushroom soup the recipe called for...but I was all out. I did, however, have two cans of golden mushroom soup, so I just used them instead.

So not the same.

Jeff couldn't even pretend he liked the dish. In fact, twenty-seven years later, he still loves to share that culinary disaster story. He's never been able to look at a can of golden mushroom soup again without cringing.

The lesson here? If you're going to do something, do it right. Do it with excellence. Don't take the easy, more convenient way and then hope it works as well as if you'd followed the exact directions. That's just asking for a less than adequate outcome. (Ask my hubby!)

This kitchen wisdom applies to the workplace, too. Whatever task you're assigned, don't just do it to get it done. Do it right and with the right attitude. Do it with excellence. Don't compromise, substitute, or take the easy way out. Instead, do everything with purpose, precision, passion, and patience. That's the recipe for success. —*MMA*

. . . .

Lord, help me always to strive for excellence. Amen.

Questions, Meetings, and Tension Headaches

Oh, that my ways were steadfast in obeying your decrees!
Psalm 119:5

There are days when I'm set to work. I know what I need to accomplish. I have everything I need...and then the phone rings. And it continues to ring all day. Between the phone calls, I get questions from coworkers. Throw in a couple of unexpected—and unproductive—meetings, and *voilà*, I have a totally wasted day, complete with a tension headache. I've been so distracted that I haven't accomplished anything.

Unfortunately, distractions come in all shapes and sizes. In the office, they're endless phone calls, long meetings, and water cooler banter. In your spiritual life, distractions can be people, fear, or the business of life. Basically, anything that keeps you from focusing on God and spending time with Him is a distraction.

As you determine to spend time with God in prayer every day, ask Him to help you prioritize your day. As you make this a part of your life, you'll begin to understand true productivity. You'll begin to differentiate the necessary to-do-list items in your life from the distractions. In time, you'll have the satisfaction of accomplishing what He's called you to do. —*GM*

. . . .

Dear Lord, thank You for showing me exactly what I need to do today—for You and at work. Help me to steer clear of distractions. Amen.

Encourage Dreams

My mouth speaks what is true, for my lips detest wickedness.
Proverbs 8:7

Did you know that every time you or I speak, we have the ability to inspire or destroy those around us? Our words are a powerful force. We can encourage our coworkers and build one another up, or we can criticize and spew words that hurt.

I once attended a writing seminar called "Writing for Children 101." I had never written for children, but God had put that desire in my heart. So, I couldn't wait to hear what the instructor had to say. Unfortunately, she had nothing edifying to share. She said: "You can't make a living writing children's books. It's very competitive, and the marketplace is already overflowing with new writers."

I wanted to jump up in the middle of class and yell, "You are a dream squasher! Shame on you!" I don't know how many budding children's writers never embarked on their careers because of her speech, but I know if God hadn't already birthed that vision in my heart, I would've said, "Hey, she must know what she's talking about. Forget this."

Be careful of your words. Keep God's Word in your heart, and let His divine words flow through your mouth. Don't be a dream squasher. Be a dream encourager! —*MMA*

. . . .

Father, use my mouth to speak Your words, not mine. Amen.

No Shortcuts

Everyone has heard about your obedience,
so I rejoice because of you.
Romans 16:19

Everyone wants to be successful. We want to be respected for what we do and rewarded accordingly. But what if there was an easier way? Sure, those books and seminars insist that the road to success is paved with diligence and perseverance, but if someone suddenly offered to pluck you out of obscurity and give you a pat on the back, a raise, and a more prestigious title...who would turn that down? Not many. But the road to success is rarely easy. We must be productive, hardworking, and willing to follow our employer's rules to truly be successful.

The spiritual life is the same. We can't casually throw up a prayer and treat God like a benevolent Santa Claus and expect to receive His blessings. He wants us to be diligent in our faith, determined in our calling, and obedient to His Word. That's when He'll use us mightily. As I heard one minister say, "Don't try to get through prayer what you can get through obedience."

So as you diligently and obediently work to achieve success in your job, be just as diligent and obedient for God's kingdom. Then you'll know true productivity and success. —*GM*

. . . .

Father, I pray that I would be diligent, faithful,
and obedient to You and Your Word. Amen.

An Honest Day's Work

*Moses inspected the work and saw that they had done it
just as the LORD had commanded.
So Moses blessed them.*

Exodus 39:43

K nock, knock...can I come in?" she asked, peeking her head
into my office.

"Uh...sure," I said hesitantly.

It was her—Tammy Talk-a-Lot. Once she entered your
office, you could count on at least a fifteen-minute distraction.

While it seems harmless enough, talking at length with others during the workday is the same as stealing time from your
company. As Christians, we should go the extra mile when it
comes to integrity. We should make sure that we give an honest
day's work for an honest day's dollar. We should have the courage
to say, "I'd love to talk with you after work, Tammy, but right
now, I need to get back to my assignment."

Granted, this response won't make you the most popular gal
at work, but sometimes you have to be willing to ruffle a few
feathers in order to do the right thing. It is possible to walk in
love and integrity at the same time. And rest assured, God will be
pleased with those steps. —*MMA*

. . . .

*Lord, help me to stand up for what I believe—
even if it's not the most popular thing to do. Amen.*

Time for Strength

*You must remain faithful to what you have been taught
from the beginning. If you do, you will remain in fellowship
with the Son and with the Father.*

1 John 2:24 NLT

Have you ever caught yourself treating the time you spend
with the Lord like an obligation, a task to cross off your
daily list, instead of an honor? I have, but I was reminded recently
that it is so much more.

Sitting in a church service, I was listening to a minister talk
about his trip to Israel. Out of all the sites he'd visited, he said
he'd found the garden of Gethsemane the most touching, because
it was where Jesus, during His private time with God, found the
strength to endure the cross. I felt duly convicted.

If you're like me and sometimes you struggle to prioritize
the things in your life, decide to take time out for God. Trust me;
it'll make a *huge* difference. Spend some quiet time praying and
worshipping Him. Let Him soothe your mind and arrange
your day. Your time with Him will be so much more satisfying
and your day so much less overwhelming. —*GM*

*Heavenly Father, I want to spend time with You today,
not out of obligation but because I consider it an honor.
Let Your will be done in my life and work. Amen.*

Patience, Please

Be patient, bearing with one another in love.
Ephesians 4:2

How do you react when one of your coworkers acts ugly toward you? Before you get too aggravated, put yourself in his or her shoes. Better yet, try to see that person through the eyes of Jesus.

I recently heard a pastor tell about his encounter with a woman who manned the phones at a local pizza place. He shared that he frequently called that establishment to order pizzas, and the first thing they always asked him for was his phone number. So, knowing the routine, he simply gave his phone number as soon as the woman answered. She said, "Sir, I didn't ask you for your phone number. I'm not ready for it, and when I get ready for it, I'll let you know." In fact, she spoke so ugly to him that he was tempted to order twenty pizzas and cause her to make dry delivery runs to fake addresses all over the city. Instead, he chose to respond in love. By the end of their conversation, she was throwing in hot wings and two-liter sodas and coupons for free pizza. He had won her over through the love of Jesus.

Why not follow his example? Go that extra mile and respond in love. God will reward you, and He gives even better gifts than free hot wings. —*MMA*

. . . .

Lord, help me to always respond in love. Amen.

Dance of Joy

Oh, visit the earth, ask her to join the dance! Deck her out
in spring showers, fill the God-River with living water.
Paint the wheat fields golden. Creation was made for this!
Psalm 65:9 MSG

Do you remember the 1980s sitcom *Perfect Strangers*? The premise of the show was simple. Two distant cousins lived together in Chicago. Larry was an uptight American; Balki was an ex-sheep herder from the Isle of Mypos. Together, they got into all sorts of jams. One of the things I remember most was Balki's dance of joy. Whenever something exciting happened, Balki would grab Cousin Larry and begin a festive shuffle that included kicking out their legs to each side in sync.

While this may not seem like the most spiritual application in the world, I do think that everyone needs a dance-of-joy kind of friend, someone who will get excited when something good happens. When a friend or coworker has good news, get excited for her. Instead of comparing your successes to hers and silently wondering why it wasn't you, celebrate the fact that something exciting has happened. That kind of selflessness is part of encouraging others in the blessings God has given them. And just as He blesses them, He'll bless you, too, because He's got enough joy to go around. —*GM*

. . . .

Lord, thank You for Your blessings.
Let me be an encouragement to others. Amen.

What-ifs

Wait patiently for the LORD. Be brave and courageous.
Yes, wait patiently for the Lord.

Psalm 27:14 NLT

"Courage is not simply one of the virtues," C. S. Lewis said, "but the form of every virtue at the testing point."

There are moments in your work when you need courage. Maybe you've been given a tough assignment, earned a much-desired promotion, or have to give a big presentation. Whatever it is, you're more than a little nervous about it.

Well, take a deep breath; you're not alone. Everyone has faced situations where they weren't sure they could accomplish what they'd been asked to do. A thousand *what-ifs* may be racing through your mind—what if I stammer, what if I fail, what if they're sorry they hired me, what if, what if, what if?

If you're doing what God has called you to do and you're on the career path that He's laid out for you, then you're going to be fine. It doesn't mean that everything will always be easy, but you can relax knowing that the Lord is with you. —*GM*

. . . .

Dear Lord, thank You for going before me and being with me.
Help me to have courage and to trust You to show me
everything I need to do. Amen.

Build a New Climate

Be imitators of God...and walk in love.
Ephesians 5:1–2 NKJV

I was fresh out of college with a journalism degree and no place to use it. I had interviewed with a few area newspapers, but no one was hiring. So a local optometrist took mercy on me and hired me to do receptionist work. Eventually he even taught me how to pretest patients on his expensive equipment. He showed me how to do a frame selection with patients. He helped with billing when I couldn't get the numbers to add up. He had great patience with me. In fact, he looked for ways to compliment me. (And the Lord knows, there weren't many things he could choose from—I was clueless to this type of work!) I've never forgotten his kindness.

You know, we can take a lesson from this generous man. We should look for the best in our coworkers and subordinates. We should find ways to encourage them. We should be patient when someone drops the ball. We should help one another and point out one another's strengths instead of magnifying each other's weaknesses.

When you sow good things into your coworkers, you'll reap a harvest of good things—kindness, mercy, grace, patience, and more. Look for ways to build up your coworkers today and watch the climate of your office change. —*MMA*

. . . .

Lord, help me to build others up, not tear them down. Amen.

Admit It

*You can't whitewash your sins and get by with it;
you find mercy by admitting and leaving them.*
Proverbs 28:13 MSG

Okay, so you missed it. You dropped the ball. You made a whopping big mistake. It happens. You're only human, and you're going to miss it once in a while—that's normal. How you handle your mistake is what's important. Your first instinct might be to hide under your desk or figure out a masterful way to defend yourself. Neither is the best course of action.

Proverbs 28:13 tells us not to whitewash our sins and try to get away with them. In other words, we need to take responsibility for our mistakes. Go to your boss and say, "Hey, I messed up. My intentions were good, but I missed it. I'm sorry." Not only are you able to better fix what is broken the sooner you address it, but you will be known as a person of integrity who owns her own mistakes.

See, if we are quick to admit our mistakes and ask for forgiveness, we open up the door for a second chance. God is a God of mercy. He wants to see you prosper and succeed in your endeavors, but you must be honest and sincere with Him and others. Freely admit when you are wrong. He will reward your honesty. *—MMA*

. . . .

*Lord, help me to be quick to admit my shortcomings
and just as quick to receive Your mercy. I love You. Amen.*

Wait

*Since before time began no one has ever imagined,
no ear heard, no eye seen, a God like you who
works for those who wait for him.*

Isaiah 64:4 MSG

Do you remember the story of Sarai, Abram, Hagar, and Ishmael? God told Abram that He would give him a son, and that his offspring would outnumber the stars in the sky.

No doubt he shared the news with his wife, Sarai, who desperately desired to give Abram an heir. But she was getting too old to bear children, and she grew tired of waiting. So she convinced Abram to sleep with her maid, Hagar. Hagar became pregnant and eventually gave birth to a son—Ishmael. But Ishmael wasn't the promised heir. If Sarai had waited on God, she would've discovered that God already had a good plan—a plan for Sarai to become pregnant and give birth to Isaac, the promised heir. I'm sure every time Sarai looked at Ishmael, she was reminded of her mistake. Sure, God still gave her Isaac, but only in *His* time.

Have you birthed any "Ishmaels" at the office lately? Have you been so impatient, waiting on God's perfect plan for your life, that you've jumped ahead and worked out a plan of your own? If so, go back to God. Wait on His plan. It's a really good one! *—MMA*

. . . .

Lord, help me to wait patiently on Your plan for my life. Amen.

Blessing

The LORD bless you and keep you; the LORD
make his face shine on you and be gracious to you;
the LORD turn his face toward you and give you peace.

Numbers 6:24–26

The Lord gave the above blessing to Moses. He instructed Moses that this was how Aaron and his sons should bless the Israelites. One of my pastors has used this blessing at the end of his sermons for years, and I love it. Each week, these words are like a warm blanket that he wraps around his congregation to remind them of the Lord's love and favor.

As you go through your day, remember this blessing. Recite it to yourself, write it down, or enter a reminder in your phone so you'll be able to see it. These words weren't man's creation but God's. This is His blessing to His people. It is for you and me and every other believer. If there are people in your office who don't know the Lord, pray that they'll come to know Him so that this blessing can become theirs and "the Lord will make his face shine upon" them, too. —*GM*

. . . .

Lord, thank You for Your favor and blessing.
Thank You for blessing and keeping me, for making
Your face to shine upon me and being gracious to me,
and for turning Your face toward me
and giving me peace. I love You. Amen.

Detours

*The LORD himself goes before you and will be with you;
he will never leave you nor forsake you.*

Deuteronomy 31:8

There came a point in my career when I just wanted a change. I had worked in the same field for over eight years, and though I had a great relationship with my boss, there was no longer any challenge in my job. So I started looking for something new.

I received a call from an employer in a new field, and I excitedly accepted the position. It wasn't long after I started, however, that I discovered the job wasn't for me. I didn't care for the duties or the corporate structure. At first glance, that job change might have looked like a false step, but I have come to see God's hand in the whole process. Through that short detour, I found the courage to do what I really wanted to do. Without that detour, I wouldn't have had the guts to try.

Sometimes situations arise that leave you thinking you've made a wrong turn. But remember: just because something is hard, it can still be in God's plan. His Word says that He goes before you and will never leave you. With Him, how can you ever really fail? —*GM*

. . . .

*Lord, I trust You with every step I take, because I know
that You go before me and will never leave me
nor forsake me. Amen.*

Take Off the Limits

I am the LORD, the God of all mankind.
Is anything too hard for me?
Jeremiah 32:27

I recently read an inspiring quote by Mary Kay Ash that said, "Don't limit yourself. Many people limit themselves to what they think they can do. You can go as far as your mind lets you. What you believe, you can achieve."

I love that quote. Mary Kay Ash might be the first one who spoke it, but as Christian working women, we are called to live it! You should be excited about that, because God is limitless. In other words, He has removed the limits where you're concerned. The only thing stopping you is you. Don't let your lack of confidence stand between you and your dreams. Know that if God called you, He will equip you. No job is too hard. No task is too big.

On those days when you feel less than capable, remember this: We don't go by our feelings, we go by our faith. Our feelings can be (and often are) wrong, but our faith in God can move mountains. That's what the Word of God says, and it's never wrong.

No matter what awaits you at work, no matter what deadlines are looming, no matter what unexpected challenges arise— have faith in God and have faith in yourself. Wake up. Pray. And slay! You've got this. —*MMA*

. . . .

Lord, I put my career in Your hands. I know nothing is too big
for You. Help me to be confident and really go for the dreams
You have placed in my heart. Amen.

DAY
111

Mentors

*I always thank my God for you because
of his grace given you in Christ Jesus.*

1 Corinthians 1:4

We all have mentors—the people we look up to in our professions. During my stint as a sportswriter at a daily newspaper in Indiana, I had such a mentor. Bob was (and still is) the hardest working newspaperman in the business. He didn't just go the extra mile; he went the extra *hundred* miles. I am so thankful for the time I had to work with him. Though he'd never discuss it because he's too modest, Bob has won just about every journalistic award you can win. In fact, he was inducted into the Sportswriters Hall of Fame and the Indiana Basketball Hall of Fame. I always say, "I earned my journalism degree from Indiana University, but I learned the craft of writing from Bob." He worked with me. He coached me. And, yes, at times he was hard on me. But he made me a better writer and, in the end, a better person.

In a world of slackers, moochers, and yes-men, it's so wonderful to have the privilege to work for someone who gives his all every day. Why not take a moment today and thank those men and women who have impacted your life as a working woman? Drop them a note or give them a call. —*MMA*

. . . .

*Thank You, Lord, for placing such marvelous mentors in my life.
Please bless them today. Amen.*

Did You Hear That?

I will listen to what God the LORD says.
Psalm 85:8

I was going through old journals one day, and I found a quote from one of my favorite Bible teachers, Dr. Billye Brim. She said, "There's an 'ear' in the middle of your heart." And I stopped to think about that.

There's a lot of truth in that observation. As Christians, we need to hear with more than just our ears—we need to hear with our hearts, too. And that isn't always easy to do.

In the midst of office craziness, training seminars, and water cooler gossip, it's hard to hear God's voice, isn't it? But it's not impossible. Jesus says in John 10:27, "My sheep know my voice" (CEV). Well, if we're born again, we're His sheep. So we should know His voice. But in order to hear His voice, we have to make time to listen. We need to quiet ourselves before Him every day and listen for His voice.

The Lord's voice can be drowned out by many distractions in the office and the home, but don't allow it. You can't be the best version of yourself—at work or at home—if you don't spend time listening to God on a daily basis. He has all the answers. He knows the future. He has all the wisdom you'll ever need. So tune out the world and tune in to Him.

And don't just listen with your ears; listen with the ear in your heart. That's where you'll hear that still, small voice. —*MMA*

. . . .

Lord, help me to hear You more clearly.
I long to know You more. Amen.

Working for Jesus

If I were still trying to please people,
I would not be a servant of Christ.

Galatians 1:10

Don't you just love to receive compliments? I do. It's nice to hear things like, "I know I can count on you." And it *really* means something when the compliment comes from someone who doesn't give them often.

A friend once worked for a boss who was hard on her. Sometimes during a trying time, she would escape to my office. During those moments, she would shake her head and say, "I work for Jesus, not her." At the time, I didn't completely understand what she was saying, but now I do.

Compliments, though nice to receive, aren't why we should do our jobs well. If a compliment can pick us up, then a slight or an insult can tear us down. In truth, our self-worth should only be dependent on God. That doesn't mean we shouldn't enjoy a compliment, but we should perceive ourselves through God's eyes, not man's. So the next time you receive a compliment or an insult, keep it in perspective. Ultimately, you work for Jesus, not man. —*GM*

. . . .

Lord, thank You for loving me just as I am.
Help me to see myself through Your eyes and not be bound
to what others think of me. Amen.

Big Plans

"I know the plans I have for you," says the LORD.
"They are plans for good and not for disaster,
to give you a future and a hope."
Jeremiah 29:11 NLT

Being in a meeting with her was pure torture because I knew she was going to take her best shot at making someone—maybe even me—look bad before the meeting was over. She used words like darts, aiming at anyone who might come between her and the boss's ultimate approval.

One day I saw her chatting it up in the boss's office, and an eerie feeling shot down my spine. *She's setting somebody up,* I thought. I worried all day that it might be me. By that night, I was a mess. As I went into my prayer time, the Lord reminded me that she couldn't stop the plans for my life that He had already ordained, only my doubt and unbelief could mess that up.

I felt ashamed. I'd had my eyes on her, not on God. I was so worried she might sabotage my position that I never once figured in the God factor. No one can stop God's plan for your life—not even that coworker who's always trying to make you look bad. Get your eyes off her and back onto God. He's got big plans for you! —*MMA*

. . . .

Lord, help me to keep my eyes on You. Amen.

Ah, Youth!

*Be joyful. Grow to maturity. Encourage each other.
Live in harmony and peace.*
2 Corinthians 13:11 NLT

Growing up, my older brother and I had a bad habit of keeping tallies of who did what. If my father asked me to do something, I added it to my "I've done more than you" list. The next time I was asked to do that task, I gleefully responded, "I did it last time." Ah, youth...

It's funny though, because this same type of who-did-what exists in the workplace. If someone has to work harder, she grumbles about picking up the slack.

It reminds me of the story of Martha in Luke 10:38–42. Martha usually gets a bad rap for working while Mary sat at Jesus's feet, but she was a hard worker. She welcomed Jesus into her home and probably wanted to prepare a special dinner for Him. But her hard work wasn't the problem; her attitude was. Instead of listening to Jesus, she became consumed with doing things and compared her work to Mary's.

Working hard is important. In fact, Proverbs 14:23 says "all hard work brings a profit" (NLT), but don't get caught up in comparing your work with someone else's. It's better to work harmoniously with others than to demand equality. —*GM*

. . . .

*Lord, help me to live in peace and be of one mind
with my coworkers. Amen.*

Something to Work With

How long will this wicked community grumble against me?
I have heard the complaints of these grumbling Israelites.
Numbers 14:27

Nobody knows the trouble I've seen. Nobody knows the sorrow..." Have you been singing the blues lately? Have you been complaining about your job? Your coworkers? Your life? When you open your mouth, are you spewing words that could be the chorus for a bad country song? Listen, I get it. We all go through difficult seasons, and it's easy to grumble our way through those valleys. But there's a better way. No matter how bad your situation is at work, you need to find something positive and praise God.

Have you ever heard the expression "Complain and remain or praise and be raised"? It's really true. Complaining never changes anything for the better, but praising changes the condition of our hearts and the atmosphere of our workplace. Not to mention, God appreciates our praise.

You have to give God something to work with in order to change your situation. Your negative words and sour attitude can tie God's hands. C'mon, now. Take off those dark glasses. Put away that harmonica. Stop singing the blues. Give God praise and give Him something to work with today! —*MMA*

. . . .

Father, I praise You today for all that You've done in my life,
and I praise You for all that You're going to do.
I love You. Amen.

Intuition? Maybe.
Discernment? Oh Yeah!

The heart of the discerning acquires knowledge;
the ears of the wise seek it out.

Proverbs 18:15

Have you ever had a feeling about taking a course of action but didn't know why? You just sensed it. Some may consider this intuition, but for the Christian, it goes beyond that. Somehow, in our spirits, we just know the right thing to do or how to handle a situation. This is discernment. And when it comes to working with people, you just can't beat discernment. It can help you accomplish your goals more quickly and effectively.

This verse says it all: "The heart of the discerning acquires knowledge; the ears of the wise seek it out." You can't get much clearer than that. As wise, working women, we should seek discernment. In fact, if we're smart, we won't be able to help but turn to God to do our jobs better.

If you need to work effectively and efficiently with others, ask God for discernment. Listen when the Lord leads you to handle things a specific way. As you rely on His Spirit, you'll enjoy more success. —*GM*

. . . .

Lord, thank You for giving me discernment.
I want to see things the way You see them. Amen.

Putting Out the Flames

When you walk through the fire, you will not be burned;
the flames will not set you ablaze.

Isaiah 43:2

Firemen aren't the only ones who put out fires. At times I've felt like I was one crisis away from donning the red hat and fireproof jacket. Okay, so maybe part of me just wanted to climb down the nearest ladder to get away from the flames.

No matter what position you hold, there are days when you'll feel that you've accomplished nothing more than standing in your office holding an imaginary hose to put out the projects that inexplicably combust. When those days come, don't let feelings of failure, anger, or panic get the best of you. Remember, God will give you the wisdom you need to prioritize your work, handle the crisis, and get the job done. Step back and take a breath. Collect your thoughts. Don't just react but pray and ask God for wisdom.

Some days, your job is to put out fires. But when the day is over, take the time to thank Him for giving you inspiration and keeping you calm. More than anyone else, He's with you, not as a silent partner but as the One who helps you work things out and be a success. —*GM*

. . . .

Lord, thank You for Your wisdom and Your peace.
Regardless of what comes across my desk,
I will give You thanks for it. Amen.

DAY
119

Facets

Let the loveliness of our Lord, our God, rest on us,
confirming the work that we do.
Psalm 90:17 MSG

Women know that life is a balancing act. Many of us work to keep our professional lives intact while doing what we need to do in our personal lives. But what about fun? Often we think we don't have time for fun—but actually, without a little fun, we lose the thrill of doing our jobs and caring for our families. No one is meant to work all the time.

Consider a diamond. A diamond shines the best when it has as many facets as possible. That's the only way light shines through it so that it can glimmer brightly. Similarly, we need facets in our lives. We need those different aspects—work, church, family, friends, fun—to make our lives shine.

On the road to success, make time for fun, even if you have to enter it into your schedule. This isn't a frivolous treat; it's a necessity for success and the ability to enjoy that success. Yes, life is a balancing act, but don't just limit it to the must-dos on your to-do list. Make time for fun so that you can shine brightly for Jesus. —*GM*

. . . .

Lord, let Your loveliness rest on me.
Let me balance my life and work so that the work
of my hands is pleasing to You. Amen.

Supernatural Favor

*The LORD had made the Egyptians favorably disposed
toward the people, and they gave them what they asked for;
so they plundered the Egyptians.*

Exodus 12:36

Do you know that God can cause people who don't particularly like you to do nice things on your behalf? It's true.

When the Israelites left Egypt, headed for the Promised Land, they left in a hurry. But on their way out of town, they asked the Egyptians for articles of gold and silver and for clothing. Now the Israelites and the Egyptians weren't exactly bosom buddies, yet the Israelites were given all they asked for and more!

I can just imagine the Egyptians loading up sacks of silver and gold to give to the Israelites and saying, "I don't know why I am giving these precious items to you, but enjoy them. Have a good trip!"

See, God can cause even your enemies to treat you favorably. He can cause that supervisor who despises you to recommend you for a raise. He can prompt your grouchy boss to grant you those vacation days you requested so many months ago. Just honor God. Obey His voice and thank Him for His supernatural favor that is causing your enemies to bless you. —*MMA*

. . . .

*Lord, I thank You that even my enemies desire to bless me
because of Your supernatural favor. Amen.*

A Little Coffee
and a Whole Lotta Jesus

*You will receive power when the Holy Spirit comes upon you.
And you will be my witnesses, telling people
about me everywhere—in Jerusalem, throughout Judea,
in Samaria, and to the ends of the earth.*

Acts 1:8 NLT

Many people, when they hear the word *evangelism*, automatically think about knocking on strangers' doors or going on mission trips. But you are an evangelist everywhere you go—even in the workplace. Though what you can say might be limited, you can still share God's goodness and joy through your attitude.

People will see a difference in you. They'll know there's a peace in your life that they're missing. Don't assume that, because you're not standing behind a pulpit, you can't minister. Sometimes just by showing kindness, you can impact someone's day. And hopefully, one day they'll ask what makes your life different.

You *can* effect change in others just by sharing the goodness that God has shown you. Ask someone who needs a friend to lunch. Take a cup of coffee to someone who's stressed. Those little niceties will go a long way in sharing the love of Jesus with the lost. —*GM*

. . . .

*Lord, I lean on the power that Your Holy Spirit has given to me
to be a witness for You in the workplace. Amen.*

The Dream List

*Write the vision and make it plain upon tablets,
that he may run who reads it.*

Habakkuk 2:2 NKJV

Years ago, I made a list of things I wanted to do in my life-time. It included sailing around the world, attending the Olympics, going on a cruise, and traveling Europe by train with my husband. I haven't accomplished all of them, and some, like skydiving and hang gliding, I'm no longer interested in doing. (Pretty much anything that has the potential of me plummeting to my death is off the list.) Still, it's fun to review the list and see how many I've accomplished, which ones I no longer want to do, and others that are still to come. And, of course, there are always new adventures to add.

Writing down a vision—whether personal or professional— is a great way to keep your dreams in front of you. As time passes, your list can be a great encouragement. During those times when you feel like you're going nowhere, your list can remind you of all you've accomplished. Then you can thank God for giving you the desires of your heart, because He is the author and fin-isher of your life. —*GM*

. . . .

*Lord, thank You for giving me dreams and visions.
I dedicate them and my life to You. Amen.*

Faithfulness

*The master was full of praise. "Well done, my good
and faithful servant. You have been faithful in handling
this small amount, so now I will give you many more
responsibilities. Let's celebrate together!"*
Matthew 25:21 NLT

*F*aithfulness. Easier said than done, eh? Being faithful means being loyal and consistently doing your best regardless of the circumstances. Even if your boss is asking you to accomplish way more than anyone else in your department, faithfulness means you will give it your all. If you've been passed over for promotion time and time again, faithfulness means you still show up for work and do your best. When your new team lead talks to you like you're a total moron, faithfulness means you work hard to make her look good.

God honors faithfulness.

You give God something to work with when you're faithful. In fact, when you're faithful, you put yourself in position to be blessed and promoted. You see, when you're faithful in the little things, you earn God's trust. Once God knows He can trust you—look out! Rejoice in that fact and praise God for your job. Praise Him that He is maturing you as you stand faithful. Praise Him for what's to come. —*MMA*

. . . .

*Lord, help me to be faithful—no matter what.
I am trusting You for promotion. Amen.*

Translate This

If any of you lacks wisdom, let him ask of God,
who gives to all liberally and without reproach,
and it will be given to him.

James 1:5 NKJV

Sitting across from my new boss, Karen, I listened as she gave me promising points about the position that I had just accepted. She rattled off how successful I would be as her newest manager. *Sign me up,* I thought.

Unfortunately, what she said and what was reality were miles apart—but I didn't discover that truth until later.

When she said, "Your staff is set for growth," she actually meant, "All but two employees have quit." When she said, "Your sales goals are on track," she meant, "Last week was the first time in eighteen months that we've even come close." Not quite the translation I was used to.

There are times in the workplace that you'll be misled. It's a fact. When it happens, turn to God for wisdom. His Word says that when you ask for wisdom, He'll give it to you liberally.

Many times, I've thrown myself on God's mercy, begging for wisdom. Thankfully, I've always received it, and you will, too. He'll show you what to do and say, leading you in wisdom the whole way. —*GM*

. . . .

Lord, I need Your wisdom for my situation.
Please show me what to do and say. Amen.

Only One Thing

*"Martha, Martha," the Lord answered, "you are worried
and upset about many things, but few things are needed—
or indeed only one. Mary has chosen what is better,
and it will not be taken away from her."*

Luke 10:41–42

In today's world, women are expected to bring home the bacon, fry it up in the pan, and then find time to run on the treadmill to burn off those bacon calories. Seriously, there are a lot of demands on us, aren't there?

If you're like me, you don't do anything halfway. I am a classic type A personality, taking on way more than one person can handle, then working crazy hours to accomplish everything. Then, of course, I feel guilty for neglecting my family, so I'll spend quality time with them, sacrificing sleep, ordering pizza (because who has time to cook?), and skimping on my time with God. Sound familiar?

Well, like Martha in the Bible, we're worried and upset about many things, when only one thing is needed—spending time at the feet of Jesus. I desire to become more like Mary, but my nature is very much like Martha's. So it's a constant battle. But guess what? When I actually spend quality time at the feet of Jesus, everything else in my life is better. So go ahead. Do the bacon thing, but don't neglect your time with God. —*MMA*

*Lord, help me to become more like Mary and less like Martha.
I love You. Amen.*

Duck!

Answer me when I call to you, my righteous God.
Give me relief from my distress; have mercy on me
and hear my prayer.

Psalm 4:1

Have you ever worked for a difficult boss? I have. One in particular was known for being tough on her staff. She demanded excellence of herself and everyone around her. On the positive side, she never grew complacent. She continued to learn and pushed her staff to do the same. On the negative side, she was merciless when it came to mistakes or less-than-stellar results. She also did not accept excuses, even valid ones. People throughout the organization trembled at the thought of getting in her way. Though I was fortunate enough to never receive her unleashed wrath, I was aware that I was only one incident away from the line of fire.

If you work for a difficult boss, the kind who has everyone ducking to miss her angry arrows, pray. It's not easy, and you may never see a difference in her, but pray. Avoid complaining and pray. Prayer is the only thing that will give you insight into her personality, teach you how to communicate with her, and show you how to gain her favor. It may not be easy, but it's your best defense. —*GM*

. . . .

Lord, I need Your help. Please show me how to have
favor with my boss. Amen.

Tattletale

*The Pharisees and the teachers of the law who belonged
to their sect complained to his disciples,
"Why do you eat and drink with tax collectors and sinners?"*
Luke 5:30

Remember when you were in elementary school and someone would tattle on another student? The teacher would say, "Why don't you just worry about yourself, and I'll handle the other classroom concerns." I was in fifth grade with a guy who thought it was his job to report the wrongdoings of every child in the school. Needless to say, he didn't have many friends.

Well, unfortunately, little tattletales can grow up to be big tattletales, and maybe one of them works in your office. Or maybe it's you. Young or old, there's no excuse for complaining and tattling about somebody else. It certainly doesn't create a very positive workplace environment.

If you're a complainer or tattler by nature, ask God to change you today. After all, who are we to judge someone else's actions? We see only snippets of life, while God sees the big picture. Whenever I begin to look at someone else's faults, I am reminded of Matthew 7:3: "Why worry about a speck in your friend's eye when you have a log in your own?" (NLT).

I don't know about you, but I have enough specks in my eyes to keep me busy for years! —*MMA*

. . . .

*Lord, help me to focus on Your work in my life,
not on others' faults. Amen.*

She Meant Well

*At that point Peter got up the nerve to ask,
"Master, how many times do I forgive a brother or sister
who hurts me? Seven?" Jesus replied,
"Seven! Hardly. Try seventy times seven."*
Matthew 18:21–22 MSG

I had been teaching my little heart out at a writers' conference, and I was really tired by day five. As you might imagine, there was little time to eat. So rather than dive into a full-course meal, I opted for a Snickers and a Diet Coke. In fact, I'd had that same meal a few times throughout the week.

As I headed up the dining hall steps, a woman approached me. She said, "I've been watching you all week. You give so much to others." I smiled, feeling pretty good about myself. Then she continued. "I've also been watching your eating habits, and I'm worried for you." I thought that was a bizarre statement, but I kept listening. "So," she said, "I have something for you." I smiled, thinking another conferee had a gift for me—until she whipped out a diet plan and said I should prayerfully consider it.

Okay, I hadn't seen that one coming.

I wanted to dump my Diet Coke on her head! Sometimes it's difficult not to be offended—especially when a coworker over-steps boundaries or says something that's clearly offensive. But you can ask God to help you not be easily offended. And have a Snickers on me! *—MMA*

. . . .

*Lord, help me not to become easily offended.
I love You. Amen.*

Who's Too Old?

I am certain that God, who began the good work within you,
will continue his work until it is finally finished
on the day when Christ Jesus returns.

Philippians 1:6 NLT

So, I have a divine bucket list. I'm not talking about the items still on my regular bucket list, like running a half marathon, but rather the things I feel God has called me to do. He has put dreams in my heart that I've journaled about, prayed over, and treasured—but not yet accomplished.

I was panicking over this recently, wondering if I was too old to accomplish all the items I had yet to check off. But God patiently reminded me that He is in control. He has written my life with twists and turns and meaning. Therefore, if He is the writer, I don't have to stress over those unchecked items and unwritten pages, because I can trust Him.

Honestly, we probably all have dreams we haven't realized yet, but here's the good news—it's not too late! You're not too young. You're not too old. You're not too dumb. You're not too poor. You're not too anything!

And neither am I.

God will bring forth those dreams in His perfect timing. Spend some time today meditating on those divine bucket list dreams. Commit to pray over them every day until they are realized. It's not too late. God is always on time. —*MMA*

Thank You, Lord, for putting big dreams in my heart.
Help me to realize them in Your timing. Amen.

Going Public

Those who speak for themselves want glory only for themselves,
but a person who seeks to honor the one
who sent him speaks truth, not lies.

John 7:18 NLT

Public speaking is one of the greatest fears among adults today. Some say it is even more prominent than the fear of death. As someone who used to dislike public speaking, I understand how overwhelming it can be. Through practice, my fear lessened. I came to understand that if I had an idea or comment to share, the goal wasn't to elevate myself but rather to get the job done in the best possible way.

If you're terrified of public speaking, begin looking for ways—at church, work, or other organizations—to practice and overcome your fear. Know that when you hold back from speaking up in a meeting or at work, you're withholding the talents God has given you. What you have to share is as worthwhile as that of your coworkers. Ask God to help you gain confidence, overcome your fear, and practice your technique. Through practice and prayer, you'll succeed in ridding yourself of that fear. —*GM*

. . . .

Father, I pray that You'll teach me to speak Your words
in every situation. Amen.

Small Beginnings

*Do not despise these small beginnings,
for the LORD rejoices to see the work begin.*
Zechariah 4:10 NLT

When God impressed on the hearts of my sister and her husband to start a church in their hometown in Indiana, they were excited. He had been a pastor years before, but he'd been building houses and just preaching here and there for some time. My sister, an interior designer, worked with him in his homebuilding business, but she also believed God was calling them to start a church. When they caught the vision for the church, they thought it would happen overnight, but no doors opened. Rather than trying to knock down those doors, they put their vision on the shelf and took another opportunity—working for a worldwide ministry in Texas.

My sister was hired as a communications coordinator. Sounds impressive, but it was really a glorified gofer position. It was not a very glamorous job, but she worked at it faithfully. Eventually, she was promoted to an important position. Meanwhile, her husband remodeled houses and did other odd jobs. It wasn't until seven years later that the doors began to open for their own church.

My sister worked that gofer position with a joyful heart. She and her husband worked and prayed and waited on God with anticipation. They didn't despise their small beginnings, and now they are walking in their dream.

Maybe you're in the waiting season. If so, rejoice! God hasn't forgotten your dream; He just knows the best time for it. —*MMA*

. . . .

Lord, help me to rejoice in small beginnings. Amen.

Tidal Waves

Surely, LORD, you bless the righteous;
you surround them with your favor as with a shield.
Psalm 5:12

Have you ever noticed that when you're good at your job, you tend to be given more responsibility? That isn't a bad thing, but it can lead to overload. As new projects come up, your boss—who is constantly impressed by your efficiency and good attitude—gives them to you without considering the five hundred other assignments on your desk. You're flattered, but it's kind of hard to keep swimming when tidal waves are slamming against your desk.

Ah, the price of good work ethics! As women, we're notorious for believing that if we just reorganize or reprioritize, we can handle immense loads—but we need to be realistic and honest, both with ourselves and our bosses. When your work responsibility becomes overwhelming, pray for direction and, if the Lord leads you to, speak to your boss.

When you need to address a sticky situation, prepare yourself with prayer. Then remember that, just like this verse says, God will "bless the righteous" and "surround [you] with favor as with a shield." —*GM*

. . . .

Lord, thank You again for Your favor.
Please direct me in how to handle the load. Amen.

Supernatural Peace

*May the Lord of peace himself give you his peace at all times
and in every situation. The Lord be with you all.*
2 Thessalonians 3:16 NLT

*T*he peace that passeth all understanding...yes, that's what I need
today. How about you? If your company is in the midst of
restructuring, if you've just been switched to a different job with
new challenges, if it's time for your annual review, if you're experiencing some trauma at home that is making it impossible to
concentrate at work—you need that supernatural peace, too.

Many things come against us in life to steal our peace, but
they can't take our peace if we don't let them. You see, the kind of
peace I am talking about only comes from our heavenly Father.
You can't get His peace from aromatherapy, massage sessions, or
relaxing music. His supernatural peace only comes from above.

Even if your life is turned upside down right now and peace
seems an impossibility, God's peace is available to you. See, His
peace isn't affected by circumstances or outward distractions. If
you aren't experiencing the peace of God today, why not seek it
right now? Ask the Lord for His peace and then thank Him for
it. Peace out! —*MMA*

. . . .

*Lord, I need Your peace today.
Thank You for removing my frantic feelings
and replacing them with Your everlasting peace. Amen.*

Competitive or Jealous?

And now these three remain: faith, hope, and love.
But the greatest of these is love.
1 Corinthians 13:13

Are you competitive by nature? I am. My husband loves to tell how I would never let our young daughters beat me when we played board games during their growing up years. (I don't think that's entirely accurate, but I did like to challenge them.) Now that they are grown and we play euchre, I still don't let them beat me... at least not on purpose. If I'm playing, I'm playing to win.

A competitive nature can work to a person's advantage; it definitely makes me work harder in my chosen career. However, it can also cause a person to behave in a ruthless manner. Apparently, I've been guilty of that, too. I wasn't aware of it until my then-supervisor handed me a copy of a book entitled *Competitive Jealousy* and said, "I just read this book. I think it will also benefit you." Ouch.

Well, like the saying goes, the truth hurts sometimes. If you're struggling with competitive jealousy or a ruthless competitive drive, don't worry. God created you, and He knows just how to correct that competitive spirit so that it works *for* you and not *against* you. He wants you to succeed—but not at the cost of others.

The Lord has prompted me to read 1 Corinthians 13, the love chapter, on a regular basis. Why don't you join me? I promise it will take your love walk to a whole new level. Suddenly, winning at life won't seem nearly as important as winning the lost. —*MMA*

. . . .

Lord, increase my ability to love others. Amen.

Illusions

*May the Lord our God show us his approval
and make our efforts successful.*
Psalm 90:17 NLT

"Time management is an illusion," the corporate trainer said. "You can't manage time; you can only manage what you spend your time doing." He then recommended setting limited daily goals and accepting the fact that only so much could be accomplished within a workday. He was right, but at the time, visions of throwing his daily planner out the window filled my mind. The last thing I needed was someone confirming what I already knew: I couldn't get it all done. The best that I could hope for was to keep the engine running as smoothly as possible.

We all have limitations, but knowing and accepting them are two different things. Yes, God has called us to be productive, but He doesn't expect us to overload ourselves or constantly beat ourselves up for not accomplishing all that needs to be done.

Accept that God has called you to do your best. Ask Him to show you how you can work more effectively, then trust Him to work though you. Realize that the most you can give is your best—at work and at home. Then ask Him to bless and multiply your efforts. —*GM*

. . . .

*Lord, I dedicate my day to You and ask that You bless
my efforts so that they are successful. Amen.*

Take the High Road

Do not seek revenge or bear a grudge against anyone among your people, but love your neighbor as yourself.
Leviticus 19:18

Okay, it doesn't happen often in the publishing business, but it does happen. Once in a while, another writer will knowingly steal your ideas. Gena and I wrote another book together before this one. During that time, we discussed our book with two other writers who were very enthusiastic about our project. We thought they were being supportive, but now we know they were pumping us for information. Just a few months later, the two of them embarked on a book *very* similar to ours.

When Gena and I found out, we felt betrayed, violated, and aggravated. "How could they do this to us?" I asked. I wanted God to zap them or something.

But you know what? Gena and I had to totally give that situation to God. We couldn't let our ill feelings toward them stop our stuff. In other words, we weren't willing to stop our blessing flow from heaven by staying mad at them—even though we felt justified in our anger. As Christians, God expects us to take the high road in every situation—even the ones that hurt our feelings.

Even if you've been betrayed, choose the high road. —*MMA*

. . . .

*Lord, help me to always take the high road,
no matter how hard it may be. Amen.*

What's Right, Not What's Wrong

Indeed, the very hairs of your head are all numbered.
Don't be afraid; you are worth more than many sparrows.
Luke 12:7

Recently I watched an interview with a famous female makeup artist. The interviewer asked the makeup artist for her top beauty tip. The artist said that her best tip wasn't about makeup at all. "When you look in the mirror, see what's right about yourself," she said, "not what's wrong."

Her comment struck me. As women, we can be very critical of ourselves. We think we're not thin enough or attractive enough, maybe we think we don't dress well enough. In the workplace, we berate ourselves for making mistakes or not speaking up or not making the best decisions. We beat ourselves down without anyone else ever saying a word.

If you constantly think about what's wrong with yourself instead of what's right, remember that you are one of God's lovely creations. He doesn't see you as anything other than His precious child. He gave you specific attributes and talents, and He loves you just the way you are. —*GM*

. . . .

Lord, thank You for loving me just as I am.
Help me to see myself through Your eyes
and to stop being so critical of myself. Amen.

DAY
138

Between a Rock and a Hard Place

My mouth will speak words of wisdom;
the meditation of my heart will give you understanding.

Psalm 49:3

My new boss was out of the office, and trouble was stirring. Though he came with an impressive resume, his personality and work style weren't gelling with our office culture. He didn't fit in.

While he was gone, his boss—my *big* boss—began calling each of his employees, asking about his performance. How was he doing? Did he follow through with assignments? Was he helping or hindering the office? I had a bad feeling about it. Some of the employees were diplomatic; others were not.

When it comes to speaking out against someone—even a questionable coworker or boss—be careful. Though you may tell the truth, you could find yourself on the short end of retribution. It's good to heed today's Scripture: "My mouth will speak words of wisdom; the meditation of my heart will give you understanding." Notice that the verse talks about words of wisdom. Do yourself a favor: speak the truth *wisely.* This will protect you from steamrolling over others or being perceived as launching your own full-out assault. —*GM*

· ·

Lord, help me to speak words of wisdom
and to have understanding when I do speak. Amen.

Pork Chops

Do not throw your pearls to pigs. If you do, they may
trample them under their feet, and turn and tear you to pieces.

Matthew 7:6

Has God shown you a glimpse of your future? Has He placed big dreams in your heart? Isn't it exciting? I remember the first time I really heard God's voice concerning my career. It was during praise and worship at church. He showed me that I'd someday have books published, and that I'd be teaching at writers' conferences around the world. At the time, that just seemed ridiculous. I was a magazine journalist who knew nothing about writing books. Yes, I had attended a few writers' conferences, but speak at them? Are you kidding? Still, I held that vision close. I wrote about it in my journal and shared it with my family. I should've stopped there.

Instead, I was so excited about what God had shown me that I told a coworker, too. Can I just share she wasn't nearly as excited for me as I thought she'd be? In fact, she spent our entire lunch hour telling me how difficult it would be to ever make it in the book business. As I listened to her trample "my pearls," like it says in Matthew 7:6, all I heard was "Oink. Oink. Oink." Lesson learned.

Be careful. Don't share your dreams with just anyone. They're too precious to waste on oinkers. —*MMA*

. . . .

Thank You for my dreams, Lord. Help me to keep them
quiet until You're ready for me to share. Amen.

On the Brighter Side

She is clothed with strength and dignity;
she can laugh at the days to come.
Proverbs 31:25

For quite a while, I worked with two women who had a gift for seeing the humor in almost any situation. "Stacy" had an outspoken wit. She said—in a very funny way—what everyone else thought. She had a gift for speaking the truth in a way that completely disarmed others. "Amber" was much more under-stated, but equally funny. A true Southern belle to the core, she saw situations from a different perspective and found the humor in them.

I'm thankful for both women.

When the time comes to either laugh or cry, wouldn't you rather be laughing? I think we all would. When pressures start to mount, look for the person who sees the humor in the situation. That doesn't mean someone who can never be serious or who wields sarcasm, no. Look for someone who can joyfully rise above a situation. Those people are blessings, and you can learn a lot from them.

The next time your work has you down, ask God to help you find the humor in it. You never know who He might send your way. —*GM*

. . . .

Lord, thank You for helping me see the humor in things
so that I can stay positive in my life and job. Amen.

Workloads

What you are doing is not good. You and these people
who come to you will only wear yourselves out.
The work is too heavy for you; you cannot handle it alone.

Exodus 18:17–18

Have you ever heard the expression, "Two heads are better than one"? That can be very true. When you're assigned a project at work, don't be afraid to ask for your colleagues' input. Who knows? One of them may have the final puzzle piece you've been struggling to find.

Why do we have such a hard time asking for help? Do we fear that we'll have to share the credit with somebody else? Are we afraid that we'll be admitting we're not perfect if we reach out for help? Are we afraid of appearing needy and weak? Well, we do need help.

Even Moses needed help when his workload became overwhelming. He was sitting as judge over the Israelites, helping them settle disputes from morning until nightfall, and he was exhausted. His father-in-law suggested that he appoint some godly men to help him judge the simple cases and leave only the difficult ones for Moses. The plan was a God idea, and it worked beautifully. See, teamwork is of God. He never told us to go it alone. So ask for help today. —*MMA*

. . . .

Lord, I give my fears to You.
Give me courage to reach out for help. Amen.

Love Me Some Correction

Listen to advice and accept discipline,
and at the end you will be counted among the wise.
Proverbs 19:20

It was my first Christian writers conference ever. I entered a piece to be critiqued, not mentioning that it had already been published and praised by others. I was confident that writing guru Dr. Dennis Hensley would be duly impressed.

Then the critique came back. I had never seen so much red ink on one page. I glanced at the edits through suppressed tears. That night, I shared the disastrous critique with my husband and told him I might not return for day two of the conference. Jeff looked at me and said, "So, you didn't want to go and improve; you just wanted someone to tell you how great your writing is? Is that right? You could've stayed home and saved a lot of money for that. I can give you compliments, if that's all you want."

Ouch. As usual, he was right. I licked my wounds, read over Doc Hensley's thoughtful and brilliant edits, and went back for day two. Fast-forward nineteen years, and I'm now serving as an adjunct professor, teaching a course at Taylor University where Doc runs the professional writing program. I've come a long way—but I wouldn't have arrived here if I hadn't taken constructive criticism along the way.

Be thankful for correction; without it, we wouldn't grow or improve. Every constructive critique is a chance to learn. Every blunder helps pave the way to ultimate success. The journey of learning and growing and becoming better is one worth taking. —*MMA*

. . . .

Thank You, Lord, for Your correction and for putting people
in my life who care enough to offer constructive criticism. Amen.

My Very Own Cube

Give thanks for everything to God the Father
in the name of our Lord Jesus Christ.
Ephesians 5:20 NLT

Do you know what I find ironic? They tell you to think out-side the box, and then they put you in a boxlike cubicle for eight hours a day. Silly, isn't it?

When I worked for a monthly magazine, we had green "cubes." They were small, and they weren't very attractive. But you could always tell the positive folks in the group, because they decorated their little cubes with great pride. One woman had pearls hanging down over the corners, with lace doilies and satin ribbons everywhere. She was obviously going for a Victorian cubicle look. Another woman had chosen an animated theme, with Poohs, Piglets, and Eeyores all over her Hundred-Acre cubicle. Very cute!

Instead of whining about not having an actual office, my cheery coworkers made the best of the situation. They may not have loved working in a cube all day, but you never heard them complaining about it. They were determined to enjoy every day on the job.

Maybe you're in a cubicle kind of situation today, feeling unimportant and depressed. Don't give in to grumbling and complaining. Instead, start thanking God that you have a job that comes with your very own cubicle. Make the best of your journey—even the cubicle rest stops. —*MMA*

. . . .

Lord, help me to make the best of every situation. Amen.

Distinguished Favor

*Deborah, the wife of Lappidoth, was a prophet
who was judging Israel at that time.*

Judges 4:4 NLT

I love Deborah, don't you? She was a woman who enjoyed favor with God and man. She was a prophetess, judge, and military leader for Israel. Judges 4:5 says that the people went to her "to have their disputes decided." Obviously, they trusted her. Though Deborah was married and possibly a mother, she still worked for the good of her people. She was vital in freeing her people from the tyranny of Jabin, king of Canaan. When the fight for freedom came, she went with the army and counseled Israel's commander.

Did she accomplish these feats on her own? No, she was a godly woman who sought God's will and did what He told her to do.

We can learn from Deborah. She was strong, smart, courageous, and deeply devoted to following God's commands. She didn't allow difficult situations to keep her from serving Him. She didn't spend her days complaining because her people were oppressed. Instead, she rose above the circumstances, followed God, and helped her people

As you go about your work, remember Deborah's example. Work hard. Help people and love God. As you follow God's wisdom, you'll find His favor waiting for you, too. —*GM*

. . . .

*Heavenly Father, thank You for Your favor and honor.
Like Deborah, I want to be a person who works hard for You,
looks to You for direction, and points others to You. Amen.*

Positive Perceptions

Everybody we saw was huge.... Alongside them
we felt like grasshoppers. And they looked down on us
as if we were grasshoppers.

Numbers 13:32–33 MSG

How is your perception? Do you have a positive perceiver or a negative perceiver? In Numbers 13, Moses sent out twelve spies to survey the land God had promised the Israelites. The Bible says that all twelve spies saw exactly the same thing—a land flowing with milk and honey; large, scrumptious grapes; rich, fertile soil...and some very large giants. Ten of those spies were wearing their negative perceivers. They came back and reported how impossible it would be to take over the land due to the resident giants. But two of the spies were wearing their positive perceivers. They came back and said, "Hey, we're well able to conquer those giants and possess the land!"

Basically, ten had faith in the giants, and two had faith in God. They all saw the same thing, but only two men saw the situation through God's eyes. Which perceiver are you using today? Are you looking at your work situation through God's eyes or yours?

Through faith, decide right now that you're going to use your positive perceiver in all situations. Keep your eyes focused on God by staying in the Word. —*MMA*

. . . .

Lord, help me to keep a positive perception,
no matter what. Amen.

Follow the Leader

When the Spirit of truth comes, he will guide you into all truth.
He will not speak on his own but will tell you what he has heard.
He will tell you about the future.

John 16:13 NLT

You want to move up. You want the promotion, but the odds are against you. Maybe you haven't been at your job very long or maybe there is stiff competition, but you know that you could do the job. So, other than working hard and trotting out your accomplishments, how do you go about gaining management's confidence? By listening to the Holy Spirit.

Many assume that God doesn't get involved in business, but if you're involved, He's involved. Ask Him to show you what to do. Don't be afraid to turn to God and His Holy Spirit for answers. Ask Him to help you put your best foot forward and to give you fresh ideas.

God is interested in your success, so if you know in your heart that a job is yours, ask Him to give you the direction you need to wow your boss. Then trust Him to lead you, regardless of the outcome. Whether the job becomes yours or not, continue to trust Him. He knows best, and He knows you best. He won't forget about you or your dreams. He's still on your side! —*GM*

. . . .

Lord, I lean on Your Holy Spirit to guide me in all truth.
Please show me what to say and do. Amen.

Let Me Be Heard

I will speak only the message that God puts in my mouth.
Numbers 22:38 NLT

Have you ever noticed the differences in the way men and women communicate? According to experts, a woman's style of communication is generally much more touchy-feely than that of her male counterparts. We might say "I feel" or "I believe," instead of "I think." We are also more likely to turn statements into questions, like, "I like the production schedule, don't you?" We're more likely to add disclaimers to our statements, such as, "Correct me if I'm wrong, but..." And we are less likely to interrupt others while they're talking. While these differences are fascinating (have a listen in your next meeting), both women and men can be effective communicators and leaders.

Of course, our communication is most effective when we speak what God has shown us. No, we don't need to bow our heads before making every statement, but as we follow the leading of the Holy Spirit and pray about our jobs beforehand, we can be more confident and secure in what we say.

If you're looking for a way to improve your communication skills with your colleagues, ask the Lord for help and for His take on your situation. He can give you the strength, insight, and confidence you need to speak clearly and be heard well. —*GM*

. . . .

Lord, help me to speak Your words in every situation. Amen.

For Such a Time as This

*Who knows but that you have come to your royal position
for such a time as this?*

Esther 4:14

Esther was a risk taker. A strong, faithful woman, she stood for what she believed, even though she knew it could cost her life. It might have been easier to remain silent, but she knew that silence wouldn't save her from danger. Eventually, it would have arrived at her door, so she persevered.

Standing for what you believe in or what is honorable can cost you a lot. You run the risk of losing your job or being banished from the company's inner circle. You might even find that future promotions are unavailable. Are these worthwhile risks? Only you can decide, but living with integrity comes with a price. Unlike some of your coworkers, you have a moral code that surpasses anything written in a policy manual.

The good news is that God blesses obedience. Deuteronomy 28:1 says, "If you fully obey the LORD your God and carefully follow all his commands I give you today, the LORD your God will set you high above all the nations on earth." So don't fear your bosses or coworkers, because when you stand for God's commands, God stands for you. —*GM*

. . . .

*Lord, I trust You to show me how to follow Your commands
with integrity and to stand for what is honorable. Amen.*

An All-Nighter with God

My help comes from the LORD,
the Maker of heaven and earth. He will not let your foot slip—
he who watches over you will not slumber.

Psalm 121:2–3

Ever pull an all-nighter? In college, I basically lived on NoDoz and Diet Mountain Dew in order to stay up and study. Now that I'm in my forties, staying up all night is much harder. (And it takes a whole lot more concealer to camouflage my dark circles.) But sometimes an all-nighter is the only option.

My youngest daughter had just gotten married in the mountains of Tennessee, and as mother of the bride, I had put my life on hold to plan, decorate, and enjoy that special season. I'd also put off work, and that now needed my immediate attention. I ended up staying up all night to turn around a freelance assignment for *Guideposts*, while my hubby and our two dogs snoozed. I felt very alone.

As I prayed for direction about writing the lead to that story, it hit me—God is awake! Somehow that made staying up all night much easier. It was like having a study partner. Isn't it comforting to know that God is always there?

No matter how much work you have on your plate today, God can help you accomplish it. You don't need Diet Mountain Dew or NoDoz—all you need is Him. —*MMA*

. . . .

Thank You, Lord, for being on call, day and night. Amen.

Bite Your Tongue

Do everything without grumbling or arguing.
Philippians 2:14

Have you ever worked for an incompetent boss? I don't mean a boss who occasionally makes bad decisions, but one that leaves you shaking your head every time you deal with him. When he gives his opinion, you think: *That's the most ridiculous (or wrong or dim-witted) thing I've ever heard.* And meetings are really fun, because you get to cringe the moment he starts bestowing his vast wisdom on others.

I've had the unfortunate privilege of working for one of those bosses. It actually got so bad that my coworkers and I made a pact not to complain about him—and that was something we had elevated to an art form. When he pulled out his bag of absurd tricks, we had to bite our tongues. A lot.

Incompetent bosses can prevent us from performing at our best, but the best decision we can make is to refuse to complain about them. Not complaining won't change their incompetence, but it will make work more bearable because you won't be reliving every situation. Complaining can only make a difficult situation worse, so determine to work without complaining. It will help you make the most out of difficult situations. —*GM*

....

*Lord, forgive me for complaining about the things I can't change.
Teach me to stay quiet even in crazy situations. Amen.*

A Short Road

You shall not hate your brother in your heart.
Leviticus 19:17 NKJV

There is an Italian proverb that says, "Short is the road that leads from fear to hate." In the workplace, there are many chances to become afraid. There is the fear that another employee will influence the boss or take over our job. Fears like these can quickly lead from fearing that person to hating everything they do and everything about them. It's a short road.

That's why it's so important to determine to do our very best, while we remind ourselves that God is in control of our future and that we work for God's approval more than man's. That's how we avoid getting caught up in comparing our place in the office with theirs. That's how we protect ourselves from traveling the short road to hate.

If you've found yourself drifting toward fear, jealousy, or hate, ask forgiveness from God and possibly that other person. Don't let your feelings become roadblocks in your professional or spiritual life. Remember that God directs your every step, and nothing that person does against you will have eternal effect. God is your ultimate employer, and He will take care of you. —*GM*

. . . .

Lord, help me to love others the way You do.
Keep me from fear and hatred and teach me to trust You
with everything in my life. Amen.

Drama Queen

*You have made them a little lower than the angels
and crowned them with glory and honor.*

Psalm 8:5

I saw a T-shirt the other day that had *#Dramaqueen* printed on the front of it. I almost bought it, because I've been known to be a drama queen from time to time. How about you? Do you have a little theater blood running through your veins, too?

Sure, we all go through our drama-queen stage in life, but by the time we enter the workforce, we should have outgrown that phase. However, that's not always the case. Whether you have a lingering drama queen inside of you or you work with one, you know that drama-queen syndrome disrupts an office. In fact, it can destroy an otherwise smooth-running workplace. There's no place for drama in the office.

If you wear the drama-queen crown from time to time, ask God to help you become more consistent in your Christian walk. Ask Him to help you grow in the fruit of the Spirit. The Bible says that God has crowned you with glory and honor. You don't need that drama-queen crown anymore! —*MMA*

. . . .

*Lord, help me to become more like You and less like
a drama queen. Amen.*

Don't Go It Alone

As iron sharpens iron, so one person sharpens another.
Proverbs 27:17

It's interesting to notice how many people try to do everything themselves. They want to believe that they don't need anyone else, but actually, others help strengthen them. Maybe they can earn success on their own, but they'll work harder for it and won't have others to celebrate with them once they achieve it. Just ask those who have spent all their time grasping for success without taking time to invest in others. Most would trade some of the success for real friendship and love.

God never meant for any of us to travel through life alone, not personally or professionally. He has given you family members, mentors, and Christian brothers and sisters to make the journey easier, more successful, and more fulfilling. Even Jesus had friends and companions in His ministry, and after He died, those companions—His disciples—continued the work He had begun. So as you work, take time to invest in the people around you. Though it may seem like a sacrificial effort at first, in the end, you will reap the reward. —*GM*

. . . .

Lord, help me to remember to invest in others.
Show me those with whom I could develop
true friendship. Amen.

He Wants to Do What?

*By [the help of] God I will praise His word; on God I lean,
rely, and confidently put my trust; I will not fear.
What can man, who is flesh, do to me?*

Psalm 56:4 AMPC

There is nothing quite as unnerving as a new boss who wants to make radical changes. When an organization has been doing things one way for a long time, mixing things up can cause widespread panic.

I've experienced this a few times. New bosses. New procedures. New insecurities. People either didn't know what to do or were so protective over their areas that the office was one scuffle away from selling ringside seats. Some of the changes I handled with ease; others left me a nervous wreck.

If you're facing new procedures or a new boss, try to keep a cool head. Avoid becoming one of the malcontents (because there will *always* be malcontents) and take plenty of deep breaths. Continue to praise God and rely on Him. As you continue to honor the people in authority over you and trust God with your fears and insecurities, you won't get sucked into the boxing ring. Change may still be hard, but you are more than up to it. You'll be able to do your job with confidence, knowing that you don't need to fear what any man can do. —*GM*

. . . .

*Lord, I rely on You and praise Your Word. I will not fear,
regardless of the situation. Amen.*

What? Forgive?

Bear with each other and forgive one another
if any of you has a grievance against someone.
Forgive as the Lord forgave you.

Colossians 3:13

Is there someone in your office who has offended you so deeply,
you just can't let it go? You see that person, and your stomach
immediately ties into a knot or your heart races. The feelings of
hurt and anger continue to hang on.

Yes, you've been wronged, but you'll never find peace until
you forgive her. You might protest, "You don't know what she
did!" True, I don't know, but God does. And He doesn't tell us to
forgive some of the time. He simply tells us to forgive.

You may have to forgive her several times before it becomes
real. You'll decide to forgive her, but the next time you see her, the
anger and hurt rise again, so you have to forgive her again. Not
only is it important for your spiritual health, but it's important
for your emotional health, too. Until you forgive and let go of the
pain and anger, you'll never have the peace that God wants you
to have. So determine to forgive that person—not only for her,
but also for you. —*GM*

. . . .

Lord, I choose to forgive this person just
as Your Word instructs me to do. Please heal me
from these feelings of hurt and anger. Amen.

F.O.G.

May the LORD smile on you and be gracious to you.
May the LORD show you his favor and give you his peace.
Numbers 6:25–26 NLT

Have you ever heard the expression "walking in the F.O.G."?
The acronym stands for "walking in the favor of God." I
use this expression a lot, like when I find that my seat at a literary
luncheon is right next to the editor I'd been hoping to meet for
several years. I immediately thank the Lord for saving that seat just
for me, and I think to myself, *Yep, I'm just walking in the F.O.G.*
My friends and family and I deliberately look for opportunities to
thank God for His favor.

Have you ever intentionally looked for God's goodness and
favor in your life? If not, why not start today? It's fun, and you
know what? Once you start praising God for His favor that's
operating in your life, you'll start walking in much more favor.
God appreciates that you notice the nice things He does for you
each day.

So when your boss says, "Why don't you take the rest of the
day off today—you've been working so hard," take a moment and
thank God for His favor. Start walking in the F.O.G. today! —*MMA*

. . . .

Thank You, heavenly Father, for the F.O.G.
I praise You for all that You do for me.
You're awesome! Amen.

Courageous Steps

GOD hasn't quite walked out on us after all!
He still loves us, in bad times as well as good!
Ruth 2:20 MSG

Have you ever made a big change in your life? Maybe you've accepted a new position, changed employers, or entered a new field. Maybe you've even moved to a new city for that new job. You don't know what's waiting for you, but you have a peace about your decision nonetheless. Those can be exciting and scary times. You have to trust that you're doing what God wants you to do.

Ruth was a woman who took a chance and changed her life. She left everything she knew—her culture, home, and family—to follow her mother-in-law back to Bethlehem. She didn't know what awaited them, but she trusted that it was the right thing to do. Thankfully, God was faithful. He led her to the exact place she needed to be.

Whether you're on the verge of making a big change in your life or you already have and are waiting to see how it plays out, continue to trust God. If you believe that He directed you to do something different, trust Him to complete His work. Just as He didn't walk out on Ruth, He won't walk out on you. —*GM*

. . . .

Lord, thank You for not walking out on me.
I'll continue to follow Your leading in all that I do and trust
that You'll provide for me. Amen.

Your Dream Job

Not one of all the LORD's good promises...failed;
every one was fulfilled.
Joshua 21:45

I have good news for you—there is no such thing as a glass ceiling where God is concerned. There are absolutely no limits to how far you can go in your career. There is only one roadblock that can stop you on the path to your God-given dreams. No, it's not your boss. No, it's not that nasty coworker who is always sabotaging your work. No, it's not the state of the economy.

It's your mouth.

That's right. Only *you* can stop what God has for you. If you speak doubt and unbelief, you tie God's hands. With every negative confession, you move another roadblock smack dab in the middle of the road. So don't fall into that bad habit. Instead, use your mouth to praise God for all that He has done and all that He is going to do.

Maybe you're not working in your dream job right now. That's okay. God has a plan. Just keep being faithful and only say what He says about your situation, keep working, striving, and focusing your efforts and pretty soon you'll have that dream position. Begin each day saying, "Thank You, Lord, for my dream job. I know it's on the way." Get excited! —*MMA*

. . . .

Lord, keep a watch over my mouth.
Help me to only speak positive things. Amen.

Cheaters

*Cursed is the cheat who has an acceptable male
in his flock and vows to give it, but then sacrifices
a blemished animal to the Lord.*
Malachi 1:14

She had already given her two-week notice. I was sorry she
was leaving, so I told her I'd treat her to a good-bye lunch.
We laughed and talked and enjoyed one another's conversation.
The clock ticked away the minutes too quickly. As our lunch
hour came to an end, I just figured we'd walk back to our offices
together. Instead, she joined another table of friends. "I'm taking
an extended lunch today," she said. "What are they going to do,
fire me?" She was right—the company couldn't do anything to
her. But that was the wrong attitude.

See, when we take a longer lunch break or spend fifteen minutes on a personal call or do some Facebook stalking or post-
ing on social media while on the job, we're actually cheating our
employers. If they are paying us for an eight-hour day, we ought
to give them eight hours of work, right? As Christians, our goal
should be to go the extra mile of integrity. If you do, you won't
go it alone. God will walk with you. —*MMA*

. . . .

*Lord, help me to be a person of integrity in all situations.
I love You. Amen.*

Still Not Listening

Everyone will have to give account on the day of judgment
for every empty word they have spoken.
Matthew 12:36

The office gossip. Yep, it seems every workplace has one. Isn't it amazing how quickly she can move her lips? Of course, she can go through stories pretty quickly, since she only tells half-truths.

I have a good friend who was greatly hurt by one such person. The office gossip started a rumor that my friend was seeing another coworker outside of work, even though both were married to other people. It simply wasn't true! I knew it. My friend knew it. I think even the office gossip knew it, but she didn't care. It made for good storytelling, so who cared? Thankfully, my friend's husband believed her, and their marriage survived the vicious rumor, but it was a challenging time. They ended up in marriage counseling, while the office gossip received a gentle slap on the wrist for her misdeed.

Gossip—whether you're the one telling the lies or the one listening to them—is flat-out wrong. Don't participate in office gossip. Don't fan the office gossip's flame by showing any interest in her words whatsoever. Ask God to help you keep your lips and ears closed whenever you encounter the office gossip.

Here's an idea: why not tell her about Jesus and give her something really worth talking about? —*MMA*

. . . .

Father, protect me from the rumor mill, and help me
to never participate in office gossip. Amen.

Faith Eyes

*The seventh time the servant reported, "A cloud as small
as a man's hand is rising from the sea." So Elijah said,
"Go and tell Ahab, 'Hitch up your chariot
and go down before the rain stops you.'"*

1 Kings 18:44

Remember the story of Elijah and the small cloud? There was a terrible drought in the land. God told Elijah to present himself to evil King Ahab, and He would send rain. Elijah did as God instructed. Still, there wasn't a cloud in the sky. Elijah kept praying and sent his servant out seven times to look toward the sea for signs of rain. Finally, after seven tries, the report came back: "A cloud as small as a man's hand is rising from the sea." Elijah knew it was God and basically told Ahab to get ready for a toad strangler.

Elijah had his faith eyes on.

When you get ready for work each day, do you remember to put on your faith eyes? No, I'm not talking about some new miracle cream that diminishes wrinkles. (But if you have any of that, bring it on!) I'm talking about a state of mind—a faithful way of thinking. It's one of the most important things you can put on each day. A woman's not really dressed for success without her faith eyes. —*MMA*

. . . .

Lord, help me to keep my faith eyes in focus. Amen.

Discerner Malfunction

With their words, the godless destroy their friends,
but knowledge will rescue the righteous.

Proverbs 11:9 NLT

I thought she was my friend. We had shared several long phone conversations while working on the same project. We had even prayed for one another. When questioned about her integrity and work ethic, I went to bat for her, putting in a good word with the vice president of the company. She seemed like such a nice person. Whoa, was my discerner off!

She turned out to be not such a nice person. In fact, once she'd attained her new position, she acted really ugly to me and tried to weaken my credibility as a writer within the company. Wow! I *so* didn't see that one coming.

Have you ever been blindsided by someone? Did a coworker that you trusted turn out to be a rat fink? Yep, we've all been there. It hurts. And sometimes it hurts for a while. But God is the healer of all hurts, and He cares about you. Give God your hurts. Allow Him to mend your broken heart. And ask Him to give you better discernment in the future. Don't trust your gut instinct. It's faulty. Trust only your God instinct. It works every time! —*MMA*

. . . .

Lord, please give me better discernment
and heal my hurting heart. Amen.

Break Out of the Mold

There are different kinds of gifts, but the same Spirit.
1 Corinthians 12:4

Have you ever had a hard time fitting in at work? You've worked as hard as you could to fulfill your boss's wishes, work with excellence, and get along with coworkers, but after all that, you still don't seem to fit. Sometimes it's the result of differing personalities. Other times it's a culture clash. And sometimes, it has nothing to do with you at all. There are dynamics happening within management that affect everyone. You're merely a bystander.

If that's where you find yourself, remember John the Baptist. As special as he was, he didn't quite fit the mold of his day either. Here was this wild man who came out of the wilderness, wearing camel's hair, and eating locusts and wild honey. He was different, but God still anointed him for what he was called to do.

If you don't fit into a specific mold, don't second-guess yourself or hold yourself to an unreasonable standard. If after praying and possibly talking to your boss, you believe that you've given your best, then relax. Make any adjustments you can, but relax. You may not fit someone else's mold, but you will always fit God's. —*GM*

. . . .

Lord, I'm struggling to fit in at work right now.
Please give me wisdom for what to do
and help me to see myself through Your eyes. Amen.

Sinner vs. Sin

*Jesus said, "Father, forgive them,
for they do not know what they are doing."*
Luke 23:34

Have you ever heard someone say, "Hate the sin, not the sinner?" That can be difficult, can't it?

When people are cruel or unfair, it's hard to separate their actions from their person. I've struggled with this at times. I have a hard time getting past the fact that someone has been rude to me or a loved one. Eventually, though, I feel convicted and have to take my emotions to God. I won't say that's always a pleasant or easy thing to do, but I try to forgive and move past the hurt. I know that even though what they did was wrong, I still need to forgive.

But can you imagine how Jesus must have felt? After being falsely accused, tortured, and hung on a cross, He still had the strength to say, "Father, forgive them, for they do not know what they are doing." He separated His accusers' sinful actions from their need for forgiveness.

As you face difficult people, remember Jesus's example. Try to separate the sin from the sinner and bless those who mistreat you. It won't always be easy and it might not even be appreciated, but whether they know it or not, they need your forgiveness. —*GM*

. . . .

*Lord, please help me to distinguish between the sinner and the sin.
Remind me of all that I've been forgiven, and give me
strength to forgive those who offend me. Amen.*

Get the Work Done

*From him the whole body, joined and held together
by every supporting ligament, grows and builds itself up in love,
as each part does its work.*

Ephesians 4:16

Everyone has a job to do. And without everyone working together, things wouldn't run smoothly or, possibly, at all. Imagine a grocery store. What would happen if those who ordered the food didn't do their jobs? How about the cashiers and stockers? Each person plays a role in getting the work done.

It's the same way in the body of Christ. Everyone has a job. If you're called to teach others, you've got one job. If you're called to help administrate, you work behind the scenes, but your role is still important. If you're called to prayer, your work may be done completely in secret, but that doesn't make it any less important.

We're all part of the team of the body of Christ, and your role is just as important as anyone else's. As long as you are doing what God has shown you to do, then you are successful. Take your job—your work and your ministry—seriously. In both, you're part of getting the work done. —*GM*

· ·

*Lord, thank You for calling me to be part of the body of Christ.
Help me to accomplish all You need me to do. Amen.*

On Call

Is anyone among you in trouble? Let them pray.
James 5:13

If you're feeling insecure about yourself and unsure of your abilities, I have good news for you. You don't have to know all the answers. You just have to know the One who *does* know all the answers. If you're lacking wisdom; if you're overwhelmed with responsibilities; if you're having trouble at work—go to God.

James 5:13 tells us to do just that: "Is anyone among you in trouble? Let them pray." Prayer changes things. Have you been hitting your knees on a regular basis? If not, you're missing out. God has all the answers. He knows the exact information you need for your meeting tomorrow. He knows how you can win over your difficult client. He knows it all! And what's more, He's willing to share it all with you.

Prayer is your connection to the Creator of the entire universe. Not only that, you have access to Him twenty-four hours a day, every day of the year. You just can't beat a deal like that! Why not put in some prayer time today? After praising Him for all of your blessings and putting in all of your requests, make sure you take time to listen. God may want to impart some wisdom to you this very day. —*MMA*

. . . .

Thank You, Lord, for being on call 24/7. Amen.

I Thought I Had It Tough

It is strength that endures the unendurable and spills over into joy,
thanking the Father who makes us strong enough to take part
in everything bright and beautiful that he has for us.
Colossians 1:11–12 MSG

Everyone goes through periods of feeling discouraged and frustrated at work. When that happens, we often dream of doing something else—pursuing a dream, finding a different job, entering another field, or going back to school. Though these are fine pursuits and quite possibly God-given desires, we may simply need to remind ourselves that we're part of a greater work. If we're a teacher, we're investing in our students. If we're in sales, we're helping others find what they need. If we're in the medical field, we're assisting others as they cope with their ailments.

Today, think about the greater work that you do. Don't focus on your immediate to-do list. Instead, concentrate on how you help others. Then consider how God has provided for you and your family through your work. Spend time thinking and praying about these things. Though you may eventually find another job or even begin training and preparing for a new one, be thankful for what He's given you right now. —*GM*

* *

Lord, thank You for my job. Help me to remember
the big picture, the ways I help others. Amen.

Unpleasable

*I know that you are pleased with me,
for my enemy does not triumph over me.*
Psalm 41:11

There are times when no matter what we do, someone will not be pleased. Some people won't return our friendship. Some bosses won't trust us completely. Some people will never believe that we measure up. That's why our confidence must be based on what God says about us. For everyone else, we can only do what God's Word instructs us to do.

I received a phone call one day from a friend who was devastated by the loss of an important relationship. Jealousy, pettiness, insecurity, and emotional instability on the part of her friend had whittled away their friendship until nothing was left. In time, with much prayer and soul searching, my friend recognized that this relationship she had valued so much had been emotionally abusive. She had spent years giving in to her best friend's emotional whims, riding them up and down like a roller coaster.

I spent most of that conversation building up my friend's morale and reminding her that she was a smart, kind, and capable person.

If anyone—a boss, friend, husband, pastor, mentor, or boyfriend—has you questioning your value, turn to God. If necessary, talk to an objective third party who is a Christian. Remember that you belong to God's family, and your value depends on Him, not anyone else. —*GM*

. . . .

*Father, thank You for Your love that never changes.
Help me to seek Your favor above anyone else's. Amen.*

A New Way

Many are the plans in a person's heart,
but it is the LORD's purpose that prevails.
Proverbs 19:21

Well, that's the way we've always done it."
Ever heard that one before? Doesn't it just make you want to run out of the conference room screaming? So many times I've wanted to raise my hand and interrupt the meeting to say, "Just because that's the way we've always done it, doesn't mean it's always been the right way!"

Just think...if we hadn't embraced computers, we'd still be writing on typewriters and using that Wite-Out stuff to erase our mistakes instead of just hitting the Backspace key.

When we become inflexible and stubborn, we hinder growth. Yes, there may be times when the old way is still best, but don't automatically dismiss another idea simply because it's different. If you struggle with change or if new ideas make you nervous, ask God to help you embrace change with hope and a positive attitude. Don't be the office ogre who's known for saying, "But, that's the way we've always done it." Instead, be open to new ideas. Start seeing change as a chance to grow. God may have all kinds of new and exciting things in store for your office. —*MMA*

. . . .

Lord, help me to be flexible and embrace change
with hope, not fear. Amen.

A Personal Mission Statement

*Then the Lord answered me and said, "Record the vision
and inscribe it on tablets, that the one who reads it may run."*
Habakkuk 2:2 NASB

A mission statement sums up a company's vision and purpose and answers the question, *Why are we here?* When I moved from a nonprofit Christian organization to a for-profit company in the beauty industry, I struggled to find purpose in the new company's mission statement. The nonprofit's vision had focused on encouraging Christians in their faith. This one focused on selling beauty products. One dealt with eternity, the other with sales.

I wanted to be successful at my new job, but I struggled to find motivation. I had to find a greater purpose than just selling beauty products. Then one day, I worked with a client who was struggling to see her own worth. The time we spent together made her feel special and valued. It changed her, but it changed me too. I found a new personal mission statement: I was to make my clients feel valued and cared for.

Ask God to show you the larger purpose in what you do. He'll help you develop a personal mission statement, and when He does, write it down and make it plain. Regularly remind yourself of why you do what you do, and trust Him to use you along the way. —*GM*

. . . .

*Father, give me a vision, a personal mission statement,
for my work. Then help me keep that vision in mind,
so I never forget why You have me where I am. Amen.*

Have Mercy

Shouldn't you have had mercy on your
fellow servant just as I had on you?
Matthew 18:33

Have you ever made a big mistake at work? Not a little oops but a full-blown *oh no!* kind of mistake? I have. Once in the midst of developing a direct mail piece, I left off a crucial piece of information, a last-minute special guest appearance at an international convention. After my boss's boss called to ask why it wasn't on the final piece, I dove into my notes, only to discover that I had accidentally left it off. I swallowed my pride and admitted my mistake. Oh, that was a painful phone call. She could have yelled, threatened, fired, or placed a letter of reprimand in my personnel file, but amazingly, she was merciful. She began brainstorming about other ways to advertise the appearance. Disaster averted.

If you've ever received mercy, then you can understand the parable of the unmerciful servant (Matthew 18:21–35). You know how thankful you are to receive mercy and how important it is to extend it to others. It's part of the favor and grace that God, through His Son Jesus, showed to you, and it's a reflection of the favor and grace that you should show to others. —*GM*

. . . .

Dear heavenly Father, thank You
for Your mercy, grace, and forgiveness.
Help me to show that same grace to others. Amen.

Holy Rollers, Unite

*Blessed are those who are persecuted because
of righteousness, for theirs is the kingdom of heaven.*
Matthew 5:10

In our day and age, many of us don't think much about being persecuted for our faith. Living in countries that protect religious freedom, we don't face life-and-death persecution. But that doesn't mean we don't face a different type of persecution. If your coworkers top off their workweeks by partying or flirting with immorality, you could be perceived as a holy roller because you refuse to participate. If you walk away from gossip or decline to join the occasional bashing of an absent coworker, you may be labeled as self-righteous. These are types of persecution.

You are living by the standards of your Christian integrity. Others will see that and try to bring you down.

Stand strong. Don't allow the allure of pleasing others make you lower your standards. Understand that persecution is part of living the Christian life. Second Timothy 3:12 says that "everyone who wants live a godly life in Christ Jesus will be persecuted," and the above Scripture says those who are persecuted are blessed. So take heart—you know that God is on your side. —*GM*

. . . .

*Lord, I will stand for You regardless of what others say.
Thank You for Your blessings in my life. Amen.*

Standing at the Cross

Near the cross of Jesus stood his mother, his mother's sister,
Mary the wife of Clopas, and Mary Magdalene.
John 19:25

Women are a resilient bunch. I mean, come on—we endure childbirth, which in itself is an award-winning feat. But in everyday life, too, many of us balance families, friendships, and work, all while keeping a cool head. At home, we cook dinner, talk on the phone, and balance a baby on one hip. At work, we juggle multiple projects, referee opposing sides, and still find the energy to work out with a friend during lunch. We do what needs to be done.

That's why it comes as no surprise that women remained at the foot of Jesus's cross. They were devoted to Him and ready to remain until the end. Even in the midst of brutality and the devastating loss of someone they admired and loved, these women kept their eyes on Jesus and remained.

When challenges come—whether unexpected or the everyday variety—keep your eyes on Jesus. Place yourself at His feet and ask Him to show you the big picture. Let Him give meaning to what you're facing. And remember, you have a God-given strength and resilience to handle whatever comes your way. —*GM*

. . . .

Lord, help me to remain at Your feet and to keep my eyes
on You through any challenge. Amen.

Growing Fruit

If it is possible, as far as it depends on you,
live at peace with everyone.

Romans 12:18

Of course you're not going to *automatically* get along with every coworker in your office. Getting along takes real effort, and from everyone involved. I mean, even the disciples had problems with each other.

In Acts 15:36–41, we learn that Paul and Barnabas had a fight over another coworker, John, who was also called Mark. It seems that Paul didn't want to take Mark along on a ministry journey because Mark had previously abandoned them in Pamphylia, but Barnabas insisted he come along. So Paul and Barnabas parted ways. Paul took Silas to Syria and Cilicia, while Barnabas took Mark to Cyprus. Interesting, isn't it? Both Paul and Barnabas were godly men. They were committed to doing God's work. They were part of the chosen group—yet they had strong differing opinions at times.

Strife happens. Maybe it's happening at your workplace. If so, don't join in the strife fest. Instead, walk away. Turn to God and ask Him to help you be the peacemaker of the group or at least protect you from the war zone. View these strife-filled times as a chance to grow in the fruit of the Spirit. God will use this time in your life to take you to a higher place with Him. —*MMA*

. . . .

Lord, help me to grow in the fruit of the Spirit
and walk in peace. Amen.

Comparison Trap

*It is good to give thanks to the LORD,
to sing praises to the Most High.*
Psalm 92:1 NLT

Do you love to attend home shows? My coauthor, Gena, and I love to go. When we both lived in Texas, we used to tour the finest homes in Fort Worth. There's just one problem. After an afternoon of seeing the finest furnishings and the finest flooring and the most divine accessories, it was hard to go home. Suddenly, everything in my house made me want to redecorate immediately! I looked at my walls, and I wished I had more artwork. I looked at my carpeting, and I wanted hardwood floors. I stared at my countertops, and I desired granite.

You know what? It's the same way in the workplace. The minute you start comparing the size of your office to your coworker's office, you're in a heap of trouble. One comparison leads to another, and before you know it, you're unhappy, ungrateful, and unmotivated.

Instead of comparing, start praising. Be thankful that you have a parking spot that's close to the office building. Be grateful that you have several vacation days each year. Be thankful that you have a job. Bottom line—be thankful. As Psalm 92:1 says, it is good to give thanks to the Lord. It will immediately lift your spirits, and God appreciates it, too! —*MMA*

. . . .

*Lord, help me to be content in my job and stop
comparing myself to my coworkers. Amen.*

Joy Robbers

He will once again fill your mouth with laughter
and your lips with shouts of joy.
Job 8:21 NLT

Have you been robbed lately? No, I don't mean robbed of material things. I'm talking about something else—your joy. See, there are joy robbers in every company. They sneakily cozy up to you, only to steal all of your joy, leaving you drained and depressed. Some joy robbers skillfully put you down. Others give a negative report. Still others criticize you on a personal level. And they are trained to come at you when you least expect it.

When I sold my first devotional book, I shared my joyful news with a colleague who said, "You sold your manuscript to *that* company? I guess it's fine for you, but I wouldn't want my name on the cover of the poor quality books they produce. Of course, that's just me." Nice, huh? Yes, I had encountered a joy thief.

First, never be a joy thief. Seriously. Don't. If you are dealing with joy thieves in your workplace, ask God to help you guard your joy level. You need joy, because the Bible tells us "the joy of the Lord is our strength." Dive into God's Word today and get a joy refill. It's even better than a power shake! —*MMA*

. . . .

Lord, help me to avoid the joy robbers in my life.
Keep me filled up with Your joy, Lord, that my strength
might be renewed. Amen.

DAY
177

Keeping the Peace

Love one another deeply, from the heart.
1 Peter 1:22

My husband, Jeff, was my high school sweetheart, so we practically grew up together. However, during our first year of marriage, we found out that we didn't know each other nearly as well as we thought we did. I couldn't believe how moody he was, and he had no idea that I was so high maintenance. (Okay, he'd had some idea...) We had to learn the true meaning of the word *compromise* or we never would have made it through those first twelve months. Now, over twenty-seven years later, we're still compromising and finding that middle ground, and that's a main reason we have such a happy marriage.

You know what? It works the same way in the office. No, you're not married to your coworkers, but you are with them at least eight hours a day. Spending that much time together is an absolute breeding ground for strife. You're going to disagree with your coworkers—it's a fact of life. But how you handle those disagreements will determine the happiness level of your work relationships. Choose your battles wisely. Be willing to compromise. And look for that middle ground in every situation. If you do, God will take you to a higher ground. —*MMA*

. . . .

Lord, help me to find that middle ground
in every situation at work. Amen.

Hijacked

May the God of peace...equip you with everything good
for doing his will, and may he work in us
what is pleasing to him, through Jesus Christ.
Hebrews 13:20–21

Have you ever handled an assignment differently than the norm? It might have been a better, more efficient, or more effective way, but new procedures and ideas can cause panic and incur a boss's wrath. When confronted, you can be left feeling hijacked. You were flying along doing your work, when suddenly, out of nowhere, your boss jumps on your case about doing things differently. It's confusing and can leave you feeling frustrated and insecure.

In those times, trust God to be your God of peace. Though your boss may not be right in her assumption that there's only one way to accomplish a task, submit to her authority. Acknowledge to her that, in the future, you will communicate your plans before trying a new tactic. Try to please her, but don't let her criticism paralyze you. You *can* do your job. If after trying to please her, you feel that you need to work for someone else, trust God to direct your steps. You are valuable, and your talents will be put to good use. —*GM*

. . . .

Lord, thank You for being my God of peace
and for equipping me to do Your will in my job. Amen.

Joy Supply

Do not grieve, for the joy of the LORD is your strength.
Nehemiah 8:10

As a child, did you ever sing the song "I've got the joy, joy, joy, joy, down in my heart...down in my heart to stay"? That little song packs a powerful message.

If you've got joy down in your heart, you can accomplish anything. You can go through any circumstance and do it all with a smile. The Word tells us that the joy of the Lord is our strength. The devil knows that, so he'll try to zap your joy every chance he gets. If he can steal your joy, he can steal your strength. If he can steal your strength, he can infuse you with some hopelessness and discouragement. In fact, if he has his way, by the time he's done, you'll be so far down in a hole, you won't even be able to see out. So don't allow it! Keep your joy supply full.

Listen to praise music on the drive to work. Take a few minutes at lunch to read from Psalms and Proverbs. Make sure you're getting enough sleep. Take time to exercise and take your vitamins. (I sound like your mother, don't I?) Keep yourself healthy so that you don't give the devil an entrance. Say, "I've got the joy of the Lord down in my heart," and then act like it. —*MMA*

. . . .

Thank You, Lord, for Your eternal joy supply. Amen.

Rejoice

*May the LORD show you his favor
and give you his peace.*
Numbers 6:26 NLT

I had worked a ten-hour day, and I still had another story to write before morning. I was tired. I was discouraged. I was frustrated. And for a brief moment, I wondered if I'd even chosen the right profession. Ever felt that way? How about when you've worked like a dog all month, and when it comes time to pay the bills, you're still short? It's enough to make you want to give up, isn't it? I know.

But I have good news for you. One moment of God's favor is worth a lifetime of labor. In other words, God can turn things around for you in an instant. He can put that screenplay you've been trying to get published right into the hands of a famous director. He can orchestrate a divine meeting between you and the president of your company. (My friend, actor and author Torry Martin, calls those moments holy introductions and divine appointments.)

Don't be discouraged. Don't complain when you have to work late. Don't whine when you have to pay bills. Rejoice! Praise God that He is granting you favor with those who can help you. Just think, your moment of God's favor may happen today. —*MMA*

. . . .

*Thank You, Father, for causing me to have favor
with the right people. Amen.*

Reach Out

Share with the Lord's people who are in need.
Practice hospitality.
Romans 12:13

We had just moved from Indiana to Texas, and I knew very few people. I wasn't chummy with my coworkers yet, and I hadn't met many of my neighbors. However, as an aspiring author, I was making regular trips to a place called Max's E Z Mail in Lake Worth, Texas, to mail manuscripts to various publishers. So some of my very first Texas friends were the folks at Max's. From the very beginning, they were hospitable and made me feel special. They weren't just doing their jobs, they were reaching out to a transplanted Hoosier. When we moved back to Indiana after nine years of living in the great state of Texas, the folks at Max's remained on my Christmas card list because we had developed a true friendship—all because they took time to be friendly.

No matter your role, you have a perfect opportunity to make people feel welcome. A friendly smile goes a long way. Whatever your job, make sure you welcome people into your workplace. Go the extra mile of kindness. You may be the only Christian someone encounters all day. If your workplace is inhospitable, be the one to change your environment. —*MMA*

. . . .

Lord, help me to reach out with Your love and kindness
to all I encounter at work. Amen.

Encourage One Another

*Beautiful words stir my heart. I will recite a lovely poem
about the king for my tongue is like the pen of a skillful poet.*
Psalm 45:1 NLT

Are you a supervisor in your office? Are you rising to the top of your field? Are you on your way to changing the world? That's great! Truly, you should be very proud of yourself. But I bet you didn't do it all on your own, did you? Think back—weren't there mentors and coworkers who encouraged you along the way? If so, then it's your turn to sow good things into others' lives.

As a successful person, you have the opportunity to speak into the lives of others, so choose your words wisely. You should be writing skillfully with your mouth—just like this psalm says. Your words could make or break someone.

That's why I love speaking at writers' conferences across the nation. I meet such wonderful people, and we encourage one another. We speak into each other's lives, helping each other realize the dreams that God has put on our hearts.

Every day, you have the opportunity to speak life to others. Start using your mouth as a skillful poet today. Let God speak through you to encourage others. —*MMA*

. . . .

Lord, use my mouth to encourage others. Amen.

Blessing Blocker

My dear brothers and sisters, take note of this:
Everyone should be quick to listen, slow to speak
and slow to become angry, because human anger
does not produce the righteousness the God desires.
James 1:19–20

You know the type. He comes in late. He doesn't prepare for meetings. He always misses deadlines. His lunch hours are more like two hours. He leaves early almost every day. Yet the bosses love him! (You're thinking of that person right now, aren't you?) Okay, be honest—it makes you angry.

But guess what? As aggravating as he is, that person is not your concern. God wants you to get your eyes off others—even aggravating coworkers—and back on Him. Harboring ill feelings toward this person will only hurt you. In other words, you'll be blocking your blessings. Your anger toward this slacker may be the only thing standing between you and your dreams. So get over it!

Hebrews 12:2 reminds us to fix "our eyes on Jesus, the author and perfecter of [our] faith" (NASB). If you're focused on Jesus, you won't be focused on the guy in the office who is making you so mad. So fix your eyes on Jesus. Give Him your anger and, in return, He will give you love, peace, joy, and so much more. What a deal! —*MMA*

. . . .

Lord, help me to fix my eyes on You
and give up my anger once and for all. Amen.

Compromise

*I refuse to take a second look at corrupting people
and degrading things.*

Psalm 101:3 MSG

Have you ever compromised your faith to fit in with the workplace crowd? It's hard not to participate in the boss bashing at lunch or join the gossipfest by adding your little tidbit of information once in a while.

It's difficult to live a holy life, isn't it? Especially if you are the only Christian in the workplace. But you don't have to go it alone. God will help you. You can also help yourself by filling up with God's Word instead of with things that are contrary to the Bible.

I once heard a preacher say that we need to be careful what goes in and out of the gates that allow entrance into our spirits—the ear gate and the eye gate. That's good advice. If you're watching inappropriate movies or listening to off-color podcasts, you're filling yourself with the wrong stuff. When the opportunity to join in corrupt conversation occurs, you won't have any Word in you to stand strong. Instead, you'll have corrupt stuff to add to the conversation.

Fill up on the Word, and you'll be able to withstand any office peer pressure. Ask God to guard your ear and eye gates today. —*MMA*

. . . .

*Father, help me to fill myself with Your Word
and nothing contrary to it. Amen.*

Paging Wonder Woman...
Oh Yeah—That's Me

He gives strength to the weary
and increases the power of the weak.
Isaiah 40:29

Michelle, I'm going to need you to work late again tonight," my boss said, poking his head into my office.

I grimaced.

"Is that going to be a problem?" he asked, eyebrows raised.

"No sir," I answered, wishing I could go home at the normal hour just once that month.

Is this a familiar scenario? If so, I feel for you. It's tough to juggle all the balls that are thrown at you daily, isn't it? There are some days when I long for a hot bubble bath to soak away the troubles of the world. But in reality, I'd have to take my laptop computer into the tub with me if I were to squeeze a relaxing bath into my schedule. Life is busy—especially for the working woman. Whether you work at home taking care of your family and homeschooling your children or you occupy a cubicle at a large company and come home to your fur babies every night, balancing work and home can be tricky and tiring.

If you're feeling weary today, turn to God. No matter what you are facing, no matter how overwhelming it seems, no matter how tired you feel—God can help you. He will give you strength. Just ask. *—MMA*

. . . .

Lord, renew my strength. Help me to accomplish everything
on my to-do list. I love You. Amen.

Daddy

*I will be a Father to you, and you will be
my sons and daughters, says the Lord Almighty.*
2 Corinthians 6:18

When people work together, there is always the temptation to hold some at arm's length. You quickly learn that there are some you can trust and others you have to watch. You know they'll sell you out if the opportunity arises. It isn't necessarily malicious; it's just business.

So it's comforting to know that we can trust the Lord. In 2 Corinthians 6:18, God says, "I will be a Father to you, and you will be my sons and daughters." Through Jesus's sacrifice, we were accepted as members into the family of God. That's not a trivial thing. Before Jesus, worshippers didn't talk directly to God, nor He to them. Once a year, a priest—at his own peril—entered the inner holy sanctuary to offer amends for everyone's sins. But today, you and I can "approach God's throne of grace with confidence" (Hebrews 4:16).

If you find yourself surrounded by people you distrust, remember that God isn't one of them. He is a faithful Father who sent His Son to die for you. And He did it because you mean the world to Him. —*GM*

. . . .

*Heavenly Father, thank You for making me
Your daughter and allowing me to approach
Your throne with confidence. Amen.*

Pearls and Swine

Do not throw your pearls before pigs, lest they trample them underfoot and turn to attack you.

Matthew 7:6 ESV

You have happy news. You just received a promotion. Finally, you'll receive recognition for all your hard work. Gleefully, you tell a friend all the exciting details—how it's a dream come true and what you want to change in the position. On and on you go, but instead of encouragement, you receive a plastic grin.

When happy news happens, we want to shout it to the world. We're excited and hope that others will be just as excited for us. Sadly, that's not always the case. Instead, they could be comparing your success to their own or assuming that you're gloating.

That's why you need to use wisdom. In the above verse, Jesus warned His disciples about the insincerity of the religious leaders of the day. He wanted them to use wisdom when sharing their good news. He knew that instead of hearing the truth, the leaders would turn on the disciples. Unfortunately, it's the same with all good news.

Instead of saying everything that's on your heart, trust the Holy Spirit to show you what you can share. With this sensitivity, you're more likely to receive the response you desire. —*GM*

. . . .

Lord, help me to have wisdom when I speak,
regardless of what I'm sharing. Amen.

The Good Fight

Whoever loves discipline loves knowledge,
but he who hates reproof is stupid.
Proverbs 12:1 ESV

Ever had a boss who was especially hard on you?
I have worked with many fine editors over the course of my writing career, but one was especially tough. I dreaded turning in my manuscript to her, knowing she'd have lots of edits. In the beginning that was true, but as time went on, I was grateful for her edits because I learned from each one. With every project we did together, I grew as a writer.

Just recently, I was able to thank her for investing in me and making me a better wordsmith. Being the humble, amazing person she is, she downplayed her efforts, but it's true. She was hard on me, but that "tough love" editing is what I needed, and anytime I am privileged to have her as an editor for a project, I am thankful.

No matter what kind of work you do, or how good you are at your job, there's always room for improvement. If you have a supervisor who is especially hard on you, see what you can learn from that person. Don't be defensive. Accept constructive criticism and learn all that you can. God may be preparing you for something greater. —*MMA*

. . . .

Lord, thank You for placing people in my life who
challenge me and push me to do better. Amen.

Devil's Advocate

*Live in harmony with each other. Let there be no divisions
in the church. Rather, be of one mind,
united in thought and purpose.*

1 Corinthians 1:10 NLT

There's always one in a crowd—that person who takes it upon himself to play devil's advocate because no one else knows how things should be done, right? I worked with one of these for quite a while. "Jerry" was detail oriented, talented, intelligent, and passionate about his work. He was also completely irritating. Nothing anyone else did was ever good enough. If there was a problem to point out, he'd do it. Our team would be running with a plan, and Jerry would be standing back, shaking his head because, to him, we were clueless. As talented as he was, his constant criticism stifled his influence in the group.

If you're working on a team, support that team. No, the group isn't going to get it right every time, but you'll be able to make a bigger impact with constructive teamwork than with destructive criticism.

Working with other people can be a challenge, but if we recognize that we don't always have all the answers, we'll be more apt to recognize that others' input and talents are just as valuable as ours. —*GM*

. . . .

*Lord, teach me to work in harmony with others
so that we can be united in thought and purpose. Amen.*

Unstable

*Conduct yourselves in a manner worthy of the gospel of Christ.
Then...I will know that you stand firm in one spirit...
without being frightened in any way by those who oppose you.*
Philippians 1:27–28

I once worked closely with a talented but very angry woman. After several uncomfortable situations arose where this coworker seemed about to lose her cool, my boss and I agreed that I should limit my contact with her. In response, the woman accused me of being jealous of her. Her accusation took me aback. *Was I jealous of her?* I didn't think so, but I couldn't decide what about her affected me so much. After some soul-searching, it hit me: she intimidated the daylights out of me. It wasn't her talent; it was her anger and her ability to look like a victim in any situation. She scared me, and I questioned her mental and emotional stability.

When dealing with someone who is emotionally or mentally unbalanced, tread carefully. Be aware that you are not dealing with a rational person, so your comments and actions are likely to become twisted in their mind. Inform your manager or HR of the situation. Keep your interactions professional, well documented, and pleasant, but refrain from trying to win the person over. It probably won't be possible anyway and could exacerbate the situation. Finally, pray. Pray for wisdom, pray for protection, pray for truth to come to light, and pray for healing for the person. Prayer is always your best strategy. —*GM*

. . . .

*Lord, help me to conduct myself in a manner worthy of You,
and please heal this person. Amen.*

Rain

Anyone who listens to my teaching and obeys me is wise,
like a person who builds a house on solid rock.
Though the rain comes in torrents...and the winds beat
against that house, it won't collapse, because it is built on rock.
Matthew 7:24–25 NLT

Recently someone made a point about the parable of the wise and foolish builders that I hadn't heard before. In the lesson, both men built homes—one on solid rock, the other on sand. The example teaches us to build our lives on Jesus, our solid rock, so that we can live with certainty. And yet, regardless of how you build your house, Scripture says the rains *will* come.

Often we want to find the equation to a content, happy life that is free from any problems. In reality, building our lives on Jesus only means that we have the tools to withstand the storms when they come, not that we'll never face them.

If you're looking for the key to living an easy life—or an easy career path—you probably won't find it. But, if you're looking for a way to rise above challenges, Jesus will be there to help. Instead of praying for the trouble-free path, trust Jesus to show you how to live. It may not be the simplest way, but it will be the best. —*GM*

. . . .

Lord, thank You for building my life on You
so that I can withstand the rains when they come. Amen.

Showing Favor

Then the King will say, "I'm telling the solemn truth:
Whenever you did one of these things to someone overlooked
or ignored, that was me—you did it to me."
Matthew 25:40 MSG

Don't you love giving the perfect gift? Whether it's a Christmas present, a birthday gift, or a simple I'm-thinking-of-you gift, they're fun to give. I love to give presents to friends and family when I know it's something they're going to love—Xbox games for my sons, art supplies for my daughter, an online game subscription for my husband, or a new blouse for my mother. I love it!

It's also fun to give thank-you gifts to those whose kindness means so much. These don't have to be expensive; even small gestures can say so much—an email expressing gratitude, a handwritten card of thanks, or even a Starbucks drink.

As you go about your day, think of the colleagues you can thank. Consider the coworker who gets you what you need on time (or early), the receptionist who answers the company phone, or the office manager who keeps your workplace operational. As fun as it is to treat loved ones, it's also fun to show kindness to those you see every day at work. And remember, as you show kindness and favor to others, it is as though you are showing it to Jesus. —*GM*

. . . .

Lord, help me show favor and kindness to everyone around me,
even those I haven't noticed before. Amen.

Find Your Tribe

Therefore encourage one another and build each other up,
just as in fact you are doing.
1 Thessalonians 5:11

I read an Instagram post that really spoke to me. It said, "Find your tribe. Love them hard." Can I get an amen? You may have several different tribes—I do. My writer friends are in one tribe, and my Bible study buddies are in another. My Texas friends are a great tribe, as are my lifelong Indiana buddies. But you know the one tribe we should all have, yet most of us don't? Other women—especially other working women. Listen, we need each other. We've got to stop this petty competitive jealousy stuff and start supporting one another.

As working women, I think sometimes we're afraid to celebrate other females in the workplace for fear that our friendly support will be viewed as a sign of weakness. So we isolate ourselves. But there is power in numbers, and recent statistics show that women make up 46.8 percent of the current labor force. As we become more prevalent in the workforce, we should stand united and strong. We should take every opportunity to encourage our sisters, mentor them, help them, and promote them.

This isn't a women's lib idea; it's a God idea. Titus 2 speaks of older women mentoring and teaching younger women. Let's do that in the church, at home, and in the workplace. Find your tribe. Love them hard. Do it today. —*MMA*

. . . .

Thank You, Lord, for placing strong, confident,
capable women in my life. Help me to love my tribe
the same way that You do. I love You. Amen.

Tough Choices

*Whenever they have a dispute, it is brought to me,
and I decide between the parties and inform them
of God's decrees and laws.*

Exodus 18:16

Do you make tough choices in your work? Maybe you've had to fire someone or go against popular opinion. Good decision making is a vital part of business. Sometimes it means following the facts; other times it means going with your gut instinct.

Finding someone willing to make the tough decisions isn't as easy as it sounds. Consider Rahab, a woman in the Bible who had to make some tough decisions. At great risk to herself and her family, she hid Israel's spies. If she had been discovered, she and her entire family would have been killed for treason. Still, not only did she decide to hide them, but she also stood firm. She was courageous. In the end, she and her family were saved because of her actions.

If you're in a position that requires you to make tough decisions, rest easy. God and His Holy Spirit are there to help you. Though people may get angry and lash out, be courageous. Remember that it's easy for them to second-guess you when they aren't responsible. God has given you your position, and He's equipped you to do it. —*GM*

. . . .

*Lord, help me to follow Your leading
and make wise decisions. Amen.*

She Is You!

*She considers a field and buys it; out of her earnings
she plants a vineyard. She sets about her work vigorously...
She sees that her trading is profitable.*

Proverbs 31:16–18

Have you ever read Proverbs 31? I mean, really read it in light of your life? So often people visualize a truly godly woman as a quiet little church mouse, but if you read Proverbs 31, you'll see that she is a savvy businesswoman. She is frugal, business minded, and hardworking, much like the modern working woman. She cares for her family, buys land, expands her crops, and gets good deals.

Sound familiar? Sure it does.

She's you as you balance your career and family. She's you when you work to make the best sales and meet your employer's goals, all while serving the Lord with your whole heart.

Don't believe that because you work outside of the home, you will never attain the godly Proverbs 31 woman's image. The truth is that the gifts and talents you have are God-given, and as you use them, you are honoring Him...and that is the true vision of the Proverbs 31 woman. —*GM*

. . . .

*Dear Father, thank You for providing for me and for using me
to accomplish Your will in my family's lives and in mine.
Help me glorify You in all I do. Amen.*

DAY
196

Rules and Dress Codes

*Your obedience will give you a long life on the soil
that God promised to give your ancestors
and their children, a land flowing with milk and honey.*

Deuteronomy 11:9 MSG

Do you have a problem with stupid rules—um, I mean authority? I'll be honest: I sometimes do. I once worked for a company that had a very strict dress code. Women were expected to wear hosiery year-round. Okay, summers in Texas are insane. It's nothing to have an entire month of triple-digit temps. And you know how hot hosiery can be, right? So I used self-tanner on my cleanly shaven legs and went to work without stockings. Needless to say, I was written up before noon. I protested, stating it was too hot to wear hosiery. Besides, my dress was very long. You could only see about four inches of calves! But you know what? None of my reasons were good enough, because I had directly disobeyed my supervisor by ignoring the dress code.

God doesn't want us to obey *some* of the time. He wants us to obey *all* the time. He doesn't want our obedience just when we agree with Him. He wants our obedience no matter how we feel about it. He also wants us to honor those who are in authority over us. So if you're a bit of a rebel like me, ask God to help you follow the rules—all of them. —*MMA*

. . . .

*Father, help me to walk in obedience to You
and those in authority over me. Amen.*

Eureka!

*I came down from heaven not to follow my own whim
but to accomplish the will of the One who sent me.*

John 6:38 MSG

Many of us have things that make our lives rewarding: family, work, or other personal achievements. If we don't keep these priorities in mind, we may wake up years from now far from where we want to be.

I discovered myself in this position a few years ago while attending a Dale Carnegie seminar. The speaker asked us to list the ten most important things in our lives. I rattled them off the top of my head: God, family, health, friends, etc. Then he asked us to rank them. Suddenly, I realized that my priorities were out of whack. Certain priorities were at the top of my list, but they weren't where I spent most of my time. I believe that was a divinely appointed *eureka*.

If you are unclear whether your priorities are straight, make a list of the ten most important aspects of your life. Then rank them from one to ten. If you aren't spending your time on important things, ask God to help you rearrange your schedule so that you can accomplish what He's called you to do. —*GM*

. . . .

*Lord, help me to accomplish Your will.
You know the things that are most important to me.
Please help me to make time for them. Amen.*

Best Imitation

A new command I give you: Love one other. As I have loved you,
so you must love one another. By this everyone will know
that you are my disciples, if you love one another.

John 13:34–35

I finally had an office of my own at the nonprofit company where I worked. I couldn't wait to decorate it. I didn't have a bulletin board, so I taped a few family pictures on the back of my door. That way, I could look at my loved ones throughout the day. Well, in the midst of my gleeful decorating, my supervisor poked her head into my office.

"No, I'm sorry. You can't do that," she barked. "We don't allow the use of tape on our walls or doors."

"Oh, is that all?" I said, smiling. "The personnel office supplied me with 'office-friendly tape,' guaranteed not to damage anything."

"Still, it looks unprofessional," she added.

"But they are on the back of my door," I reasoned. "No one will see them but me."

"I want them down by morning," she ordered and walked off.

I had a decision to make. I could follow her instruction with a Christlike attitude, or I could give her the raspberries. In the end, I removed the pictures and even forced a smile when I saw her the next morning.

If you're feeling mistreated, follow Christ's example. Don't give your difficult supervisor the raspberries; give her the love of Jesus instead. God will honor your Christlike attitude. *—MMA*

. . . .

Lord, help me to walk in love every day. Amen.

Stinkin' Thinkin'

I can do everything through Christ, who gives me strength.
Philippians 4:13 NLT

I love to read. I especially love to read children's books—which is good, since I also write books for children. However, once in a while, the devil will use that simple activity to make me feel inferior. It usually goes something like this: I pick up a really great children's book. I devour it because it's so wonderful. Then I sit around wondering things like, *Why would God call me to write books for children when there are so many other amazing children's book authors?* Of course, this wondering activity leads into the whole feeling-sorry-for-myself routine, and the day usually goes downhill from there.

Pretty pathetic, isn't it? It's not only pathetic but also self-destructive. And what's more, God doesn't appreciate it. Are you also guilty of this kind of wondering? If you find yourself participating in this negative thought process—stop! It doesn't matter if you're not the very best in your chosen profession. God didn't call you to be the best. He just called you to be the best version of yourself. Comparing yourself and your work to others is never a good idea. Instead, let those who are better than you are inspire you to greatness. Learn from them; don't envy their success or talent. Use that energy to meditate on God's promises, such as: "I can do everything through Christ, who gives me strength." Now that's something worth thinking about! —*MMA*

. . . .

Lord, help me to stop my negative thinking. Amen.

Cutting Back

*People are counted as righteous, not because of their work,
but because of their faith in God who forgives sinners.*
Romans 4:5 NLT

The company was cutting back, and the trickle-down effect had reached the lowest level: office supplies. Something as simple as a ballpoint pen could usually be acquired with relative ease, but not anymore. My boss called me to her office. "We have to cut back," she said, "so here ya go." Out of her pencil drawer, she handed me a hodgepodge of capless old pens. I stood there a moment feeling confused and more than a little irritated. *I'm not even worth a decent ballpoint pen?* I wondered. I walked back to my office, sat down, and stared at the pens. *How has it come to this?* I thought and then decided to foot the bill for my own pen.

Now, a pen may seem pretty petty, but in the workplace, many things can make us feel unappreciated. Over the years, I've tried to remember that inconsideration usually isn't personal. It's just part of the system.

If you feel underappreciated, try to remember that most of the time, it isn't personal. It's just the way things work. Ask God to give you insight into management's decisions. Understanding what they're facing will help you have more compassion for their decisions. —*GM*

. . . .

*Lord, give me the insight and understanding
to take management's decisions in stride. Amen.*

For the Team

*Just as our bodies have many parts and each part
has a special function, so it is with Christ's body.
We are many parts of one body, and we all belong to each other.*
Romans 12:4–5 NLT

Not long ago, I was watching the National Cheerleading Association finals on television, and I was amazed at the skill level of the athletes. I was also sad for one squad that dropped a very important stunt. It collapsed somewhere in the middle, and down came the formation, totally throwing off the entire routine. Needless to say, that squad didn't win.

You know, we can learn from cheerleaders when it comes to our workplaces. (And I'm not just saying that because I cheered in high school and college, raised two competitive cheerleaders, coached several squads over the years, and wrote a cheerleader devotional). First off, they're cheery and they're leaders—both good qualities for the office. We can also take a lesson in teamwork from these fine athletes. See, if we get out of sync with one of our coworkers due to a disagreement or a lack of understanding, it throws off the entire office. Or if someone is relying on you and you're off doing your own thing, the whole formation will fall. So get in sync! Be a team player. If you learn to do those things, you and your coworkers will really have something to cheer about! —*MMA*

. . . .

*Father, help me to support my coworkers as we work
together to accomplish great things. Amen.*

Did I Say That?

*Friends, don't get me wrong: By no means do I count myself
an expert in all of this, but I've got my eye on the goal,
where God is beckoning us onward—to Jesus.*

Philippians 3:13 MSG

Early in my career as a newspaper reporter, I was asked to cover the filming of *Blue Chips*, a movie about basketball that was being shot, in part, in Indiana. I watched as Rick Pitino, then coach of the University of Kentucky, arrived on the set. I desperately wanted to scoop the other news outlets, so I prepared some questions in my head, then walked up and asked if I could interview him. He was gracious yet intimidating, standing there in his Armani suit. "Sure," he said. And before I could stop myself, the words "Wow, you smell really nice" rolled right out of my mouth. I wanted the floor to open up and swallow me. He smiled while I regained my composure. Thankfully, I wasn't escorted off the set.

I learned some valuable lessons that day. First, don't just formulate great questions before an interview; pray for God's guidance, too. Second, no matter how badly you mess up, God can fix it. He gave me favor with Coach Pitino, and that interview led to several others with big-name coaches and athletes. Third, leave your mistakes behind and move forward. By looking forward, I was able to concentrate on the task at hand and succeed. Looking back would not have produced the same results.

The next time you mess up on the job, remember this: God is the God of both our good and bad days. Trust Him and you'll come out smelling like a rose. —*MMA*

. . . .

Lord, help me to let go of my mistakes and move forward. Amen.

Bloom Where You're Planted

Think of all the hostility he endured from sinful people;
then you won't become weary and give up.

Hebrews 12:3 NLT

I have cute little postcards that say, "Bloom where you're planted," featuring a picture of Texas bluebonnets. I love Texas bluebonnets. I miss them, now that we've moved back to Indiana. You know what I find fascinating? Every spring, Texas bluebonnets pop up in the most unusual places. You'll even find them in the medians of highways, poking their vibrant blue heads up among the weeds and tall grass. It's as if they're saying, "Hey, we're blooming here despite the fact that no one waters us or pulls the weeds that surround us."

I want to encourage you today—become like a Texas wild-flower. Bloom wherever you are planted, despite the weeds that surround you. Maybe you're not working in a very nice environment, but you can still make the best of it. Do your best work and keep your eyes on God. He will water you. He won't let the weeds choke the life out of you. Just keep trusting Him, and pretty soon you'll be blooming in a much better environment. God has a way of transplanting us at just the perfect time. Until then, keep growing! —*MMA*

. . . .

Father, help me to bloom where You have planted me.
I love You. Amen.

The King's Own

Every animal of the forest is mine,
and the cattle on a thousand hills.

Psalm 50:10

What if your father owned the company where you work? If he did, you'd probably have some fabulous fringe benefits, wouldn't you? Yes, that would be nice. But even if your father doesn't own the place where you work, you can expect great favor. Why? Because you are a child of the King of kings. God is your heavenly Father! The Bible says that God owns the cattle on a thousand hills. Having lived in Cowtown, Texas, I can tell you—that's a lot of cows!

We serve a wealthy God, and He loves to shower blessings on His children. If you are born again, then you qualify. And if you aren't saved, we can take care of that right now. Simply pray, "Lord, I repent of my sins. Thank You, Jesus, for dying on the cross so that I might live. I make you the Lord and Savior of my life. Amen." That's it. You're in the favor club.

As a child of the Most High God, you can expect favor and blessings. Become favor minded in every area of your life— including in the workplace. Expect good things to come your way, because He has good things in store for you. —*MMA*

. . . .

Thank You, Father, for salvation, favor, blessings,
and so much more. I love You. Amen.

DAY
205

Hell's Angels and Ex-Convicts

Let the peace of Christ rule in your hearts, since as members
of one body you were called to peace. And be thankful.
Colossians 3:15

I worked at an event that catered to a rough crowd. From the outside, these people looked like former Hell's Angels—and some of them actually were! They were big, tough, and rough around the edges. Some were ex-convicts, and others would have been if they'd ever been caught. But there was something different about them now. They were completely sold out for Jesus. I've never met another group of people who were so thankful for their salvation. No one had to paint them a picture of hell; they'd seen it. Yet in their darkness, Jesus had found these amazing men and women and changed their lives.

When I think back to them, I can't do it without feeling a sense of humility. I have no doubt that Jesus changed my life; without Him, I can't imagine where I'd be. Still, the thankfulness that these people had, I sometimes forget. I sometimes take my salvation for granted.

Today, take time to thank Jesus for your salvation. Think about the goodness that He's brought into your life. Remember the changes He made. Keeping a grateful attitude will help you keep your eyes on Him no matter where you are. —*GM*

. . . .

Jesus, thank You for dying for me and changing my life. Amen.

Envy

*For where envy and self-seeking exist, confusion
and every evil thing are there.*
James 3:16 NKJV

Do you ever find yourself jockeying for position in your office? If so, you're not alone. It's a challenge to keep a go-getter attitude in balance with our mandate to do unto others as we'd have them do unto us.

I was struggling with this issue during a season of my writing career when I worked for a worldwide ministry magazine. I was praying one afternoon, when the Lord revealed to me that my drive for promotion was motivated by fear. I knew immediately what He meant. You see, I'd been entertaining the thought of applying for an editor's position, yet I really didn't like magazine layout and tedious editing, which this position entailed. I loved to write—period. But I'd heard a colleague was applying for the editor's opening, and I thought I should, too. I was afraid of being left behind. Have you ever gone after something as more of a notch on your belt than because it was what you wanted or were gifted to do?

I am so thankful we serve a patient and understanding God—a God who sees our hearts and gives us our abilities. I decided not to apply for that position. Once I searched my heart, I knew I was just being competitive. You don't have to jockey for position. Be true to yourself and work hard for the things you really want for the right reasons. Then trust God. He has the perfect position for you. —*MMA*

. . . .

Lord, help me to trust You more and walk in Your love. Amen.

Don't Blame Me

*I will put enmity between you and the woman,
and between your offspring and hers; he will crush your head,
and you will strike his heel.*

Genesis 3:15

Passing the buck is one of the greatest talents on display in the workplace. "It wasn't my fault," people say when a mistake occurs. "I was just doing what so-and-so told me to do." It's funny—more time can be spent trying to pin down the offender than correcting the problem. Sure, there are times when we need to figure out why something happened, but passing the buck is counterproductive.

Even in the Garden of Eden, Adam and Eve played the blame game. Adam's response was especially humorous. When asked about why he was disobedient, he responded, "The woman you put here with me—she gave me some fruit...and I ate it." In other words, "God, you put her here. It's kinda Your fault." Funny, huh? Of course, despite the fact that Adam and Eve disobeyed Him, God immediately implemented a plan to bring mankind back into relationship with Him. In Genesis 3:15, God referred to Jesus when He told Satan that the woman's offspring would crush the serpent's head.

When we do things that are counterproductive to the Word of God, He still tries to protect us. We may try to go our own way, but we are never abandoned. Why? Because God always has a plan. —*GM*

. . . .

Lord, thank You for always having a plan for my life. Amen.

What's Different?

*You will be his witness to all people
of what you have seen and heard.*

Acts 22:15

Thomas Payne said, "Reputation is what men and women think of us; character is what God and the angels know of us." In other words, people see our actions and words, whereas God sees our hearts. It's through our actions and words that the people around us will see the truth of our faith and know the difference that a relationship with Jesus makes.

When we decide to live for Jesus, we become His hands and feet in the world. People can either be drawn to Him or repelled from Him because of our actions. They'll know something is different, even if they don't know why. They'll know we have more hope and peace in our lives than they've known in theirs. In time, hopefully, they'll ask us about it, and we'll have the opportunity to invite them to church, pray for them, or encourage them.

Just because you're at work doesn't mean you can't be a witness for Jesus. Through your thoughtful actions, kind words, and graceful integrity, you can be a witness to everyone of what you have seen and heard and of the difference Jesus has made in your life. —*GM*

. . . .

*Lord, let me be a witness for You so that others
will want to know You. Amen.*

Laughter and Hairpins

He will yet fill your mouth with laughter
and your lips with shouts of joy.
Job 8:21

Like most women, I like to look my best when I leave the house. So when I received the worst haircut of my life, I panicked. I had a mullet, and those had not made a return to the runways. (Mullets were bad when they first debuted, and they didn't get any better decades later.) To improve my hairstyle during the growing out process, I bought some extensions that matched my natural hair. They sort of clipped into my natural hair, but it took me a while to get the hang of making them work.

Imagine this...I'm in the office of a coworker, discussing the outcome of a meeting we'd just had in the conference room. I passionately reviewed a point, and as I did so, I flipped my hair. In fact, I flipped it right off my head. My faux hair landed on the ground, near my coworker's feet. She jumped and screamed a bit. (I think she thought it was a gopher or something.) We both laughed until our stomachs hurt.

I learned a valuable lesson that day—well, two actually. First, it's good to laugh at yourself. Second, use a lot of bobby pins when securing hair extensions.

Laughing together and showing your vulnerability can be very bonding. Don't be afraid to be imperfect with your coworkers and God. They'll love you—mullet and all. *—MMA*

. . . .

Lord, help me to be able to laugh at myself. Amen.

Real Struggle

We are not fighting against flesh-and-blood enemies,
but against evil rulers and authorities of the unseen world.
Ephesians 6:12 NLT

The spiritual world is more real than the physical," I once heard someone say, and I've tried to remember that. Workplace struggles are often chalked up to differences of opinions or personalities. Everyone assumes that the parties simply viewed things differently, but there are times when the struggles are more spiritual than physical.

In 2 Kings 6, the prophet Elisha, who was targeted by the Aramean army, stood his ground. When his servant asked, "Oh, sir, what will we do now?" "Don't be afraid," Elisha replied. "There are more on our side than on theirs!" He then prayed for his servant's eyes to be opened so that he could see the heavenly horses and chariots of fire that were protecting them.

Of course, that doesn't mean spiritual forces are involved in every difficult situation, but you can watch and pray to know the difference. Pray for sensitivity and wisdom. Pray for the truth, and pray for the person's peace of mind and salvation. Through prayer and sensitivity, you can be more tuned in to what's going on around you. —*GM*

. . . .

Lord, help me to see the truth about the struggles
I face each day—whether they're spiritual or physical.
Give me the wisdom to deal with them accordingly. Amen.

Approval

Before I formed you in the womb I knew [and] approved of you.
Jeremiah 1:5 AMPC

I had never felt so intimidated. I looked around at all the other conference speakers and thought, *What am I doing? I'm not worthy to sit next to these authors. They write life-changing books, that sell millions of copies. I should just leave...no one will notice.*

It was my first year to teach at a writers' conference. I'd gone from conferee to staff member in less than two years, and I wasn't sure God had promoted the right person. But what I failed to realize in my panic is that every single person on faculty had also once been a first-timer at some point. Comparing myself to someone who had been in the industry for many more years was unfair. Sure, I can see that now, many years later, but at that juncture, I was paralyzed with fear that I wasn't good enough to share that stage.

But God wouldn't have opened that door for me if He didn't think I was capable of fulfilling that calling. I'm so thankful I didn't let the fear of not measuring up keep me from my destiny.

So here's my question to you: Are you in comparison mode too, afraid to walk through the door of opportunity that God has opened for you? What have you talked yourself out of for fear that you're not good enough? Today is your day to change all of that wrong thinking. Say out loud: "I am called. I am capable. I am enough." —*MMA*

. . . .

Lord, help me to love myself the way that You love me. Amen.

Stop the Rain

*I have told you these things, so that in Me you may have
[perfect] peace and confidence. In the world you have tribulation
and trials and distress and frustration; but be of good cheer...
I have overcome the world.*

John 16:33 AMPC

Into each life a little rain must fall." Ever heard that expression?
Yeah, well, there have been days in my life when that "little
rain" was a torrential downpour. I've wondered if the flood would
simply carry me away—never to be heard from again. Maybe
you're there today. If you've had your share of rain lately, let me
encourage you.

Though it's tempting, crying in your office won't change
your negative circumstances. (Plus, your eyes will get all puffy,
and that's bad, too.) Instead, meditate on this—you have Jesus
living on the inside of you, and He has already overcome every
kind of trouble there is. Now, that doesn't mean you aren't going
to experience pain and loss in this world, but it does mean you
don't have to experience it alone. God will be with you through
it all. No matter how difficult your circumstances may seem—
maybe you're having marital problems or maybe you just learned
that your hours are being cut or maybe your teenage son is in that
rebellion stage—God can handle it.

There is nothing too big or too hard for our God. Cast your
cares on Him today. Tell Him all about the rain you've been experiencing and then thank Him for the sunny days ahead. Be of
good cheer; you are an overcomer! *—MMA*

. . . .

Lord, thank You for my impending victories! Amen.

Part of the Whole

*For there is one body and one Spirit, just as you
have been called to one glorious hope for the future.*
Ephesians 4:4 NLT

A pastor once said, "Relational joining is necessary in order to enjoy the fullness of what God has to offer." By relational joining, he meant that God doesn't want us to focus solely on ourselves and our individual salvation. Instead, God wants us to be part of a whole. As someone who is leery of joining groups, this was a good message for me.

I don't always feel in sync with other women in the church because of my career. I've attended women's retreats, only to be so exhausted from my workweek that I wanted to sleep—a big no-no at women's retreats. Or I've attended church classes and found little to talk about with the other women. Eventually, though, I found other career-minded Christian women who shared my interests. Their friendships are some of the closest of my life.

Don't give up on finding other Christian women with whom to connect. Even if it seems like a hopeless task, make the effort. As you connect with other women in the body of Christ, you will enhance your faith. —*GM*

. . . .

*Lord, help me to find close Christian friends
with whom I can share my walk and grow. Amen.*

DAY
214

Is There a Doctor in the House?

We understand these things, for we have the mind of Christ.
1 Corinthians 2:16 NLT

Do you get intimidated easily? I do. I sort of fell into a speaking ministry, and now I teach at women's conferences and writers' conferences across the United States. I never dreamed I'd be speaking in front of thousands of people, but God knew. I guess that's why He had me minor in speech communication at Indiana University all those years ago. I just thought I was minoring in speech because it was easier than minoring in earth science.

Even today, though, I still feel queasy each time I stand up to speak. Shortly after I began my speaking career, I was asked to teach a continuing education course for a national pharmaceutical group. My audience? A bunch of brilliant pharmacists. As I glanced over the roster of speakers, I realized I was the only one without a "Dr." before my name or a whole lot of initials after my name. You might say I was a tad bit intimidated.

So I prayed, "Lord, Your Word says I have the mind of Christ, so I am calling upon that wisdom right now. Help me to speak with excellence." And guess what? He did help me. I actually sounded like I should have a lot more initials after my name than I do. God always comes through.

Don't be intimidated. Even if you feel you can't do it, know that God can do it through you. —*MMA*

. . . .

Thank You, Lord, for giving me courage to be excellent. Amen.

Work Perks

Praise the LORD for his love
and for the wonderful things he does for all of us.
Psalm 107:21 CEV

I once heard actress Reese Witherspoon share about the perks of playing Elle Woods in the *Legally Blonde* movies. Her favorite perk? She was able to keep some of Elle's shoes! Talk about a work perk!

I'm sure if you think hard enough, you can think of a few work perks you have. Okay, so maybe your job doesn't have a cutest-shoes-ever allowance, but surely you have some perks. Maybe you have flextime. Maybe you have four-day work weeks. Or maybe you have casual Friday every day. Whatever the perks, be grateful!

The next time your annual review rolls around and you're asked for feedback, take a minute to thank your company for the office perks. Better yet, why not write a note to the head of your company, thanking him for the perks that you enjoy? Bosses like to be bragged on once in a while. Company presidents like to feel appreciated by their employees. (Now that I'm a company president, I can say this from experience.) And God likes it when we honor those that He has put in authority over us. So why not perk up someone's day and thank your boss for your work perks! —*MMA*

. . . .

Father, help me to always have a grateful heart. Amen.

Leave a Legacy

I have fought the good fight, I have finished the race,
and I have remained faithful.
2 Timothy 4:7 NLT

My late mother-in-law, Martha, was an amazing lady—not just because she raised a godly, awesome son, but also because she made every place better just by being there. At age eighty-four, she was still working part-time until the day she went into the hospital, battled a short illness, and eventually went on to glory.

At her funeral, hundreds of folks—many past and present coworkers—waited in line to pay their respects, and as they shook our hands and offered their condolences, they shared stories about sweet Martha. Over and over again, we heard how she was the first one to arrive at work and often the last to leave. Others remarked that she always had a smile and kind word for everyone—it made no difference to her whether that person worked as a custodian or in the front business office. One man said he'd only worked with her a few months, and then through tears, he added, "But she made an impact on me. Martha was never too busy to check on me and ask about my family. She was a dandy."

Her work ethic was inspiring. Her professionalism was impeccable. And her genuine love for life—whether at home or at work—continues to impact those fortunate enough to have known her. To me, she was the definition of a godly working woman.

I truly hope I can leave that same kind of example and legacy, and I hope you will do the same. —*MMA*

. . . .

Father, help me to be a shining example
of a godly working woman and a legacy of love. Amen.

Tough Stuff

[We are] fixing our eyes on Jesus, the author and perfecter of faith,
who for the joy set before Him endured the cross,
despising the shame, and has sat down
at the right hand of the throne of God.

Hebrews 12:2 NASB

There are times when we have to make tough decisions. We come to a crossroads, and instead of choosing the easy route, we take the hard way. It could be a change in career or relationships. It may mean going against popular opinion to stand up for morality. We all have these choices to make, and we must do what's right.

It's good to remember the choice Jesus made. He knew that in order to restore a relationship between mankind and God, He would have to sacrifice His life. We can see in Scripture that it was a tough choice, but He made the decision to endure the cross for us. Just because it was right, the lashes and crucifixion weren't any less agonizing.

If you're facing a tough choice, prayerfully consider your options. If necessary, discuss it with a strong Christian friend or your pastor. Your decision may not be easy, but it can be the right one. —*GM*

. . . .

Jesus, thank You for enduring the cross for me.
As I make tough choices in my life,
help me to make the best one—even if it isn't easy. Amen.

In Focus

In the same way, let your light shine before others,
that they may see your good deeds
and glorify your Father in heaven.
Matthew 5:16

When my daughters were in elementary school, we had the same routine every morning. As they grabbed their backpacks and headed out the door for school, I would always say, "Let your lights shine for Jesus. You may be the only Jesus some people ever see."

I think that's a good reminder for all of us, whether we're heading off to school or to a corporate environment. We don't have to wear "Jesus Saves" T-shirts or post "Got God?" bumper stickers on our vehicles to share the love of God. We can reach hearts for Him simply by living out our faith consistently in front of others. With political correctness in overdrive these days, we have to be careful about talking about our faith at work, which is why it's even more important to live our faith.

Find ways to show the love of God through little acts of kindness—those little things make a big impact on all who encounter them. I want the light of Jesus to shine so brightly in me that it warms all those around me. I hope you'll share with me in that goal and let your light shine for Jesus everywhere you go—especially at work. Remember, you may be the only Jesus some people ever see.—*MMA*

. . . .

Lord, help me to be a good witness
for You everywhere I go. Amen.

A Little Help from My Friends

*When Moses' hands grew tired, they took a stone
and put it under him and he sat on it. Aaron and Hur
held his hands up—one on one side, one on the other—
so that his hands remained steady till sunset.*

Exodus 17:12

Remember the story of Moses, Aaron, and Hur? The Amalekites had attacked the Israelites at Rephidim. Moses said to Joshua, "Choose some of our men and go out to fight the Amalekites. Tomorrow I will stand on top of the hill with the staff of God in my hands" (Exodus 17:9). So Joshua went to battle as instructed, and Moses, Aaron, and Hur went to the top of the hill. As long as Moses held up his hands, the Israelites won, but whenever he lowered his hands, the Amalekites began winning. After a while, Moses's arms became tired, so Aaron and Hur held up his arms—one on one side, one on the other. That way, his hands remained steady till Joshua overcame the Amalekite army.

Together, Moses, Aaron, and Hur were able to keep their side winning. You might say Moses needed a little help from his friends. Let's face it, we can all use a little help from our friends once in a while. Don't try to go it alone. Don't be the hero. Together, you and your coworkers can accomplish much! —*MMA*

. . . .

*Lord, help me to be willing to assist my coworkers
when called upon. Amen.*

The Downfall

Too much pride causes trouble. Be sensible and take advice.
Proverbs 13:10 CEV

If there is one quality that I've seen lead to someone's downfall, it's pride. Some talented people I've known have fallen into pride's trap. They didn't make unpardonable mistakes; they just didn't believe they *could* make mistakes. In their eyes, they were always right, and everyone else—all us other poor, unenlightened souls—were wrong.

Pride comes from many sources. Some people get puffed up because of a spiritual gift like discernment. Because they have a gift for reading situations and people, they set themselves up as the judge of everyone. Or because someone is talented at their job, they see themselves as the standard and look down on everyone else. None of us are immune. We all want to be valued for our talents, but we must be careful to keep pride out of our lives. We need to be open to others' ideas and realize that all talents are God-given.

By remaining humble and keeping pride out of your life, you allow God to work through you and use you for His glory. —*GM*

. . . .

Lord, thank You for the gifts and talents that You've given me.
Help me keep pride out of my life and remain
humble in everything I do. Amen.

Identity Crisis

*We were in our own sight as grasshoppers,
and so we were in their sight.*
Numbers 13:33 KJV

I love what I do. I truly enjoy writing children's books, inspirational books for women, and magazine articles. But as much as I love it, I have had to learn that my identity comes from the Lord—not my career.

When I gave birth to our second child, my husband and I prayerfully decided that it would be best for me to stay home with the girls for a season. So I quit my daily news reporter position and went home to write and be a mom. While I loved being a stay-at-home mom, I must admit that I missed the position I'd held at the newspaper.

After a few months of my being at home, Jeff and I were invited to a community function. As we socialized with the important folks in town, I realized just how much my identity was rooted in my career. When asked, "What do you do?" I'd mumble, "I'm a stay-at-home mom, but I used to be a journalist for the local newspaper." I wanted them to know that I could talk about more than diapers. That night I realized that I had been defining myself by what I did and how others viewed my career. But that was incomplete.

If you're in that same boat, jump ship! Your career doesn't define who you are—only God can do that. —*MMA*

. . . .

Lord, help me to find my identity in You. Amen.

Love Like Jesus

If you love those who love you, what reward will you get?
Are not even the tax collectors doing that?
And if you greet only your own people, what are you
doing more than others? Do not even pagans do that?

Matthew 5:46–47

I once heard a preacher say, "Hurting people do hurtful things." For some reason, that has really stuck with me. Now, every time I encounter a rude person in the business world, I'll think, *I wonder what that person is going through right now. I bet she is really hurting inside.* When you think that way, it's impossible to retaliate. Your flesh will cry out, "Return rudeness for rudeness. If she zings you, go ahead and zing her back." But your spirit will be filled with compassion and love for those who are hurting. You'll begin to see them through God's eyes.

If you find yourself ready to zing back at a moment's notice, it might be time for a compassion checkup. Ask the Great Physician to fill you with His love and compassion for people.

When you return rudeness with love, you totally change the situation. You don't give that rude person anywhere to go except to the Father. This will take some practice, but remember, practice makes perfect—or in this case, practice makes perfect love. *—MMA*

. . . .

Lord, help me to love people like You do. Amen.

Thank the Lord, I'm Free!

Now the Lord is the Spirit, and where the Spirit of the Lord is,
there is liberty (emancipation from bondage, freedom).
2 Corinthians 3:17 AMPC

Take a moment to consider freedom—freedom from past mistakes, freedom from spiritual and physical slavery, freedom to choose how and where to live, freedom from living up to others' unrealistic expectations, freedom from trying to keep up with the Joneses, freedom from anything that would separate us from Jesus. For those of us who live in a Western country, we sometimes take freedom for granted, but our brothers and sisters in Christ who live in other parts of the world know how precious freedom is. It's something to be treasured.

As you go through your day, thank Jesus for the freedom He's provided for you. Thank Him that loving and serving Him is the only requirement for a fulfilling life and eternal salvation. Thank Him that He's paid the price for your freedom so that you don't have to. Remember, it's because of Him that you have a freedom that can never be taken away. —*GM*

. . . .

Jesus, thank You for making me free—free from anything
that would separate me from You. Amen.

DAY
224

Now's a Great Time
for a Breakdown

*You're going to wear yourself out—and the people, too.
This job is too heavy a burden for you to handle all by yourself.*
Exodus 18:18 NLT

Emotions sometimes get the best of us. We try to handle pressure as it comes, but then we just can't keep it inside any longer. Even if we're not overly emotional, we can't keep the tears down. All the stress and frustration come to the surface, and we find ourselves crying in the bathroom or in the car.

Letting emotions out is generally healthier than burying them. Now, I'm not suggesting that you fly into hysterics or run over anyone in the parking lot, but having a good cry, hard workout, or even screaming into your pillow may be just what the doctor ordered. Once you're calm again, go to the Lord so He can comfort you. Then talk to an objective, Christian friend who can give you perspective and encouragement. Don't let the stress build into a physical or emotional ailment. God didn't make you out of stone. He created you with emotions, so instead of denying them, take them to Him and let Him help you deal with them. —*GM*

. . . .

Lord, show me how to handle the stress in my life. Amen.

Humility First

Whosoever will be chief among you, let him be your servant.
Matthew 20:27 KJV

Do you have a "me" problem? Do you think of yourself before everyone else in your office? Do you always have an agenda? You're right in line with the world's way of thinking if you do. The world says, "If you don't look out for number one, nobody else will." But God's Word says, "Whosoever will be chief among you, let him be your servant." Those two statements are in direct contradiction, aren't they?

Well, let me give you some additional reasons to go God's way. Proverbs 16:18 says, "First pride, then the crash—the bigger the ego, the harder the fall" (MSG). The Word also says a lot about humility. It says that God gives grace to the lowly and that He promises to save the humble. Sounds like He looks out for those who aren't so concerned with looking out for themselves, doesn't it?

See, you don't have to look out for numero uno because the Creator of the universe is looking out for you. Stop the "me, me, me" mentality and focus your attention on God. You don't have to do a single thing except trust in the Lord. He is your protector and defender. —*MMA*

· ·

Father, help me to get my eyes off myself
and back onto You. Amen.

Spiritual Gumbo

Praise be to the God and Father of our Lord Jesus Christ,
who has blessed us in the heavenly realms
with every spiritual blessing in Christ.

Ephesians 1:3

Have you ever spent time around someone who referred to their beliefs as "spiritual"? I'm not talking about someone using the term to define their Christianity. I'm talking about the kind of spirituality that believes nothing is wrong and we all need to just be open to whatever spiritual force comes our way. It's a kind of religious gumbo—a little Christianity mixed with a dash of Eastern mysticism and a helping of humanism.

I've spent time around people who believe this way, and I've sensed they're on a quest for truth, peace, and possibly power to deal with their lives. I'm not sure, but I pray that they'll come to know the peace, love, and joy of a relationship with Jesus.

When you encounter someone like this—and if you work outside of your home, you will—be sure to show grace. Instead of judging or belittling their beliefs, recognize that they are on a quest for truth and ask the Lord to draw them to Him. Keep an open dialogue. Ask probing questions that make them think or invite them to an event at your church. With time, patience, and possibly your influence, they may come to know Jesus. Until then, commit to being what all Christians are called to be—ambassadors of God's love. —*GM*

. . . .

Jesus, thank You for saving me and setting me free.
Please help me to be an example
of Your love and grace to others. Amen.

Thanksgiving

*Let the peace of Christ rule in your hearts, since as members
of one body you were called to peace. And be thankful.*
Colossians 3:15

Nothing puts life back into perspective like a tragedy or a
loved one's illness.

I received news that an acquaintance's young husband had
died suddenly from a heart attack. Then, out of the blue, my
own husband asked if I'd make a doctor's appointment for him
because he'd experienced some alarming symptoms. Thankfully,
his checkup was clear except for some unusually aggressive
allergies.

Until that week, I'd been focused on some frustrating personal business and disappointing career news. Things that I
thought would work out easily were not going as planned. But all
of that was put into perspective with my coworker's loss and my
own husband's scare. All of that helped remind me once again of
God's blessings.

Each of us has things for which we should be thankful. It
may be our job, our health, our family, our friendships, or, above
all, our salvation. If we think about it—and some of us may need
to think hard—God has blessed us. Take the time to be mindful
of all the blessings your heavenly Father has brought into your life
and thank Him—especially because He calls you His child. —*GM*

. . . .

*Lord, thank You for calling me to be a member of Your family
and for blessing my life with so many good things. Amen.*

It's Free!

Freely (without pay) you have received,
freely (without charge) give.

Matthew 10:8 AMPC

I can never outgive God," a friend once told me. A working mother of five, she and her husband weren't wealthy, but she freely gave to anyone who needed it. Money, clothes, time, service—whatever she had, she gave. I once witnessed her give a beautiful leather jacket—something she adored—to someone because she felt impressed to do so. Why? She understood an important truth: everything she had came from God, and if she felt the Holy Spirit leading her to do it, she should be ready to give it away without reservation.

James 1:17 says, "Every good and perfect gift is from above." It's a good reminder that our possessions don't belong to us but rather to God. He's the One who gave them to us, and He's the One who can direct us to pass them to others.

Be open to making the practice of giving a regular part of your life. The gifts you give may or may not be tangible. They could, instead, include compliments, encouragements, introductions, job leads, or something else. If you ask the Lord to show you ways to be a giver at work, His Holy Spirit will surely fulfill that request. Remember the verse above: "Freely...you have received, freely...give." —*GM*

. . . .

Lord, I realize that all that I have is from You,
so please show me how, when,
and where to give to others. Amen.

Let God Define You

Now you are the body of Christ, and each one of you is a part of it.
1 Corinthians 12:27

I was finishing up a book signing at the International Christian Retail Show (ICRS) in Orlando several years ago when I noticed a woman waiting at the edge of the *Guideposts* booth.

"We just ran out of books," I explained as I walked over to her, "but I'd be happy to mail you a copy from my personal stash at home."

"Oh, that's okay," she said. "I didn't want a book."

Just as I was about to ask what she wanted, she took my face into her hands, looked me square in the eyes, and said, "Quit saying you're not a speaker. Stop saying that you're only a writer. Did God tell you that you're only a writer and not a speaker?"

I shook my head no, trying to keep my composure.

"Then stop saying it. Only say what God says. Let Him define you."

With that, she removed her hands from my face, walked away, and I never saw her again.

How could she have known that I had just said those exact words to my husband the night before in the privacy of our hotel room, as I told him I'd been invited to speak at an upcoming women's conference?

It was a turning point in my journey. It was the day I stopped defining myself and started allowing God to define me. So, how have *you* been defining yourself? Are you letting God define you, or are you letting others tell you who you are and what you're called to do? —*MMA*

. . . .

Lord, I only want You to define me. Amen.

Alien Invasion

And the peace of God, which transcends all understanding,
will guard your hearts and your minds in Christ Jesus.
Philippians 4:7

Sooner or later, everyone loses their cool because of pressure and stress, and I'm no different. I've found myself being irritable toward people, worried about assignments, or fearful that things wouldn't be accomplished. It's one of the pitfalls of gaining added responsibilities. There's nothing like a promotion with additional duties, a better title, and a higher salary to give you the chance to lose your cool. I've worked with many people whose personalities were altered by work pressures. Their calm rationale was replaced by harsh frenzy, as though some alien creature had taken over their bodies.

The good news is that none of us have to cave to the pressure. In the midst of crazy days when things don't go right and people get on your nerves, you can still have inner peace. You can still have God's perspective on your work and life. It requires spending time with Him and sometimes taking a moment in the middle of a crazy day to pray and focus on Him, but you can do that. As you do, you'll be able to bring your emotions, thoughts, and actions back into alignment with Him so that His peace prevails. —*GM*

. . . .

Heavenly Father, I pray that Your peace will
guard my heart and mind in Christ Jesus. Amen.

God Is in the Details

*O GOD, God of Israel, there is no God like you in the skies above
or on the earth below who unswervingly keeps covenant
with his servants and relentlessly loves them as they sincerely
live in obedience to your way. You kept your word....
You did exactly what you promised—every detail.*

1 Kings 8:23–24 MSG

You know how important paying attention to detail is. When drafting a contract, every clause must be considered. When counting money or balancing books, every column must balance. Even something as simple as a few pennies in the wrong place can wreak havoc. As you are promoted to higher positions and incur more responsibility, the details become even more important.

In fact, in every area of our lives, the details matter. So it's nice to know that God is interested in the details. He doesn't just want the high points, He wants *every* point. And He isn't just interested in your church life or what you do wrong. He's interested in everything about you—home, work, relationships, well-being, health, hopes, disappointments—all of it.

If you've always assumed that God isn't interested in the details, think again. He wants to be a part of the good and the bad, the beautiful and the ugly of your life. —*GM*

. . . .

*Lord, thank You for being a personal God,
for being interested in every part of my life. Amen.*

A Good Witness

*In the same way, let your light shine before others, that they may
see your good deeds and glorify your Father in heaven.*
Matthew 5:15

I sat across from an editor at a writers' conference and listened in shock as he flatly said, "Before you start your little book proposal pitch, my answer is already no. It's your responsibility to change my mind to yes." As you might imagine, that just made me want to jump right into my presentation. (Go back and read that line with a hint of sarcasm for the full effect!) He was a tough guy with a stern look, and my energetic, somewhat peppy personality didn't exactly make him his favorite person. However, by the time I was done with my peppy pitch, he actually cracked a small smile, and he asked me to send him my book proposal. Yay!

You know, I think our coworkers feel much like the book editor I described above. I think they've seen too many Christians behave badly, and they've already decided that their answer to Christianity is no—unless you can convince them otherwise. I don't mean they want us to shove Scriptures down their throats every day in the office. I mean, they are watching us closely. If they see something in us that they like—if they see Jesus in us— they might just crack a smile, too. Be a good witness today! —*MMA*

. . . .

*Father, help me to be a good witness
for You day in and day out. Amen.*

Celebrate Women

Dear friends, since God loved us that much,
we surely ought to love each other.
1 John 4:11 NLT

I admit it. I admire strong women. I admire them for their lively conversations, devoted friendships, headstrong determination, and humorous observations about life. They work hard, love intensely, and keep their sense of humor through it all. Even through the tough times, they never give up believing that, with God's guidance, they'll be okay. They're the ones who have shaped my life, and I hope that you've had a few of them in your life, too.

Take time to honor the women who have meant so much to you—your mother, grandmother, aunt, neighbor, mentor, friend, coworker, boss. Don't miss the opportunity to give back to them, whether a gift or a note of appreciation. Let them know how special they are. These women have taught you so much through their example and friendship. They are gifts from God, people He brought into your life to teach you, love you, and be your friend, so honor them today. Because of them, you're who you are. —*GM*

. . . .

Dear Lord, I pray that You would bless the women
who have meant so much in my life.
Let them sense Your presence today. Amen.

Hurtful Words

I tell you anyone who is angry with a brother or sister
will be subject to judgment.
Matthew 5:22

A re you the queen of the zinger? Do you retaliate with a witty, sarcastic remark when someone hurts you? I'm not like that. Instead, I cry a lot and think about what I should've said. Oh yeah, I can really tell somebody off...like, two hours later.

Although I'm not very good with one-on-one confrontation, I'm quite skilled at firing off wicked emails. I can compose a scathing, tell-somebody-off email like nobody's business. This, of course, is a very bad thing. It's so easy to hit that Send key and walk away satisfied. But later, when I go back to my computer and reread my hurtful email, I feel sick right in the pit of my stomach. By that time, the Holy Spirit has had time to deal with my heart, and I wish I'd never sent the email. Ever been there?

Words, whether uttered or written, can wound a person. Even if you're reacting to a hurtful remark hurled at you, you have no right to return a hurtful comment. Go ahead, hit the Delete key. The only thing we should be sending is our love. —*MMA*

. . . .

Lord, help me remember that it's better to think before
speaking (or writing) than spend my life regretting. Amen.

See the Potential

One generation commends your works to another;
they tell of your mighty acts.
Psalm 145:4

Are you ready to be a mentor, to share what you've learned about your field, about life? Are you ready to answer questions or give encouragement to those who want to learn?

As a professional writer, people often ask me questions about my field. Most are passing questions from people who dream of one day writing a book. Recently, however, I had the chance to sit down one-on-one with aspiring writers, people who were truly interested in pursuing a writing career. They came with thoughtful questions like how to outline a book, how to work with clients, and how to get their work published. As I sat listening to these women, I got excited. There was so much potential in front of me. I answered their questions, made suggestions, and encouraged them in their journey. It was invigorating, my chance to give back to these women the way others had given to me.

Next time you come across someone less experienced than you in your field, take a moment to recognize the potential in front of you. Your kindness and willingness to share your experience could change that person's life. You might help them avoid a misstep or give them the encouragement they need to grow professionally, personally, and/or spiritually. What a gift—not only to them, but to you as well. Don't miss it! —*GM*

Lord, help me to be a mentor to those around me.
Help me to teach them and encourage them so that
they can do all You've ordained for them to do. Amen.

Forget It

*Joseph named his firstborn Manasseh and said,
"It is because God has made me forget all my trouble
and all my father's household."*

Genesis 41:51

Remember the story of Joseph? His brothers resented him because he was his daddy's favorite, so they sold him into slavery. But Joseph had favor wherever he went and eventually became a ruler in Egypt. Still, he had to endure much in his lifetime. Not only did his brothers sell him into slavery, but also he spent time in prison for a crime he didn't commit.

When Joseph's wife gave birth to their firstborn son, Joseph named him Manasseh, which means "made to forget." He did this as a tribute to God because the Father had done so much for him, even causing him to forget his past hurts and mistreatment.

Maybe you feel you should change your name to Manasseh today because of all the challenges you've endured at work and in your life. Let me encourage you—no matter how many hurts you have to forget, God will make them up to you. He hasn't forgotten you. Honor God with your decision to let the past be the past and press forward into your bright future. You have much to look forward to! —*MMA*

. . . .

*Lord, help me leave behind my past hurts
and move forward with You. Amen.*

Cheerleader

*I long to see you so that I may impart to you some
spiritual gift to make you strong—that is, that you and I
may be mutually encouraged by each other's faith.*

Romans 1:11–12

Everyone needs a cheerleader, a friend who believes in them when everything seems to be falling apart. Thankfully, I have one of those friends, and I hope you do, too. When she or I are hit by career disappointments, harsh coworkers, or family trauma—sometimes all at once—we meet for lunch, which must include a *huge* smothered-in-chocolate dessert. Then we remind each other that God loves us and has called us for this time. It's the best kind of therapy.

If you need a cheer from a special friend but don't have one nearby, let these Scriptures encourage you. They are specific words that your heavenly Father has said about you: He loves you (John 15:9), and nothing you have ever done or ever will do will separate you from His love (Romans 8:38–39). God knows everything about you and considers you valuable and precious (Luke 12:7). You are chosen by Him to be used for His glory (Ephesians 1:11). Every step you take is ordered by Him, and He delights in you (Psalm 37:23). Ponder these verses today, because they are part of God's personal cheer to you. —*GM*

. . . .

*Lord, thank You for Your love, acceptance,
and direction in my life. Amen.*

Please Tell Me This Isn't So

I cry out to God Most High,
to God, who vindicates me.

Psalm 57:2

Have you ever whispered, *Dear Lord, please tell me this isn't all that there is?* You've been doing your job long enough that you've started to feel the walls closing in around you. You want to be challenged in new ways.

At times, I've been very restless in my work. I might have loved the job at first, but after doing it for *y-e-a-r-s,* it lost its appeal. I wanted to do more but couldn't figure out what. I've learned to turn to God in those moments, and I hope you'll do the same. When I did, I felt led to determine what it was I wanted and loved. It took time, but eventually I got the insight and courage to step out.

If you're worried that you're never going to do anything more than you're doing right now, start talking to God about it. Look at your options and prayerfully consider what you want to be doing and what it would take to make your dreams a reality. God will give you the wisdom and insight to make a change and grow. —*GM*

. . . .

Lord, You know my dreams and talents.
Please fulfill Your purpose in my life. Amen.

Beacon of Joy

You are the light of the world.
A city that is set on a hill cannot be hidden.
Matthew 5:14 NKJV

My father suffered four strokes over a two-year period, and I spent many hours with him in various hospitals and rehabilitation units. After a while, you start to notice things. For instance, I learned quite a bit of medical terminology. I also learned something else: a good nurse makes for a pleasant stay, while a bad nurse makes every second seem like an eternity.

My father had one nurse named Joy, who was appropriately named because she was a light in our time of darkness. She just bubbled with the love of Jesus, and she was a great encouragement to my father. You could tell that she truly enjoyed her work. She didn't have to announce to the world that she was a Christian. Her life told the story. She was kind and helpful to everyone.

I don't know about you, but I want to be more like Joy. I want to be a beacon everywhere I go. I desire to walk the walk, not just talk the talk. Just as I observed Joy, people are observing us every day. Let's give them something worth watching. Let's shine with the love of Jesus as we go about our workday. —*MMA*

. . . .

Lord, I want Your light to shine through me
as I go about my work. Amen.

Thanks for the Favor

Let the favor of the Lord our God be upon us.
Psalm 90:17 NASB

Okay, so you desire the favor of God in your life, but you're just not sure how to get it, right? Favor comes through prayer, faith in His Word, and obeying His leading. Bottom line—favor comes when you spend time in God's presence.

When I was looking for a publisher for *Living the Love Chapter*, I submitted it to many places and received more than a few rejection letters. About this time, I was introduced to this favor principle, and I began praying favor over my book proposal. I also thanked God that I had favor with whichever editor opened my email. Guess what—I sold that book! Later, when I met with the publisher to sign the contract, he said, "You know, it's a miracle I even received your book proposal. You sent your email to an account I never check anymore. But for some reason, I knew I was supposed to check that account the very day your message came through. Funny, huh?"

I smiled and said, "That's my God! He does favors for me all the time." And you know what? He'll do favors for you, too. He loves doing nice things for His children. So go ahead and expect favor in the workplace—not in an arrogant way but as a grateful child of God. On your way to work, pray over the client calls you'll be making that morning. Pray over your assignments before you turn them in. Thank God for His favor before you go into the afternoon meeting.

Give your day to Him and thank Him for His favor. It's the only way to live! —*MMA*

. . . .

Thank You, Lord, for Your favor. I love You. Amen.

A Change of Attitude

God is with you in everything you do.
Genesis 21:22

I absolutely loved my boss. He was gentle. He was kind. He was brilliant. And he was quick to offer assistance. Basically, he was the perfect boss. So when I changed jobs and encountered the exact opposite of my beloved former boss, I panicked. Everything I had respected about my former boss—his dedication to the craft, his backbone, his humor, his willingness to share his gift, his humility—was absent in my new boss.

I was just about to call my former boss and beg for my old position back when I remembered a verse I'd learned in Vacation Bible School many years before: "God is with you in everything you do." The more I thought about it, the more encouraged I became. I realized that, even though I no longer had the perfect boss, I still had God, and He promised to work alongside me in everything I did. That was good enough for me.

My situation didn't change for the better, but my attitude did. And that made all the difference. If you're unhappy in your job, change your attitude. Praise God that you have a job and remember that He is with you today and always. —*MMA*

. . . .

*Thank You, Lord, for my job. Please change my attitude
so I can honor You in my work. Amen.*

Work of My Hands

"But you did not listen to me," declares the LORD,
"and you have aroused my anger with what your hands have made,
and you have brought harm to yourselves."

Jeremiah 25:7

I've always been goal oriented. It's a trait I received from my mother. Early on, she taught me the value of setting a goal and working toward it. I learned that, though it takes time and patience, it brings rewards. In college, I set about studying business with visions of position and money dancing in my head. It wasn't until after I graduated and began working that the Lord redirected my goals. Since then, I've learned the value of following His path for my life. And though money is still a concern— I mean, come on, we gotta eat—it's no longer the main one.

God gives us talents and desires that can lead to great things in our work, but more than anything, He wants us to love and serve Him. We have to be careful that our goals are about serving Him and using our abilities to honor Him, regardless of what our jobs are. And though there is nothing wrong with gaining position and money, we must also be careful not to worship our own work. Remember, your work is what you do, not the sum total of who you are. —*GM*

. . . .

Lord, I love and serve You. Direct my work
so that it glorifies You. Amen.

Keep Swinging

*Watch out that you do not lose what we have
worked so hard to achieve. Be diligent
so that you receive your full reward.*

2 John 1:8 NLT

I heard a story about a man who had a huge boulder in his backyard. He couldn't lift it because of its massive size, so he decided he would try to break it into smaller, more manageable pieces. Every day, this diligent man swung at the boulder with a large hammer. Weeks went by, but nothing happened. Then one day, that huge rock split right down the middle and into several pieces. The man couldn't believe it—he hadn't swung any harder that time, but there was the broken boulder.

It wasn't one remarkable hammer hit that destroyed the boulder; it was a cumulative effect. You might say that man's diligence finally paid off. And guess what? Yours will, too. Is there a big boulder you'd like to destroy in your life? Maybe it's financial debt. Maybe it's past hurt. Maybe your boulder is made up of years of work frustrations. No matter what it is—it's not too big for God. Keep swinging the Word of God at your boulder. Keep being diligent in your prayer life. Keep being faithful in your tithing. Keep doing all that you know to do and watch that boulder begin to break. —*MMA*

. . . .

Lord, help me to be diligent. Amen.

Fruits?

The Holy Spirit produces this kind of fruit in our lives:
love, joy, peace, patience, kindness, goodness,
faithfulness, gentleness, and self-control.
Galatians 5:22–23 NLT

Have you ever noticed how we try to split up the fruit of the Spirit? We think: *Well, I've got love covered now, but patience and self-control still need some work.* I know I have. Just ask me after I've inhaled a big bowl of pasta with cream sauce and followed it with a hot fudge brownie sundae. That's when I think I need to work on my self-control!

But notice that the Scripture above doesn't say *fruits*; it says *fruit*. So we can't develop just love, joy, or peace and not develop kindness, faithfulness, and self-control. They're all part of the same package.

If you're struggling to develop the fruit of the Spirit in your life, ask God to show you how to do it. You could even make it a joint study with a friend so that you can keep each other accountable. Though none of us is perfect, through prayer, the leading of the Holy Spirit, and diligence, we can develop this fruit so that others will see the difference Jesus makes in our lives. —*GM*

. . . .

Lord, thank You for Your Holy Spirit.
Please help me to develop the fruit of the Spirit
so that others are drawn to You by my example. Amen.

Savor the Success

*That's exactly what Jesus did. He didn't make it easy
for himself by avoiding people's troubles,
but waded right in and helped out.*

Romans 15:3 MSG

There's a sense of satisfaction that comes from having earned everything you have, isn't there? If you're one of the many who didn't come from wealth or had to overcome great opposition, you know what I mean. Maybe you put yourself through college. Maybe you're a single parent who has alone provided for your children. Maybe you've survived an abusive past or destructive habit. Regardless, you savor every success.

But even as you savor your success, remember Jesus. Think back to when you got the job that turned your life around or when you met the person who helped you. Remember the close calls when things could have gone wrong but didn't. These memories should remind you that you didn't make it alone. Jesus was there. Whether you realized it or not, He was drawing you to Him. Take time to thank Him for your salvation—and not just the moment you made the commitment but the path that got you there. He was there then, and He's still here now, partaking in your every success. —*GM*

. . . .

*Dear Jesus, You're so merciful.
Even when I didn't realize You were there,
I know that You were with me. Thank You! Amen.*

High Road

*Therefore, as God's chosen people, holy and dearly loved,
clothe yourselves with compassion, kindness,
humility, gentleness, and patience.*

Colossians 3:12

Wouldn't it be nice if everyone treated each other with kindness? Happily, most of my coworkers have been pleasant, but every so often I've come up against Cruella de Vil's mean sister. Once, after I moved to a new position, a coworker decided I was her enemy. For two weeks, I endured her belligerence.

Though I'd love to say that I was the picture of calm rationale, the truth is, I wanted to be just as catty to her as she was to me. Fortunately, two things stopped me. First, she knew that I was a Christian, and I didn't want to ruin my witness. Second, a pastor friend encouraged me to take the high road. Though I wanted to get just as rude with her, I was determined to walk out of the situation with no regrets.

None of us are perfect. We all have weak moments when we want to hurt someone the same way they've hurt us, but as Christians, we must act like God's chosen people. We must be clothed with compassion, kindness, humility, gentleness, and patience. In short, we must take the high road. —*GM*

. . . .

*Lord, thank You for choosing me. Help me to clothe myself
in compassion, kindness, humility, gentleness, and patience,
so that my actions are pleasing to You. Amen.*

Respect

*By this everyone will know that you are my disciples,
if you love one another.*

John 13:35

"You're so stuck up that if it rained, you'd drown."
I remember hearing this expression more than once when I was growing up. It took me a few days the first time to figure out exactly what it meant, but when I realized the person who'd said that to me thought I had my nose in the air, I was horrified! I really didn't think I was better than anyone else. In fact, most of the time, I felt quite inferior.

Do you ever accidentally give off the wrong impression? When your coworkers talk about you, would they say that you're stuck up? Would they say you think better of yourself than those around you? As Christians and professional women, we need to be keenly aware that we are under constant scrutiny. That's why the Word of God tells us that people will know we're Christians by the way we love other people.

Be sure that you treat your coworkers with respect. Go the extra mile. Ask God to make you sensitive to their feelings. Read 1 Corinthians 13 on a regular basis. Ask the Lord to develop the fruit of the Spirit in your life. Soon you'll be known for His love and nothing else! —*MMA*

. . . .

Lord, help me to treat others with respect and love. Amen.

Dark Path

Don't sin by letting anger control you.
Think about it overnight and remain silent.

Psalm 4:4 NLT

Have you ever gotten angry at work? Sure you have—it's all too normal. Someone treats you badly or overturns one of your decisions, and you want to take them to the woodshed. Or thoughts of walking out the front door flash across your mind. Boy, if you haven't been there, then you're more mature than I am.

Everyone has irritating days. It's how we deal with those days that separates us from the world. As Christians, we should avoid the dark path—the one filled with revenge, hostility, or verbal assault. Instead, we should find our peace in the Lord. We should take our anger to Him before we say anything to others. Then we should take a deep breath and deal with the situation with grace. That's not to say we should always roll over and take abuse, but we should keep our emotions from ruling our actions and words.

If you're facing situations that leave you livid, take them to God. Let Him help you filter through your emotions so that you handle them in the most constructive way. Then you'll continue to be an example for Him, even in your anger. —*GM*

. . . .

Lord, I'm angry, and I need Your help.
Help me to handle my emotions in the best way. Amen.

Diva on the Loose

Do to others as you would have them do to you.
Luke 6:31

Compromise...easier said than done, eh? But in order to have a happy and productive life, you have to find that middle ground. As a writer, I am constantly battling with the art department. They *always* need more white space, meaning I have to cut my articles substantially to accommodate their layout. Those of you who are creative types will understand my frustration with this routine. I mean, I feel like I've given birth to every paragraph of that article. I hate to see any of it cut, especially for the sake of more white space. I just don't get it. But guess what? I don't have to get it. In fact, it's not my job to get it. It's my job to compromise and not be the diva with an attitude, demanding my way in every situation.

Be honest...are you the office diva? Do people call you Mariah behind your back (and not because you have Ms. Carey's amazing vocals)? If so, it's time for a change. Ask God to help you become more agreeable in the office. Look for ways to find that middle ground. Choose your battles wisely and do unto others as you'd have them do unto you. Your boss will be pleased, and so will God. —*MMA*

. . . .

Lord, help me to treat others as I'd like to be treated. Amen.

Sweet Dreams

Yes, you will lie down and your sleep will be sweet.
Proverbs 3:24 NKJV

Okay, I admit it. By nature, I'm a worrier. I don't intentionally worry. In fact, my worrying usually starts as wondering,
which leads to reasoning, which leads to worrying, which almost
always leads to sleepless nights. Maybe you can relate.

You're lying in bed. The lights are off. Everyone else, including the dog, is asleep, but you can't turn off your brain. It continues to crank, trying to figure out how to solve some crisis at
work. Slowly, the tension headache begins, creeping up your neck
and spreading over your entire head. That's it. Now you're wide
awake and in pain. So you start binge-watching *Friends* reruns on
Netflix, and the clock ticks into the wee hours of the night.

I have spent more nights living out that scenario than I'd
like to admit. But worrying about those problems at work never
changed a single one of them. Now if I happen to have a restless
night, I spend it in prayer. I thank God for watching over me. I
thank Him for wisdom. I thank Him for favor with my boss. And
I fall asleep in peace—no headaches, no worries. God promises
us sweet slumber in Proverbs, so hold Him to it. Sweet dreams,
sister! —*MMA*

. . . .

*Thank You, Lord, for giving me
peaceful, restful nights. Amen.*

On the Way

Humble yourselves therefore under the mighty hand of God,
that he may exalt you in due time:
casting all your care upon him; for he careth for you.
1 Peter 5:6–7 KJV

Have you ever wondered who actually works in those really cool jobs? Like, who gets to be the taste tester for new Lay's potato chip flavors? Or who gets to name all the latest OPI nail colors? Or who gets to test ride a wild new roller coaster? Or who gets to go to the finest spas in the world and write those reviews? Those are pretty awesome jobs.

Okay, so maybe you don't have the most glamorous job. Maybe you don't have the most enjoyable job. Maybe you're not yet working in your dream job—but the key word in this sentence is *yet*. What are you doing to make that dream job your reality? Are you working toward that dream?

So what if you're the custodian? God can make it happen—in spite of your current work situation. Trust in God's Word. It says He has a good plan for you (Jeremiah 29:11), so you can hold on to that promise. Keep believing for your dream job, but all the while, do your very best in your current position. Pretty soon you'll be walking in your dream! Oh, and if you get that taste testing position for Lay's, call on me! I'll be happy to help. —*MMA*

. . . .

Lord, help me be content with where I am on the way
to where You are taking me. Amen.

A Change of Heart

The king's heart is like channels of water in the hand
of the LORD; He turns it wherever He wishes.

Proverbs 21:1 NASB

I interviewed a man named Pete who had lived a life of crime and ended up in prison. He was serving his debt to society for armed robbery and had exhibited excellent behavior in prison. The guards liked him. His fellow prisoners liked him. He was a light in a dark place because, while he was in prison, he'd become a Christian. He was a perfect candidate for early release, but every time his parole hearing came around, the chairperson of the parole board denied his request without letting him speak.

The Lord took Pete to Proverbs 21:1, and he immediately began praying that God would change the chairperson's heart. When his next parole hearing rolled around, Pete was allowed to speak for the first time. Amazingly, the chairperson was kind to him. Shortly after, Pete walked out of prison a free man.

Do you work for someone who obviously dislikes you? It's not easy. But don't worry. God can change your supervisor's heart.

God's Word is powerful, and if there's someone at your workplace who doesn't like you for whatever reason, you can pray Proverbs 21:1 over that situation. Begin to praise God and speak things that be not as though they were—begin to praise Him that He is changing that person's heart where you are concerned. God will either change that person's heart or give you a new position. Either way, you'll be free just like Pete. —*MMA*

. . . .

Thank You, Lord, for changing hearts, and thank You
for Your supernatural favor. I love You. Amen.

Stay Grounded

Because of the three great sins of Israel—make that four—
I'm not putting up with them any longer.
They buy and sell upstanding people. People for them
are only things—ways of making money. They'd sell a poor man
for a pair of shoes. They'd sell their own grandmother!

Amos 2:6 MSG

Did you recently get promoted? Receive a pay increase? Recognition? Did it change you? Money, fame, and promotion aren't bad, but they have a way of changing folks. The attitudes that sometimes accompany success can be destructive.

If the extra income you're now earning has changed you or made you insensitive to people and their feelings, ask God to give you a heart overhaul. Praise Him for your increase and make sure that your tithe reflects your new financial status. Ask the Holy Spirit to keep you grounded so you don't become too pleased with yourself. Proverbs 16:18 says that "pride goes before destruction, and a haughty spirit before a fall" (NKJV)—and you don't want to fall on your face.

The Lord loves to give His children blessings, but He wants us to use those blessings to bless others, not let them go to our heads. Let's make sure we pass the test so that we can keep moving up with God. *—MMA*

. . . .

Lord, help me to keep a humble and sensitive heart. Amen.

Tornado Watch

*The men were amazed and asked, "What kind of man is this?
Even the winds and the waves obey him!"*
Matthew 8:27

I had walked into a tornado. Excited about my new promotion, I didn't realize what awaited me. What I expected to be an exciting time where I could strategize for greatness went out the window. With few staff members, an untested computer system, unrealistic expectations from corporate, and a lack of training, I was equipped for nothing. I felt like I'd been sucked into a tornado funnel. Around and around I went, and only God knew where I was going to land.

Have you ever felt like you'd been sucked into a professional tornado, too? Maybe you're there now, struggling to keep up with your job, struggling to learn new systems, struggling to live up to expectations, just...struggling. If so, you know how important it is never to give up.

For me, God used that position to clarify my professional goals, to illuminate what was most important to me, and to comfort me with the realization that He was still in control. If you're in the midst of a tornado, I invite you to turn to Him. He'll give you wisdom to face the storm. He may calm it, or He may help you come through while it rages on. Either way, you'll know He's there with you. —*GM*

. . . .

*Lord, I feel like I'm in a storm. Please help me stay strong
as I trust You in every area of my life. Amen.*

The Mission Statement

*He said to them, "Go into all the world
and preach the gospel to all creation."*
Mark 16:15

Every company or organization has a big picture, the thing that drives the services they provide. Often it's written in a mission statement so that there's never a mistake about what the company is supposed to be doing. While an organization's purpose can, of course, change over time, in general, the mission statement is a great way to keep everyone on track.

In our spiritual lives, we have a mission, too. Jesus told the disciples, "Go into all the world and preach the gospel to all creation." That is still relevant today. Some get nervous that God will call them to be missionaries in Zimbabwe (and He just might!), but you can impact your community right where you are. In your work and your neighborhood, you can fulfill the mission. Perhaps your office is your mission field, and the lives of your coworkers will be changed by your faith and behavior. As long as you're doing your part to share the gospel, you're right on track with Jesus's mission statement. —*GM*

. . . .

*Jesus, I want to be used to tell others about You.
Please show me how to do that in the best way. Amen.*

DAY
256

Loyalty

Don't urge me to leave you or to turn back from you.
Where you go I will go, and where you stay I will stay.
Your people will be my people and your God my God.
Ruth 1:16

I love the story of Ruth and Naomi. Naomi's husband had died, and so had her two sons, leaving her with two daughters-in-law, Ruth and Orpah. Because there was a famine in Moab, where they lived, Naomi decided to return to her homeland. She wished the best for her daughters-in-law, telling them that they should go back to their families and find new husbands. Orpah kissed Naomi good-bye and did as instructed, but Ruth wouldn't budge. She basically said, "I'm with you till the end." Her loyalty to Naomi was precious.

You know, loyalty is hard to come by these days—especially in the workplace. People trade company secrets like baseball cards. Let's be the exception. Let's be the ones our companies and coworkers can count on—no matter what. Let's be the ones who work hard and give our best, day in and day out. Let's be like Ruth and do things God's way. Things turned out pretty great for her, and they will for us, too. —*MMA*

. . . .

Father, help me be loyal to You, to my family, to my friends,
to my coworkers, and to my employer. Amen.

Super Weakness

But he said to me, "My grace is sufficient for you,
for my power is made perfect in weakness."
Therefore I will boast all the more gladly about my weaknesses,
so that Christ's power may rest on me.

2 Corinthians 12:9

I used to love to watch superhero cartoons when I was a little girl. My absolute favorite superhero was Wonder Woman, with her awesome invisible jet and her cool magic lasso. I dreamed of growing up and looking just like Lynda Carter. (I think I'm about as tall as one of her legs.) I was pretty jazzed when the *Wonder Woman* live-action movie debuted in 2017!

You know what I've learned from years of watching superhero cartoons? Even superheroes have weaknesses. (Ask Superman about kryptonite.) So, if superheroes aren't invincible, why should we mere mortals expect to be any freer from weakness?

I have many weaknesses—some more evident than others. How about you? Well, I have good news! God's power is made perfect in our weaknesses. When we are weak, that's when God can really show Himself strong. So even our weaknesses aren't liabilities when we've got God—our secret weapon. When we are at our weakest point, God is at His strongest. Leave that invisible jet in the garage and call on God today. —*MMA*

. . . .

Thank You, Lord, for showing Yourself strong
when I am weak. Amen.

Coming Up Roses

"No weapon that is formed against you will prosper;
and every tongue that accuses you in judgment you will condemn.
This is the heritage of the servants of the LORD,
and their vindication is from Me," declares the LORD.
Isaiah 54:17 NASB

Has something ever happened at work that left you feeling persecuted and victimized? Isn't your first instinct to defend yourself? That's usually how I react. I want to move into lawyer mode and present my side of the story, fact by fact, in my defense. But that's almost never the right way to handle the situation. See, the more you defend yourself, the guiltier you look—even if you are innocent.

Gena, my good friend and coauthor of this book, always says, "Don't worry. It'll all come out in the wash." She's right. No matter what kind of craziness is going on in your office, the truth will eventually be known. So don't sweat it. That doesn't mean you shouldn't keep good files and document situations, but in the end, trust in the Lord and allow Him to be your defender. Memorize Isaiah 54:17 and say it every morning. Remember, God's Word says that no weapon formed against you shall prosper. That promise is better than the most expensive, high-powered lawyer you could hire. God's law is on your side. —*MMA*

• •

Lord, I am trusting You to be my ultimate defender.
Thank You for watching over me. Amen.

Apples and Oranges

But in fact God has arranged the parts in the body,
every one of them, just as he wanted them to be.
If they were all one part, where would the body be?
As it is, there are many parts, but one body.

1 Corinthians 12:18–20

Have you ever heard the expression "You can't compare apples to oranges"? While apples and oranges are both types of fruit, they are very, very different. They have different peels. They have different textures. They are different colors. And they certainly have different tastes.

As Christian working women, we also have different areas of expertise, different strengths, different callings, different talents, and more. So why do we compare ourselves with each other? It's like comparing apples to oranges. The devil would love to get us focused on our shortcomings instead of our strengths. He'd love to convince us that we have nothing to offer compared to the other talented women we know. He wants us to get our eyes off Jesus and onto our inabilities. Don't go there!

Instead, ask God to help you focus on your strengths and abilities. Ask God to help you see yourself as He sees you. Maybe you've always wanted to be an apple, yet you were born to be an orange. Take heart! You're the apple of God's eye! —*MMA*

. . . .

Lord, help me to see myself as You see me. Amen.

Wish Me Luck

*This is My commandment: that you love one another
[just] as I have loved you.*
John 15:12 AMPC

Do you know the song that goes, "What the world needs
now is love, sweet love"? I've always loved that song. It's not
just a great little melody; the lyrics pack a powerful message. You
know, the world really does need love...but not the kind of love
the world offers. That love is temporary and artificial. The world
needs God's love—everlasting, unconditional love.

Just a guess, but I'd bet your workplace could use a healthy
dose of love, too. No matter how ugly people are acting today,
answer them with love. Yes, it's tough, but you can do it with the
Lord's help. I speak from experience.

On my last day of work at a monthly magazine, one of my
coworkers poked her head in my office and said, "Just wanted to
wish you luck and say that I'll always remember you as the girl
who *way* overdressed for work." Nice, eh? Nothing like getting the
last word in. I so wanted to say something ugly back, but the Lord
wouldn't let me do it. See, God wants us to answer low blows by
taking the high road of love. Take that walk today. —*MMA*

. . . .

Lord, fill me up with more of Your love. Amen.

Big Tasks

Lord, you establish peace for us;
all that we have accomplished you have done for us.
Isaiah 26:12

Have you ever had to do something but knew you needed help? The task took determination and hard work, but it was bigger than one person.

In the Old Testament, three men were given a task like this. After years of captivity in Babylon, God was allowing Israel to return to Jerusalem. Since the city had been destroyed, the process took almost a hundred years. First, Zerubbabel returned to Jerusalem with over 42,000 people. Then seventy-nine years later, Ezra returned with 1,754 men. Finally, thirteen years after Ezra, Nehemiah returned as governor to rebuild the city.

Imagine a task like this—the rebuilding of God's holy city. It was daunting; but so is growing a company, managing a diverse and creative workforce, or even raising your children. Whatever the task, remember that if God has called you to do it, then it is doable. Don't assume that just because it's part of your calling, you can't have help. God called Zerubbabel, Ezra, and Nehemiah to rebuild Jerusalem, but He gave them help. As they set out to accomplish their tasks, they had many workers with them.

With God's guidance and the help of the people around you, you can accomplish your task, too. —*GM*

. . . .

Lord, accomplish through me and those around me
all that You want to do. Amen.

Workplace Bully

He [will] defend the afflicted among the people
and save the children of the needy.

Psalm 72:4

Do you have a scary boss? One of those Attila the Hun types? People are afraid to tell him anything because he'll either yell, degrade, or retaliate. Or maybe he just seems to have it in for you, and just entering his office makes you nervous. These people make life at work difficult. It doesn't matter whether they treat everyone that way or just you, it isn't easy.

If you've got one of these leaders in your life, know that God will help you work to the best of your ability. A frequent assurance in the Psalms is that God will defend the afflicted, and if you're working under an unfair tyrant, you may well find yourself afflicted. Pray for God's wisdom. Pray for that person. Then trust God to help you overcome the situation successfully. You don't have to be afraid of a workplace bully. Instead, focus on what God has given you to do and trust Him to defend you. —*GM*

. . . .

Heavenly Father, You know the conditions under which I work,
so I trust You to help me through. Please give me wisdom,
bless those who try to frighten me,
and defend me from their attacks. Amen.

DAY
263

Happy Thoughts

*Finally, brothers and sisters, whatever is true,
whatever is noble, whatever is right, whatever is pure,
whatever is lovely, whatever is admirable—
if anything is excellent or praiseworthy—
think about such things.*

Philippians 4:8

Martha Washington said, "The greater part of our happiness or misery depends on our dispositions, and not upon our circumstances." In essence, our thoughts determine our contentment. If we ponder doom and gloom, then we will only see doom and gloom, but if we think about God's goodness and blessings, we will see His goodness and blessings.

Today's verse is especially powerful when you consider that the apostle Paul wrote it when he was in prison. Over the course of Paul's ministry, he was beaten, mobbed, and stoned. Yet he continued to focus on joy. He didn't let the harshness of life overwhelm his attitude. He remained thankful for his salvation and focused on God's blessings.

As you search for joy and contentment in your life and work, focus on those things that are noble, right, pure, lovely, and admirable. There will always be things that don't quite measure up, but by focusing on the good, you'll find more contentment and joy than ever before. —*GM*

. . . .

*Lord, today I commit to think on things that are noble,
right, pure, lovely, and admirable.
I trust You to take care of everything else. Amen.*

Renewal

Great is his faithfulness; his mercies begin afresh each morning.
I say to myself, "The LORD is my inheritance;
therefore, I will hope in him!"

Lamentations 3:23–24 NLT

What a beautiful reminder of the Lord's character. This verse shows us once again that God is merciful and faithful to His people, and our hope is in Him. It's interesting that this passage was written after a very dark time in Israel's history. The city of Jerusalem was in ruins, yet the prophet Jeremiah, who lamented the loss, still acknowledged God's kindness.

Aren't you glad that the Lord's mercies are new every day for you, too? I know I am. It's comforting to know that even on our darkest days—days when we totally and completely miss the mark—God is faithful. He is ready to give us a fresh start. He never abandons or leaves us to get ourselves out of the messes we create. Instead, His mercies are new every day, and we can put our hope in Him.

If you are struggling to accept God's forgiveness because you feel that you are too far gone, meditate on this Scripture. Allow it to become real to you so that you know He is faithful. His mercies are new every day, and you can hope in Him. —*GM*

. . . .

Lord, thank You for Your faithfulness
and Your renewed mercies. I love You! Amen.

New People

*Now to each one the manifestation of the Spirit
is given for the common good.*
1 Corinthians 12:7

I'll never forget the one group of coworkers I loved most. We looked out for each other, encouraged each other, and celebrated each other's successes. We approached problems with unity, trying to find the best solution for everyone. Unfortunately, that bliss was only for a season. Eventually, they all took other jobs or went home to spend more time with their families, and I was left behind. When new people arrived, I quickly realized things weren't going to be the same. The spirit of the department had changed. It wasn't necessarily bad, just different. It took time for me to adjust, and to be honest, a part of me never did. Some of the joy of doing my job was gone.

As you work, coworkers will come and go. With some, you'll click. With others, you'll coexist. Though they may approach things differently, they aren't necessarily wrong. It could be that God needed new talent in the department or maybe He's fulfilling someone's calling elsewhere. When that happens, trust Him to help you make the transition. Ask Him to show you how to gel with the new people. They may be different, but you might be surprised at how well they fit. —*GM*

. . . .

*Lord, help me to work well with everyone in my office
so that I can accomplish all that I need to do. Amen.*

A Dose of Joy

Always be joyful.
1 Thessalonians 5:16 NLT

Before I had a book published, I truly thought that I'd be forever happy when I saw my book on the shelves of an actual bookstore. And I'll be honest—it was pretty exciting the first time I found my book at our local Barnes & Noble. It was even more thrilling when I did my first book signing. But you know what? That happiness was fleeting. After a few months, I began worrying about my next book contract. I worried I might be a one-book wonder. I worried that I wasn't doing enough to promote my current book. Just like a new toy loses its appeal after a few hours on Christmas morning, my shiny new book had lost its luster. It no longer made me happy.

You can't rely on career accomplishments, material things, or other people to make you happy. True happiness comes only from our heavenly Father. That kind of eternal happiness is actually called joy, and it isn't affected by outside circumstances. See, if you can't be happy taking out your boss's trash, you won't be happy even if you're promoted to boss tomorrow.

If you're lacking joy today, turn to Jesus. He has a dose of joy with your name on it, and it won't ever lose its luster. —*MMA*

. . . .

Lord, fill me with Your everlasting joy. Amen.

Faithful with Little

He said unto him, "Well done, good servant;
because you were faithful in a very little,
have authority over ten cities."

Luke 19:17 NKJV

There really is no substitute for hard work. Though unexpected blessings sometimes fall into our laps, it usually takes hard work to succeed.

In the parable of the ten minas, Jesus spoke of three workers who were entrusted with money. One didn't do anything with it. Another invested it in a mediocre venture, but the wisest of the three earned a 100 percent return. The boss was obviously most impressed by the largest return. His response was "Because you were faithful in a very little, have authority over ten cities." In other words, because you've worked hard with a small amount, I know that I can trust you with more.

We must be committed to working hard for Jesus. In whatever capacity He's called us to, we need to be faithful in little so that we can eventually have authority over much more. By giving it our all, we can prove that we're ready and able to be used by God. —*GM*

. . . .

Lord, I am committed to working hard in whatever job
or assignment You want me to do. Amen.

It's Just My Personality

As you come to him, the living Stone...
you also, like living stones, are being built into a spiritual house
to be a holy priesthood, offering spiritual sacrifices acceptable
to God through Jesus Christ.

1 Peter 2:4–5

I'll admit it—personality tests make me nervous. Though they've given me great insight into myself, I've seen people use them to one-up each other. Instead of valuing each other for their strengths and differences, they assume that certain personality types are better than others. They say, "Well, I'm a choleric (or lion or some other test's label), and that's why I'm strong willed." Or "I'm an otter (or sanguine, etc.), and that's why I'm a social butterfly." I've even heard it taken to the extreme of excusing bad behavior because "Well, that's just my personality."

When we become children of God, we're called to a higher standard than just our natural inclinations. He wants us to be "living stones" so that we become "spiritual houses" and "a holy priesthood" and "offer spiritual sacrifices acceptable to God." Yes, He made each of us different, with dissimilar attributes and tastes. Through those beautiful differences, we can grow spiritually stronger and become examples of godly integrity for Him. —*GM*

* *

Lord, thank You for allowing me to come to You.
Please help me to become a spiritual house for You. Amen.

I Have a Question

*So we fasted and petitioned our God about this,
and he answered our prayer.*

Ezra 8:23

Have you ever wanted to question God about something but weren't sure it was appropriate? Maybe it was about a life-changing event, an accepted teaching in your church, or whether you were doing what He wanted you to do. It might even have seemed good and godly—but you just didn't know if you could ask. Unfortunately, we often don't ask these questions. We assume that it's unnecessary or ungodly to question God, but really, He's the only one with the answer.

For me, one of the most freeing statements I've ever heard was "God is bigger than all your questions." I'd never considered that. I'd assumed it was wrong to question God; I'd figured some topics were just off-limits. It wasn't until that moment that I realized God really is bigger.

If you're struggling with a question that only God can answer, go ahead and ask Him. You might not always understand or even like the answer, but it's good to know that nothing is off limits with Him. —*GM*

. . . .

*Lord, thank You for always hearing
my prayers and questions. I know that You are bigger than
anything I bring Your way. Amen.*

Bring on the Blonde

Love is patient, love is kind.... It does not dishonor others,
it is not self-seeking, it is not easily angered,
it keeps no record of wrongs.

1 Corinthians 13:4–5

Believe it or not, I learned a spiritual lesson from the movie *Legally Blonde.* For those who haven't seen it, it's a comedy about a Beverly Hills ditz who decides to follow the man she loves to Harvard Law School. Because she doesn't quite fit into the East Coast Harvard persona, people don't accept her. In fact, she has to earn their respect in her own unique way, but even though people treated her badly, she never held it against them. She never wrote them off or tried to get even. Some might argue that she wasn't bright enough to think that far ahead, but to me, it just wasn't in her character. Even when they were rude, she responded with kindness.

I came out of the movie thinking, *Lord, I want to be more like that.* I want to come to a place where I don't even acknowledge or see that people are being rude, so that I can always give them the benefit of the doubt. Some may think it's an unrealistic goal, but to me, it would make loving people—even the difficult ones—so much easier. —*GM*

. . . .

Lord, help me to always be kind and never keep
a record of wrongs. Amen.

No Comparison

For who in the skies above can compare with the LORD?
Psalm 89:6

We serve an amazing God. He is the Creator of the heavens and earth, the beginning and the end. He has always existed and will always exist. Those should be reasons enough to worship Him.

For those of us who serve Him, it gets even better. He knows everything about us, and He still loves us. From the moment of mankind's first betrayal, God set in motion a plan to bring us back into relationship to Him. He sent His innocent Son to die so that we could live. And in our lives, He is a personal God. Because of Jesus, we now have direct access to God in prayer. His Holy Spirit is with us constantly, allowing us to live a holy and righteous life.

Though you know all these things, sometimes it's good just to remind yourself who you serve. No other god compares to Him. He alone is worthy of your praise. So take a few minutes to praise Him today. Thank Him for what He's done in your life and your work and for bringing you into His family. He really is a faithful God. "Who in the skies above can compare with the Lord?" —*GM*

. . . .

Heavenly Father, You alone are worthy of all praise.
No other god compares to You. Amen.

Be an Angel

Walk in the way of love, just as Christ loved us
and gave himself up for us as a fragrant offering
and sacrifice to God.

Ephesians 5:2

I was so homesick. I wanted desperately to move back to Indiana, but I couldn't tell my husband that. After all, we had just moved to Texas to accommodate my new job. I knew I was where God wanted me to be, but that didn't make me miss my family and friends in Indiana any less.

In the midst of this homesickness, I was also struggling to find my identity at this magazine. As a former award-winning newspaper writer, I walked onto the job with an attitude the size of Texas. It didn't take long to realize that my awards and experience didn't mean squat to the people at my new job. I was an emotional wreck.

I needed a touch from heaven, and that touch came through my managing editor and his wife. He was also a former newspaper reporter, so he understood my background and helped me transition into the magazine world. He and his sweet wife became family to me. God knew what I needed, and He used this sweet couple to help me. They were like angels on earth to me. I'll never forget their kindness.

Why don't you see if you can be an angel in a coworker's life today? Ask God to use you. —*MMA*

. . . .

Lord, use me to touch someone's hurting heart today. Amen.

The Least Is the Greatest

*An argument started among the disciples as to which of them
would be the greatest. Jesus, knowing their thoughts,
took a little child and had him stand beside him.
Then he said to them, "Whoever welcomes this little child
in my name welcomes me; and whoever welcomes me
welcomes the one who sent me. For it is the one
who is least among you all who is the greatest."*

Luke 9:46–48

If you're struggling to get along with a coworker today, don't
feel bad. Even the disciples—the chosen twelve—had trouble.
From this passage in Luke, we can see that they had a little jealousy going on in the ranks. They were jockeying for position.
They wanted to know who would be the greatest among them.
Notice how Jesus answered them. He said, "The one who is least
among you...is the greatest."

It's not hard to see that Jesus frowns on competitive jealousy. He wouldn't tolerate it back then, and He still won't. Why?
Because He knows it will eventually destroy us. James 3:16 says,
"For where envy and self-seeking exist, confusion and every evil
thing are there" (NKJV).

If you're striving to outshine someone else in your company
or if you're in constant strife with another colleague over who's
the greatest, end it today. Love your neighbor as yourself, and let
Jesus promote you. —*MMA*

. . . .

*Lord, keep my heart right where
my coworkers are concerned. Amen.*

Lone Ranger

*"In the last times there will be scoffers who will follow
their own ungodly desires." These are the people who divide you,
who follow mere natural instincts and do not have the Spirit.*

Jude 1:18–19

Working in a worldly workplace, you may feel like the Lone Ranger at times, standing alone for godly principles. While your coworkers party on the weekends or tell tasteless jokes, it can be tough to know that you'll never fit in.

For some, this knowledge doesn't matter. You're there to do a job, and you don't mind going against the grain. But others find it difficult. You may not be a part of the in crowd. You may be considered a prude because you won't join in their fun. Others distrust you because your standards are different. It can be disheartening—even though you know standing for Jesus is the right thing to do.

If you feel like you're on the outside looking in at work, find a group of other Christian professionals outside of work to help you deal with the isolation. If your church doesn't have a working women's group, maybe you can start one. As you build friendships with other Christian women, you'll be stronger to stand against the ungodly influences. —*GM*

....

*Lord, I feel very alone at work. There are so many ungodly
influences. Please help me to stand strong. Amen.*

My Everything

As the deer longs for streams of water,
so I long for you, O God.
Psalm 42:1 NLT

There's a beautiful worship song we often sing at church that says, "You are everything to me, Lord." That's a powerful line…but can we honestly sing it? Do we really mean it?

If we truly feel that way about our Lord, we can be content whether we're the CEO or a letter-opener-in-training. Contentment—true contentment—comes only from the Lord. Sure, we can get temporary career contentment fixes, but that lasting peace and sense of fulfillment come only from heaven.

No promotion. No pay increase. No corner office. Nothing can fill the hole in our hearts that yearns for Jesus. Only He can fill that void. Only He can cause contentment to be a way of life. That's why Paul and Silas could sing praises to God while locked up in a stinky prison. They were content—even joyful—in their circumstances. Why? Because Jesus was everything to them— period. Is Jesus everything to you today? If you've lost the passion you once had for Christ, spend some time with Him today. If He is your everything, you'll be content in everything. —*MMA*

. . . .

Lord, You truly are everything to me.
Help me never lose sight of that. Amen.

DAY
276

Do What?!

God blesses those people who want to obey him.
Matthew 5:6 CEV

Have you ever received an assignment that left you wanting to roll your eyes? Or what about the *brilliant* idea that someone has for handling a project in a way that you know won't work?

When it comes to doing what we're told to do at work, sometimes we just have to grin and bear it. There really is no other way. When it comes to our spiritual work, it's the same. God loves obedience.

Of course, if we read this verse closely, we realize it isn't only *obedience* that God desires. We should *want* to obey Him, meaning we need to have a good attitude. In fact, this verse says that He blesses us when we do.

If you are eager to have God's favor and blessings in your life, commit to living a life of eager and joyful obedience. Guard against rolling your spiritual eyes at God. As you do, you'll receive His blessings and enjoy His favor. —*GM*

. . . .

Lord, I am committed to following
Your Word and doing Your will.
As I do, I appreciate Your blessings. Amen.

A Fish Out of Water

The LORD directs the steps of the godly.
He delights in every detail of their lives.
Though they stumble, they will never fall,
for the LORD holds them by the hand.

Psalm 37:23–24 NLT

Sometimes when change comes on the scene, we think we're ready for it, but we're not. All of a sudden, we're expected to know skills we don't know, understand concepts we don't understand, meet impossible deadlines, and do it all with grace and wisdom. If recent changes in your life have left you feeling like a fish out of water, don't stress out.

Remember, God has already seen your future, and He will guide you every step of the way. God has everything you need to transition smoothly through the changes in your life. If you need wisdom, just ask Him. Proverbs 1:23 says, "Come and listen to my counsel. I'll share my heart with you and make you wise" (NLT).

Don't be afraid of having to learn and grow. Embrace it! God will never give you more than you can handle, so you're going to be just fine. In fact, you're going to be better than fine. Romans 8:37 says that you are more than a conqueror, so own that today! Change? No problem. Bring it on! —*MMA*

. . . .

Lord, help me handle the changes in my life
with supernatural grace and wisdom. Amen.

Both Feet on the Ground

*He guides the humble in what is right
and teaches them his way.*
Psalm 25:9

I would love to say that I've remained humble in all situations, but unfortunately, I can't. There have been times when I was wowed by my own accomplishments—like when one of my projects came in looking better than expected or when I accomplished a task that others didn't want to tackle or when I received a promotion. That's when I sat up a little taller in my seat and gave myself a pat on the back. Of course, there were other times too—times when I made huge mistakes or couldn't figure out a project or my suggestions were overlooked in a meeting. Those times kept my feet on the ground.

Humility is an important part of being an example of Christ to others. Face it, when we're enamored with ourselves, we're not giving Him the recognition for working through us. Instead, we're letting everyone know that we think it all depends on us.

If you've been promoted or received recognition for a job well done, thank God for it. Recognize that your gifts and talents come from Him. As you remain humble, He'll continue to guide you in "what is right" and "teach you His way." —*GM*

. . . .

*Lord, I thank You for all I have,
because I know it comes from You. Amen.*

Go to the Source

I know, LORD, that our lives are not our own.
We are not able to plan our own course.
Jeremiah 10:23 NLT

Have you ever worked on a project with no idea what you were doing? You weren't trained or given the necessary information. You had to figure it out as you went. You felt like a child, playing Marco Polo in the dark. You needed clear communication from your boss.

Similarly, you need clear instruction in your life. You need to know where you're headed and what's expected. On your own, you can feel lost and discouraged. Just as you need direction from your boss for a work project, you need direction from God, your spiritual boss, for life.

I've found that, when I begin to feel lost and discouraged in my life, that's when I've not been talking to God. I've been trying to figure things out on my own instead of getting direction from Him.

If you're feeling lost and discouraged, the answers are closer than you think. Reading your Bible and praying are the best ways to discover God's will. If you go directly to Him, you won't be left to wander in the dark alone. Turn to Him and watch as your answers come through. —*GM*

. . . .

Dear Lord, I know that my life is not my own
and I need Your direction. So please direct me;
I'm open to hearing from You. Amen.

The Road Map

*My people are ruined because
they don't know what's right or true.*

Hosea 4:6 MSG

Be honest. How often do you read your Bible? Do you medi-tate on the Scriptures so that they become written on your heart? I know it's difficult to find time to read God's Word, but it's so important. We need so much Word on the inside of us that there's not room for anything else.

This verse in Hosea really says a lot. See, if we don't know what we believe, if we don't know what is right or wrong, how will we ever be able to live a Christian life? When you're faced with an ethical dilemma at work, you need the Word to illuminate the way you should go. You need God's guidance in your life. His Word is full of wisdom and guidance, but if you don't know it, it doesn't do you much good. Neglecting the Word of God is like having a road map to your destination and never bothering to look at it for direction.

So get out your road map to life—God's Word—and study it today and every day. He will help you make the best decisions at home and at work.

He not only knows the way, He is the Way. —*MMA*

*Father, give me a craving for Your Word
and Your ways above all else. Amen.*

You Are Called

*Who knows but that you have come to your royal position
for such a time as this?*
Esther 4:14

I recently heard an interview with Christian movie director Randall Wallace, and he said something that really stuck with me: "The greatest call you can have is the one God has for you." I actually stopped what I was doing and wrote it down. I didn't want to forget those powerful words.

I don't want you to forget them, either.

See, you don't have to be behind a pulpit to have divine purpose and make a huge impact in this world.

Whether you're called to be a businesswoman, a teacher, or a mail carrier, you are important. Your life means something. God called you to fulfill that special role because He has a plan for your life. It's so powerful when you realize that you're doing exactly what you were born to do, and the devil knows this truth. That's why he will do everything he can to discourage you and get you to compare yourself with others and their callings. He's trying to convince you that your calling is not as important as theirs. Don't fall for his lies. Instead, thank God for your calling and walk in it with great enthusiasm and courage. When you do, you'll enjoy the journey, and every step toward that finish line will be purposeful. —*MMA*

. . . .

*Father, I thank You for creating me for such a time as this.
Help me to never forget the importance of my calling,
and help me to fulfill my divine destiny. I love You, Lord. Amen.*

Baggage

Forgive us our debts, as we also have forgiven our debtors.
Matthew 6:12

Have you taken any business trips lately? I have been racking up the frequent flyer miles over the past year, speaking at various conferences, book signings, and book expos. So you'd think I'd be a skilled packer, right? Not a chance. I always pack way too much. Since you're only allowed to check two free bags on my airline of choice these days, I end up taking as many carry-on pieces as the airline will allow. While that seems like a good plan, all those extra carry-ons are difficult to maneuver. I usually end up dropping a bag or fumbling with them all the way through the airport. I'm always so relieved when I reach my destination and can unload all those bags.

You know, handling too many emotional carry-on bags is a bad thing, too. Can you imagine walking through your office, juggling four or five small bags? It would be difficult, wouldn't it? Well, if you're carrying around past hurts and resentments, you are doing just that—day in and day out. You'll never be able to climb that ladder of success with all that extra baggage, so get rid of it. God made you to be more than a conqueror—not a bag lady! —*MMA*

. . . .

Father, I give You all my baggage.
Replace it with Your everlasting love. Amen.

DAY
283

His Ways Are Higher

"For my thoughts are not your thoughts, neither are your ways
my ways," declares the LORD. "As the heavens are higher
than the earth, so are my ways higher than your ways
and my thoughts than your thoughts."

Isaiah 55:8–9

In all the years I've served God, I can honestly say He never does things the way I think He will. I'm always grateful and amazed by what He does, but His ways truly are higher than mine.

Take my daughter Allyson, for example. She went to fashion design school in LA. After graduation, she paid her dues working managerial retail and visual communication jobs in shopping malls. Her heart was to work in the product development side of fashion, but her fiancé's job kept them in the Midwest, and such opportunities were scarce. It was a dilemma...but not for God.

To pay bills, she signed up to work for a temp agency, and guess where that agency placed her? Adidas. In her dream job. Using her education.

Yep, God's ways are higher. Thank goodness He orders our steps. So, if your career path seems to be going nowhere, take it from Allyson. God's ways are higher. Don't try to figure it out; just follow Him; be diligent to do all that you can do; and trust Him and His ways. You're going to love the plan He has for your life. —*MMA*

. . . .

Lord, help me to trust Your ways. Amen

DAY
284

It's a Drill!

*Be prepared.... Take all the help you can get,
every weapon God has issued, so that when it's all over
but the shouting you'll still be on your feet.*

Ephesians 6:13 MSG

Don't you love fire drills at work? You're working peacefully in your office, and all of a sudden, a loud shrill pierces the air. Often workers roll their eyes at the thought of leaving their desks for a false alarm—but if the alarm were ever real, they'd be thankful that they knew exactly where to go. Though it sometimes seems frivolous, the preparation is good.

It's good to be prepared for life's emergencies, too. Instead of being afraid or overwhelmed when challenges arise, stay close to God. It doesn't mean that you'll always avoid difficult situations, but you will be able to handle the pressure when it comes. You won't be caught by surprise when the shrill of problems comes up.

If you want to be ready for the fires of life, start preparing now by staying close to God through prayer, reading His Word, attending church, and socializing with other Christians. When you do, you'll be much more ready to take on tough situations. *—GM*

. . . .

*Lord, thank You for always helping me prepare
for the problems that come up in life. Help me to stay close
to You so that they don't overwhelm me. Amen.*

Your Helper

*I know that through your prayers and the help
given by the Spirit of Jesus Christ, what has happened to me
will turn out for my deliverance.*
Philippians 1:19

Do you ever wonder how people manage their lives without Jesus? I do. The thought of making daily decisions without His guidance is pretty scary.

But there was a time in my life when I tried doing everything myself. I made my own decisions and lived by my own rules. Boy, that was short-lived. I remember praying, "Lord, I can't do it alone. I'm Yours." I'll never forget the peace, joy, and love that filled my heart at that moment. Within weeks, the things in my life that were displeasing to Him were gone—and not by my own hand. He orchestrated all of it.

If you're struggling to do everything and make every decision by yourself, let it go. Jesus is the best coach, friend, big brother, and teammate that you'll ever have. He will never leave you, and He'll continually intercede with the Father on your behalf. Go ahead and turn your entire life—every career decision and relationship—over to Him. It'll be *by far* the best decision you'll ever make. —*GM*

. . . .

*Lord, I surrender everything in my life to You.
Direct and use me however You choose. Amen.*

The Niche

*We are God's masterpiece. He has created us anew
in Christ Jesus, so we can do the good things
he planned for us long ago.*

Ephesians 2:10 NLT

Okay, I have to 'fess up—I am hooked on some reality TV. I've watched the occasional *Dance Moms* episode, and I really kind of like *America's Got Talent*. But my favorite reality TV show of all time is *American Idol*. I have watched it ever since its debut.

During the 2003–2004 season, a contestant named John won the hearts of many. Only sixteen years old, this redheaded crooner took America by surprise. You see, he sang Tony Bennett and Frank Sinatra songs instead of pop and rock. So when he was forced to sing Latin music one night of the competition, he fell flat—literally. Simon Cowell, the notoriously mean-spirited judge, said, "John, you and Latin music go together like chocolate ice cream and an onion." Well, John was voted off after that performance, which proves one thing—you can't be the best at everything. While he could belt out big band tunes with the best, he couldn't sing a Latin lyric to save his life.

And that's okay. No one is awesome at everything, so stop beating yourself up. Ask God to help you find your niche. He has a destiny for you, and like John, it may not include singing Latin music. Whatever God has for you will be great, and you'll be great at it! —*MMA*

. . . .

*Thank You, Lord, for helping me to succeed
in my calling. Amen.*

Chapters

"For I know the plans I have for you," declares the LORD,
"plans to prosper you and not to harm you,
plans to give you hope and a future."
Jeremiah 29:11

I look at my life like chapters in a book. Looking back, I can see God's hand direct me from one phase to another. In fact, even when I couldn't see how a job or experience applied to the big picture, I eventually discovered that it did. Nothing was a waste of time. God has used every experience to mold me so that He could use me today.

And what He's done for me, He'll surely do for you.

If you are wondering whether what you're doing really matters, take heart; God is using and preparing you for the next chapter. As He said in His Word, "I know the plans I have for you." He's preparing your way. If you work retail, He may be molding your interpersonal skills. If you're in finance, He may be teaching you about financial trends. If you're in education, He may be equipping you to be a better teacher. Whatever your job, God will use your talents to glorify Him. —*GM*

. . . .

Lord, I know that You have exciting plans for me,
and I trust You to fulfill them in my life. Amen.

I Think I Can

I have strength for all things in Christ Who empowers me.
Philippians 4:13 AMPC

Remember the Little Golden Book about the little engine that could? You know the story. He tries really hard—against many odds—chugging along and puffing, "I think I can, I think I can," until he proves everyone wrong and reaches his goal. I've always loved that little book. You know why? Because it's packed with powerful teaching. If we can keep a can-do attitude, we can achieve many things.

Growing up, my daughter Abby was a power tumbler. In fact, she was a member of a competitive gymnastics team. I remember watching her and knowing as she stood at the edge of the mat whether her tumbling pass would be successful. I could tell by the look on her face. If she approached the mat with a can-do facial expression, I knew she was going to nail it. But if I saw fear on her face, I knew she was not going to give her best performance. It was all in her attitude.

Maybe, like that little engine that could, you have a goal that seems impossible to reach. Maybe you're having trouble mustering up the can-do attitude you need to accomplish the task at hand. Like Abby, fear is written all over your face. Well, God says that you can do all things through Him, so go for it! Say it out loud: "No fear here!" Keep a can-do attitude and watch your dreams become a reality. —*MMA*

. . . .

Lord, help me to have a can-do attitude. Amen.

We've Come a Long Way, Baby!

GOD's strong name is our help,
the same GOD who made heaven and earth.
Psalm 124:8 MSG

In the last few decades, there has been a huge shift in the way business is handled. Technology is so integral now that workers can't imagine functioning without it. Just imagine life without smartphones, email, text messaging, Facebook, or Instagram. At the very least, imagine life without a delete key! Think about how our mothers and grandmothers had to use correction tape and Wite-Out to correct typos.

We've come a long way, baby!

Even though business has changed and our lives in general have become much more online, God is still the same. I know there are people in the world who view Christianity as an outdated religion. They're following the "If it feels good (right) to me, do it" approach to life. But if you pay attention and if you allow God to be active in your life, you'll see how real He is. Whether it's giving you wisdom about handling a situation or helping you save a relationship, He's still there. His fingerprints are everywhere.

As times change, remember that God is still the same. Unlike technology, He will never become obsolete. —*GM*

. . . .

Lord, thank You for being real in my life.
Help me to see Your fingerprints in everything. Amen.

Play Nice

Be kind and compassionate to one another.
Ephesians 4:32

One of my go-to movies is *13 Going on 30*, starring Jennifer Garner. I love it! Not only is the movie cute, it also has a powerful message. If you haven't seen it, Jennifer's character makes a wish on her thirteenth birthday—she wants to be "thirty and flirty." She wants to be one of the popular crowd. Well, she gets her wish. She wakes up a gorgeous thirty-year-old writer, working for a successful New York magazine. She has a cute boy-friend who is a professional athlete, a closet full of cool clothes and sensational shoes, and a life she'd only dreamed of. However, she finds out that she attained that life through being a terrible person—a backbiting, overbearing, insensitive player. Over the course of the movie, she rectifies the situation, and the movie has a happy ending.

Wouldn't it be great if we could fix our mistakes just as eas-ily? Well, we can't, but God can. If you've stepped over others and made compromises in order to get ahead in your career, ask God to help you rectify those situations. Ask God to keep your heart sensitive to others' feelings. Don't spend your time plotting how to one-up a coworker. Don't take every opportunity to make your boss look bad in front of the company CEO. Remember, God doesn't want us to be players. He wants us to represent Him and play nice. —*MMA*

. . . .

Lord, help me to treat others as You would have me do. Amen.

Choose Happiness

*May the God of hope fill you with all joy and peace
as you trust in him, so that you may overflow
with hope by the power of the Holy Spirit.*

Romans 15:13

Call it hormones, an atmospheric disturbance, a lack of sunshine, or whatever—but there are days when my spirit is heavy before my feet even hit the floor. It takes a few hits on the snooze button, but eventually, I realize I'll have to consciously choose happiness for that day. Happiness really is a choice, but some days, it's harder to produce than others.

On those hard mornings, I start thinking about good things. Specifically, I choose to meditate on the goodness of God, and it works for me. It will work for you, too.

Think about the many times God has come through for you. Think about the many blessings He has given you. Think about His ultimate sacrifice—sending Jesus, His only Son, to die on a cross so that you could spend eternity with Him. He is such a good God! But sometimes it's not enough just to *think* about God's goodness. Some days, you might need to say it out loud. Okay, so this might seem odd at first, but just try it. Say, "God is so good to me!" Say it several times a day. Or maybe you'd rather sing it. You might remember this little chorus from Sunday School: "God is so good. God is so good. God is so good. He's so good to me." Try it—sing a little praise to God as you get ready for work. Choose happiness today and every day. —*MMA*

. . . .

Lord, please fill me with Your joy and let it overflow. Amen.

God's Integrity

Surely he hath borne our griefs, and carried our sorrows:
yet we did esteem him stricken, smitten of God, and afflicted.
But he was wounded for our transgressions, he was bruised
for our iniquities: the chastisement of our peace was upon him;
and with his stripes we are healed.

Isaiah 53:4–5 KJV

Take a moment today to appreciate the sacrifice Jesus made on the cross. It was neither an accident nor a coincidence. His life's purpose culminated in His death and resurrection. Because of Him, we know our God as our personal heavenly Father. We don't have to rely on priests to talk to Him for us, and we don't have to live according to a law that we have no hope of keeping. Jesus paid the price for all of that. He *is* our example of integrity and godly living.

In today's Scripture, Isaiah prophesied of Jesus years before His birth, death, or resurrection. Through Isaiah, God made a promise to His people. He assured them that there was hope and that He had a plan to save them from spiritual death. Through Jesus, God kept His word.

As you go about your workday, remember that God *always* keeps His word. If you believe you have a promise from God, don't let it go. Whether it's salvation for a loved one, healing, restitution, promotion, or wisdom, don't let go. Continue to trust Him and take Him at His word. —*GM*

. . . .

Lord, thank You for keeping Your word.
I trust You to do what You've promised to do. Amen.

Out of Time

There is a time for everything,
and a season for every activity under the heavens.
Ecclesiastes 3:1

I've read a lot of interviews of people who were dying. I've even conducted a few of those. When people are faced with death, they get pretty philosophical about life. But you know what? In not even one interview that I've read did the dying person say something like, "Well, I just wish I'd have worked a little more overtime in life. That's my biggest regret."

No, regrets usually include things like "I wish I'd laughed more and enjoyed each moment for what it was." Or "I wish I could've spent more time with my precious family." Or "I wish I could've made a difference." Work rarely comes up.

Yet some of us work way too many hours, sacrificing time with our family, our friends, and even our Lord. If you fit into this workaholic category, ask yourself why you do it. Is it a season in your life that you know will come to an end? Are you working more hours to prove something to yourself or someone else? Are you more defined by your work ethic than your faith? You don't need to prove yourself. God already approved you before you were born. Whatever your reason, God has a better way. Just ask Him. —*MMA*

. . . .

Lord, teach me to better prioritize my life. Amen.

An Affair to Avoid

You shall not commit adultery.
Exodus 20:14

Did you know that workplace affairs account for 80 percent of all marital infidelity? That's a startling statistic, isn't it? Most affairs start off innocently. A man and a woman become friends because they are coworkers. Soon they begin to have lunch together—alone. They begin confiding in each other, sharing intimate details. Suddenly, they find themselves attracted to one another. Soon the two are emotionally involved. This, in turn, leads to the physical relationship. Eventually, they both leave their spouses and children—tearing up two families. And it all started with a few harmless lunches. Amazing, isn't it?

Unfortunately, the above scenario is far too common. There may be an office affair going on where you work right now. You might even be the one taking part. If you are involved in an office romance, nip it in the bud. Run away from your co-adulterer and into God's arms. God will forgive you.

If you are happily married and thinking, "I would never do such a thing," just heed this warning: Be careful. Protect your marriage. Be clear about your marital status and commitment with male coworkers. Ask God to make you sensitive to dangerous situations. Let your conscience—the Holy Spirit—be your guide.—*MMA*

. . . .

Lord, help me to be sensitive to actions
that might promote an office affair. Amen.

If I Do Say So Myself

*Make a careful exploration of who you are
and the work you have been given, and then sink yourself
into that. Don't be impressed with yourself.
Don't compare yourself with others.*

Galatians 6:4 MSG

It's easy to become impressed with your accomplishments. You work hard and take pride in your work. People say things like, "We know we can count on you." The more praise you receive, the better you like it. On the rare occasion that you do make a mistake, others are surprised because you're usually so conscientious. Sound familiar? If you're one of the favorites or long-timers at your work, it probably does. At times I've been appreciated, too, and I have to admit that it felt great.

That's why it's good for us to remember this verse. It's pretty clear, isn't it? We should understand what we're supposed to do and then do it—with humility. We shouldn't be too proud of ourselves or hold ourselves up as the standard. We must remember that the talents we have are God-given, and if we want to see real greatness, we should look to Him. —*GM*

. . . .

*Lord, You are the One who deserves praise.
Help me keep You as my standard
and not compare myself to others. Amen.*

Plague

Repent, then, and turn to God,
so that your sins may be wiped out,
that times of refreshing may come from the Lord.

Acts 3:19

A few years ago, I made a huge mistake that involved an email and my big electronic mouth. A close friend had confided that she was having trouble with a coworker. In a moment of unrestrained cattiness, I sent an email telling my friend how I would respond to this woman's verbal assault. Here's the really horrible part: Because both women had the same last name, I ended up sending it to the other woman—not my friend. It was an ugly scene. My sin had found me out. Though I apologized, you can guess that my witness had been irreparably damaged.

Not only did I have to live with the consequences of my comment, I suffered from the guilt of having ruined my witness. It's only through a heart-to-heart with Jesus that I was able to finally put aside my guilt.

If you're struggling with guilt over a past wrong, take it to Jesus. If you need further help, talk to a pastor or Christian counselor. Whatever method He uses, either instantaneous or through a counseling process, Jesus will help you settle the situation. —*GM*

. . . .

Lord, please forgive me of my sins and help me
get rid of any guilt in my life. Amen.

Isn't It Obvious?

Serve only the LORD your God and fear him alone.
Obey his commands, listen to his voice, and cling to him.
Deuteronomy 13:4 NLT

You know that project that no one quite knows how to handle? The team comes together to discuss it. Everyone looks
perplexed...and then the observations begin. Someone says something that any sixth-grader could come up with, and everyone
nods in deep contemplation.

"Oh yes, that's true," they affirm. Then someone else says
something equally insightful and, again, everyone nods in agree-
ment. At the end of the hour-long meeting, either little has been
determined or the team has chosen the most obvious plan of
action.

The attendees aren't wrong or dense; they just don't know
what to do. It's an interesting dynamic, to say the least.

That's why it's nice to know that God always has a plan for
our lives. In the great meetings of life, He's right there in the middle, giving us truly insightful and creative ideas of what we can do
and where we can go. He's our own personal leader who is ready
and willing to lead us, if we're just ready to follow Him. —*GM*

. . . .

Lord, I serve, honor, and cling to You.
I will follow Your voice wherever You lead. Amen.

Out of My League

If you are willing and obedient,
you will eat the good things of the land.
Isaiah 1:19

Over the years, I've met many women who felt out of their league in business. Some of them have recently returned to the workplace after years of staying at home to raise their children; others have felt intimidated by new responsibilities. Each of these women were more talented than they gave themselves credit for, but they allowed their insecurities to convince them that they weren't good enough for the positions they had. The fact is, many of them could run laps around their veteran workplace sisters.

If you feel insecure because of your job or responsibilities, know that God uses those who are willing. Ask for help. Do your homework and make sure you are prepared. Then trust God to equip you to accomplish what needs to be done. Don't let fearful and doubtful thoughts plague you or hold you back from giving your all. Step back and think objectively about the talents you need and the ones you have. You're about to discover that God has prepared you more than you've ever realized. —*GM*

· ·

Lord, I am willing to do whatever You want me to do.
Please help me to be strong and confident
of the talents You've given me. Amen.

Details, Details

*But the Lord said to her, "My dear Martha, you are worried
and upset over all these details! There is only one thing
worth being concerned about. Mary has discovered it,
and it will not be taken away from her."*
Luke 10:41–42 NLT

In the midst of never-ending paperwork, office politics, possible layoffs, and office strife, it's sometimes hard to be content in your current job. I remember days when I would pull into the parking lot of my workplace and wish I could be anywhere else at that moment. But guess what? I survived that time in my life, and I even ended up liking my position.

No, my job didn't change, but my attitude did. Instead of dreading work on my drive to the office, I began praising God that I had a job. Instead of resenting the mounds of paperwork on my desk, I thanked God that my boss had such confidence in me to give me so much work. I started seeing my situation through new eyes—through God's eyes. And I stopped getting so weighed down by all the stuff. I chose to do what Mary did, and that was simply rest in Jesus. If you're weary today, rest in Him. And start looking at your job through His eyes. The view is a lot better! —*MMA*

. . . .

Lord, help me to see my job through Your eyes. Amen.

Keep Reaching

*You save the humble but bring low
those whose eyes are haughty.*
Psalm 18:27

I love to watch and read biographies about famous folks, don't you? I once watched a program about an actress whose mother is also a famous actress. When asked what piece of motherly advice had most helped her in her film career, she said, "My mom told me not to believe anything that is written or said about myself—good or bad—or it would destroy me." The interviewer said, "Well, I can understand not believing the negative press, but what about the good press and favorable reviews?" She answered, "They are just as bad because if you start believing you're all those wonderful things people say you are, you'll stop growing and believe you've already arrived."

While most of us are not in the Hollywood scene, this is still good advice. If you receive a good review at work, rejoice but don't stop reaching. If your boss compliments you, be thankful but don't be satisfied with the status quo. Keep reaching. Keep growing. Don't become haughty. If you remain humble, you remain teachable. As they say in Texas, "Don't get too big for your britches." Favor is a good thing—just don't let it go to your head. Instead, be thankful in your heart. —*MMA*

. . . .

*Thank You, Lord, for the favor I'm being shown at work.
Help me to remain humble. Amen.*

Where'd That Wrench Come From?

This is my command—be strong and courageous!
Do not be afraid or discouraged. For the LORD
your God is with you wherever you go.
Joshua 1:9 NLT

We need to stop that project to make a change," my manager called as she rushed by my door. "Grab your files and come to my office." Of course, it was five o'clock and I had an appointment, but none of that mattered because a wrench—an unexpected change—had presented itself.

After a few minutes (or days) of going through the wrench cycle—disbelief, frustration, and full-blown anger with a dash of self-pity—I picked myself up and started again. Welcome to the business world! I would love for projects to run smoothly from beginning to end, but wrenches end up in even the best-laid plans.

If you've been thrown a wrench, don't get discouraged. Changes and disappointments are a part of working with people, but you can rise above them. Stay humble and keep a sense of humor. Focus on God, then take a deep breath and move forward. When the project is completed, you'll have a sense of satisfaction, and in time you won't even remember the wrenches. You'll only remember the success. —*GM*

. . . .

Lord, give strength and courage when wrenches come my way.
Teach me to trust You for direction every day. Amen.

Making Contacts

*Earn a reputation for living well in God's eyes
and the eyes of the people.*

Proverbs 3:4 MSG

The best business contacts I've ever made have come through networking. People who know my work have introduced me to their friends, associates, and business connections. They trust me enough to recommend me, and for that I'm grateful.

Our reputation—how we handle ourselves—directly affects how well our business contacts and our friends come to trust us. Our good words, actions, and demeanor can give us a leg up, open new doors, and earn us respect.

Scripture says to "earn a reputation for living well in God's eyes and the eyes of the people." People will know us by what we say and do. That's why it's important to remember that we represent Jesus all the time. When we interact with a client, we represent Jesus. When we deal with an irate customer, we represent Jesus. When we talk to a coworker, we represent Jesus. When we work with leadership, we represent Jesus. So today, as you go about your work, be the best example of Jesus that you can be. —*GM*

· ·

Jesus, help me be the best example of You that I can be. Amen.

Give It Your All, Every Time

*I know, my God, that you test the heart
and are pleased with integrity.*
1 Chronicles 29:17

Be honest. Do you work a little harder when you know your boss is looking over your shoulder? Do you slack off a bit when you know the boss is on vacation?

If you answered yes to either of those questions, I'd say you're not alone. It's a natural instinct to work a little harder in order to impress those in authority over us; yet God wants us to do our best even when nobody is watching. God wants us to walk in the utmost integrity.

That means, even if your coworkers are surfing the Internet when they're supposed to be working, you resist that temptation and do your assignments instead. That means, even if everyone around you steals office supplies, you leave those paperclips and notepads in your office. That means you give 110 percent, whether your boss is in the office or out of town.

Do your best every single day and watch God work. Sow integrity, hard work, and loyalty, and you'll reap a great harvest. God will cause your hard work and your integrity to gain your boss's attention. You can rest assured that your Boss in heaven is taking note, too. —*MMA*

. . . .

*Lord, help me to work to the best of my ability—
no matter what. I love You. Amen.*

You Can Count on It

Strong God, I'm watching you do it,
I can always count on you.
Psalm 59:9 msg

Don't you love the people you can count on? These are special people that you know are always true to their word and stand by you. They really are the best kind of friends.

But did you know you have another friend you can count on? That's right—God is that friend. He keeps His word no matter what. If you study Israel's history, you'll see how strong God's word is. He promised Abraham that he would be the father of many nations and that his people would be God's people. Then if you follow history, you see how Israel turned its back on Him. Many times the people abandoned their faith and worshiped other gods, and yet God never gave up on them. He always remained faithful to His word and the covenant that He had made.

God continues to be faithful. He extended His mercy long before we accepted it. He loved us first, regardless of whether we returned the sentiment. Today, thank God for His faithfulness to His word. Make time to study the Bible so that you can better understand the promises He's given you. Then take a stand for those promises, knowing that He is true to His word. —*GM*

. . . .

Lord, thank You for Your faithfulness
and for always being true to Your word. Amen.

Bought and Paid For

*You were bought with a price
[purchased with a preciousness and paid for by Christ].*
1 Corinthians 7:23 AMPC

Though many people have bowed their knees to Christ and committed to follow Him for the rest of their lives, they still feel unworthy of His love. They're thankful that their sins have been washed away, but they just don't think of themselves as joint-heirs with Him. They still think of themselves as part of the lost world.

In this verse, you can see that you no longer belong to this world. Though you live in it, you are no longer a part of it. Jesus Christ paid for you. As the perfect sacrifice for all of mankind, He went to hell so that you wouldn't have to endure it. Once you committed to follow Him, anything you did in your past doesn't exist.

Whenever you begin to feel worthless or remember things you've done or the person you once were before Jesus became your Lord, remember that you were bought and paid for. You no longer belong to the world; you belong to Him. So your identity is no longer dependent on what you did in the past. It's based on who you belong to today. —*GM*

. . . .

*Jesus, thank You for paying for me and my sin
so that I could belong to You. Amen.*

Always the Same

Jesus Christ is the same yesterday and today and forever.
Hebrews 13:8

Have you ever had a friend who became mean once she was promoted? Up to that point, she was wonderful—smart, fun, encouraging, dedicated—but once she got that new title, she became harsh, withdrawn, and overly serious. It's one of the strange effects of management. But remember, she's facing new challenges and expectations, some of which may be difficult to handle. Other coworkers and managers may be constantly pulling at her, and if you're ever in a similar position, you'd want your friends to continue to support you, right? So give her a break and a prayer.

Isn't it reassuring to know that Jesus never changes? He won't suddenly turn harsh and distant when new challenges come His way. No, He's the Son of God, our Savior, and He knows exactly what to do. The Bible says that He's "the same yesterday and today and forever." He never changes. He still redeems the lost. He still forgives the sinful. He still aids the weak. He still sits at the right hand of God, interceding for us. Thankfully, He's still the same Jesus. —*GM*

. . . .

Dear Jesus, thank You for changing my life
and for always being my Savior. Amen.

Sister Perfect

Now I take limitations in stride, and with good cheer,
these limitations that cut me down to size—abuse, accidents,
opposition, bad breaks. I just let Christ take over!
And so the weaker I get, the stronger I become.
2 Corinthians 12:10 MSG

Do you have a perfect older sibling? If so, you'll understand when I say that I've always felt like I've lived in my older sister Martie's shadow—especially when it comes to spiritual things. Martie has always had the gift of gab, and I don't mean just small talk or polite party banter. No, I mean this gal can preach!

So when I was asked to speak for the first time at a ladies' luncheon in New Mexico back in 2003, I immediately said, "Oh, you must want my sister, Martie." I couldn't imagine why they'd want me. I only speak about writing and industry stuff. I'd never been asked to preach. "No, we want you to come," the voice on the other end of the line said. Before I had time to think, I heard myself utter, "Sure, I'd be happy to do it."

From that point, I had to quit comparing myself to my sister and focus on God. I knew I couldn't preach in my own strength, but I also knew that He was made perfect in my weakness. So I was giving Him a perfect opportunity to shine. And He did, through me! Let God shine through you today and stop comparing yourself to others—even your perfect older sisters. —*MMA*

. . . .

Lord, shine through me today! Amen.

DAY
308

Give Me a Dose

The joy of the LORD is your strength.
Nehemiah 8:10

Have you ever met someone and thought, *I want the kind of joy he has?* You can tell, without a doubt, that the joy of the Lord is his strength. I once had an associate pastor who had that kind of joy. He just radiated the love of God. Everyone—other ministers, the congregation, people on the street—noticed it and couldn't help being influenced by it. Then I discovered how amazing his joy really was. Not too many years earlier, he and his wife had lost their only child in an accident. For some, this devastating event could have turned them bitter and angry toward God, but not him. He endured. In fact, he more than endured. He discovered a God-given strength.

If you need the joy of the Lord, talk to God about it. Pray and consider what His joy is and how you can receive it. Ponder who God is and commit to serve Him at all costs. As His truth and character become more real to you, you won't be able to avoid getting a good dose of His joy. Then the joy of the Lord will be your strength, too. —*GM*

. . . .

Lord, I need Your joy today.
Show me how I can develop a joy that isn't affected
by anything that comes my way. Amen.

Feeling the Love

Love is patient, love is kind.
1 Corinthians 13:4

Pfsst. Ahh...the wonderful sound of a Diet Pepsi opening first thing in the morning. I've never been much of a coffee drinker. I love the smell of coffee. I love hanging out in coffee shops. I just don't like the taste of coffee. My caffeinated drink of choice? I love to mix Diet Pepsi and Cherry Pepsi for a winning combination of caffeine and fizz.

When I worked full-time for a large nonprofit, the first thing on my morning agenda was to run downstairs and fill my Indiana Hoosiers mug with ice so that I could mix my drink. One morning on my way downstairs, my supervisor stopped me and said, "You'll need to take care of getting ice before the workday begins. New rule." Now, I was a salaried employee—not a time-clock puncher, and I almost always worked more hours a week than I was required to work, so I didn't see the problem. Besides, she ran to the coffeepot that was stationed in our work area at least four times a day. I was seeing quite a double standard, and I didn't like it. I also didn't like my supervisor very much. She was constantly finding ways to make my workday miserable. I wanted to dump my cup of ice on her head, to be honest. But that still, small voice reminded me, "Love is patient. Love is kind."

Let me share, I wasn't feeling the love that day, but love is a choice. If you're struggling with a difficult boss or coworker, choose love. —*MMA*

. . . .

Lord, help me to walk in love even when
I don't feel like it. Amen.

Setback or Setup?

*We know that in all things God works
for the good of those who love him,
who have been called according to his purpose.*

Romans 8:28

As Christians, we don't have to fear failure. Isn't that great? I once heard the story about a businessman who was let go from his job of many years. But this businessman didn't let that setback destroy him. Instead, he put on his entrepreneurial hat and began working on a "God idea." That germ of an idea eventually blossomed into today's mega-earning Home Depot stores. Homeowners across America thank God for this man every night. (My husband spends so much time in Home Depot that, if he wore an orange apron, he'd be up for employee of the month.)

See, if we keep our hearts right—free from anger, bitterness, and fear—God can use setbacks to thrust us forward. If you've recently lost your job, God has another position waiting for you. If you were passed over for a promotion at your company, He has something else waiting for you. God knows exactly what you need. It is your job to work, pray, prepare, and then step out boldly in trust. His Word says in Matthew 6:32, "Your heavenly Father already knows all your needs" (NLT). So don't let disappointments depress you. Rather, see them as opportunities for God to bless you big time! —*MMA*

. . . .

*Thank You, Lord, for providing for my needs
even before I know what they are. I love You. Amen.*

Do You Love What You Do?

The LORD will work out his plans for my life.
Psalm 138:8 NLT

A friend recently asked my husband, "Do you love what you do for a living?" My husband thought about it and responded, "I love the life I have because of what I do."

Later, he explained that though he may not enjoy every part of his job, he loves his work environment, schedule, and the time he's able to spend with his family. Though it may sound simple, he's realized something about finding contentment in his work: Workplace contentment isn't based solely on the work. It's also based on the rewards associated with it, rewards that may have nothing to do with money or possessions.

No job is perfect. There will always be points of frustration, but if it's the job you want and need during this season of life, then remind yourself of why you have it and what you have because of it. Do you make a difference in people's lives? Do you make a good salary? Do you use your God-given skills? Is there room for advancement? Sure, aspects of your job are less than stellar, but by doing it well, you may be ready for the next or better position in the future. Focus on what you gain from your job, and you're sure to find more contentment from day to day. —*GM*

* *

Lord, help me remember all the good things
that I have because of my job. Amen.

Bonuses

*My God will meet all your needs according to the riches
of his glory in Christ Jesus.*
Philippians 4:19

The memo read: "Due to a financially challenging year, we will not be able to give Christmas bonuses this year."

There was outrage within the office. Many of my coworkers had been counting on that Christmas bonus to pay for their Christmas shopping sprees. In fact, several had already spent their bonus checks (on their credit cards) because they'd assumed they'd be receiving a Christmas bonus. After all, the company *always* gave Christmas bonuses—but not that year. Fear swept through the office like a swift, cold breeze. I heard, "What are we going to do?" asked many times throughout the day. Others grumbled about the company's overspending on other things throughout the year.

But you know what? I didn't join in the Grinch fest. I don't always get it right, but the Holy Spirit really comforted me that day. I knew in my heart that God would supply for Christmas (and He did). I also knew that if my company's leaders could've given bonuses, they would have. If you're in a similar situation sometime, don't grumble—praise God for His provision. He is your source, and He gives supernatural bonuses! *—MMA*

. . . .

Thank You, Lord, for supplying all my needs. Amen.

Me 2.0

In kindness he takes us firmly by the hand
and leads us into a radical life-change.

Romans 2:4 MSG

We all have times when we want to change something about ourselves. We may want to learn how to communicate more succinctly or boldly or logically. We may want to become more detailed or improve our follow-through. We may want to learn how to be taken more seriously so that our ideas can be heard.

We want to make a change. We want a kind of 2.0 version of ourselves.

Of course, there are thousands of books to help us achieve greatness at work, but since God is our Creator, doesn't it stand to reason that He can help us become more than we are now? He can help us become the person, employee, or leader that we desire to be. He can show us how to get the training we need. All we have to do is turn to Him and obey what He directs us to do. As we follow Him, He will show Himself faithful. —*GM*

. . . .

Heavenly Father, thank You for showing me
how to become the best person and employee I can be.
I give You all the glory for it. Amen.

It Isn't Who You Know

Before I shaped you in the womb, I knew all about you.
Jeremiah 1:5 MSG

I began my college career at a Christian school in Kentucky. Asbury University was small enough that you knew your professors and they knew you. In fact, the college wasn't much larger than my high school. At the time, Asbury didn't have a journalism major (only a creative writing degree), so halfway through my sophomore year, I transferred to Indiana University in Bloomington, Indiana. (Go Hoosiers!) IU is a wonderful Big Ten school, but I soon discovered I was only a number in a sea of thousands of students. My professors certainly didn't know my name. I was just a social security number to most of them.

Maybe you work in a large company where your boss barely knows your name. Maybe you feel like a number in a sea of employees. Well, that's okay. Your boss doesn't have to know you. Your Creator knows you. The Word says that He knew you before you were even born. He not only knows who you are, but He knows the number of hairs on your head. And what's more, He has a great plan for your life (Jeremiah 29:11). So don't worry if you're not a household name in your field of expertise. God knows your name, and that's all that matters. —*MMA*

. . . .

Thank You, Lord, for knowing me
and loving me so much. Amen.

Multiply My Time

*Man shall not live by bread alone, but by every word
that proceedeth out of the mouth of God.*

Matthew 4:4 KJV

On days when I have more work in my inbox than I have hours in the day, I can feel overwhelmed and out of breath. I am definitely a type A person with way too many irons in the fire, so this feeling of being overwhelmed is familiar. Can you relate?

But I've discovered something that makes no sense in the natural realm, yet it's absolutely true. When I give God my time—spending time in prayer and Bible study before work— He multiplies it back to me. It's when I neglect my time with God that I get into trouble.

I even pray, "Father, thank You for disciplining me to stay committed to this Bible study and prayer time. I ask You, Lord, to multiply my time back to me so that I can accomplish all that is on my plate today."

God is no respecter of persons, so what He does for me, He'll do for you, too. Go on—try it! Spend time with Him, and you'll discover that your work passes from your inbox to your outbox a lot more efficiently when you include God in your workday. —*MMA*

. . . .

*Lord, help me make time for Your Word
every single day—no matter what. Amen.*

On My Honor

*Obey [your superiors] not only to win their favor
when their eye is on you, but like slaves of Christ,
doing the will of God from your heart.*

Ephesians 6:6

During my on-the-job training, I learned a lot more than how to turn on the computer. Along with the technical instruction, my trainer shared company gossip and little tidbits of information she thought would prove useful. For instance, she warned: "When you're surfing the Internet, make sure you don't stay on very long all at once. They monitor us. Just be smart about it." Then she proceeded to tell me how to outsmart the watchdogs so I could slack off at work and not get in trouble. Wow!

It's a pretty sad day for us when we have to figure out ways to outsmart our bosses so we can get paid and not do any work, isn't it? God expects us to do an honest day's work for an honest day's pay. Even if you're the only one following company rules, keep doing the right thing. God will honor you for honoring your superiors. Do your best when you're being watched and even when you're not. God has called us to be excellent, so let's do it! —*MMA*

. . . .

Father, help me to walk in utmost integrity every day. Amen.

No More Spinning Wheels

*Seek first his kingdom and his righteousness,
and all these things will be given to you as well.*
Matthew 6:33

We live in a busy, busy world. And our lives are super busy, too. Making time to do everything that we need to do—work, play, eat properly, exercise, worship, relax, sleep—can seem overwhelming. I mean, how did we ever get along without smartphones or daily planners to remind us of where we need to be and when? But in all of our busyness, there is one priority that must be at the top of the list—our relationship with Jesus.

Everything else depends on it.

We can't hope to find happiness or fulfillment in our homes, work, or relationships without it. And without the peace and direction that a dedicated life brings, we're spinning our wheels.

If you find yourself so caught up in doing everything else that you can't seem to find time to pursue Jesus, then you're too busy and it's time to rearrange your priorities. Nothing else will do. When you put that priority first—above *everything* else—you'll find the peace and purpose that you desire. —*GM*

. . . .

*Jesus, I am committed to following Your kingdom first.
I love You and want You to be
the most important priority in my life. Amen.*

DAY
318

Talk, Talk, Talk

*If you listen obediently to the Voice of GOD...
your God will place you on high,
high above all the nations of the world.*

Deuteronomy 28:1 MSG

Do you work with someone who always has to be the center of attention? In meetings, he hogs the floor and talks incessantly about nothing. When you try to pin him down, to figure out what he's saying, he evades you with high-minded, vague concept statements. He doles out responsibility for his plans, trying to retain only the authority. Please tell me I'm not the only one who's sat through these long, tedious, confusing meetings.

Do you realize we can do that with God? I'll admit there have been times that I've caught myself talking incessantly to God without listening to what He has to say. I'll talk, talk, talk about something that concerns me and give Him all the reasons why my way is the best way or why I'm justified in my feelings. But if I stop to listen, many times He'll speak something very simple and piercing to my heart. In a moment, He clears up any confusion and gets me back on track.

If you find yourself talk, talk, talking to God during your prayer time and not listening, stop. Start listening. It's through listening to His voice that you'll receive your answers. —*GM*

. . . .

*Lord, I trust You with my life and am ready
to hear from You. Amen.*

An Original

*We will not compare ourselves with each other
as if one of us were better and another worse.
We have far more interesting things to do with our lives.
Each of us is an original.*

Galatians 5:26 MSG

Face it, there are times in our careers when we're on top of the world. We've got the Midas touch. Everything is wonderful. But there are also times when we can't seem to put on our eye makeup without help. We're at the bottom of the food chain, and it's a long way to the top. Can anyone relate?

Like I've mentioned before, there have been many times when I felt appreciated and admired for my work, but there were also seasons when I was barely able to hang on. For unexplained reasons, I missed things—due dates, information, files, you name it—and it all had my name on it.

It's easy during those times to look around and feel like the ugly duckling among beautiful swans, but don't give up. God can use you and teach you how to do things better. As His Word says: you are an original. *—GM*

. . . .

*Lord, help me to be the original that You want me to be.
I dedicate my work to You, ask for Your help with it,
and pray that I honor You. Amen.*

The Power of Words

The tongue can bring death or life;
those who love to talk will reap the consequences.

Proverbs 18:21 NLT

As a former sportswriter for a daily newspaper in southern Indiana, I love sports—especially college basketball (go Hoosiers!)—but I'm also partial to golf because I grew up in a golfing family. (Did I mention my late mama, Marion Medlock, was the city champ back in the 1980s?)

I once watched a special on the Golf Channel about golf legend Gary Player. In this interview, Player said that from the time he took up golf at age fourteen, he would wake up, look at himself in the mirror, and say, "I'm going to be the best golfer in the whole world." It's no wonder that in 1965 at age twenty-nine, he won golf's Grand Slam—the Masters, the U.S. Open, the British Open, and the PGA. He was the youngest competitor at that time to ever reach that pinnacle. How did he do it? He saw himself as a winner and a champion long before his talents merited such talk. He understood the power of words, vision, and dreams.

Do you understand the power of words? Why not learn from Gary Player? Wake up each morning, look at yourself in the mirror, and say: "Everything I touch prospers and succeeds. I am well able to accomplish the task that God has put before me." Speak words of victory, and you'll experience victory in and out of the office! —*MMA*

. . . .

Lord, help me to speak only words of victory. Amen.

Generalists vs. Specialists

All these are the work of one and the same Spirit,
and he distributes them to each one, just as he determines.
1 Corinthians 12:11

In business, there are generalists and specialists. The generalists are those who know a little about a lot, like the IT tech who keeps the systems running. Specialists, on the other hand, are just what they sound like. They specialize in one area, like the computer programmer who knows the ins and outs of one programming language. Both of these are necessary for an organization to run smoothly. We need the generalists to see the big picture and the specialists to make sure every minuscule base is covered. Without the generalists, the specialists may not know how to fit all the parts together, and without the specialists, something small yet important might be overlooked.

How about you? Are you a generalist or a specialist? Regardless of where you find yourself, it's beneficial to recognize and respect that you and your coworkers fall into one or the other. Management is often made up of generalists who surround themselves with great specialists who make sure every detail is covered.

Why is this important? Because we all need to work together to get the job done efficiently and effectively. God brings people into our lives, and whether they're specialists or generalists, their roles are important. When we respect that, we all succeed together. —*GM*

. . . .

Lord, help me to serve You in the best possible way
and to appreciate the gifts You've given to others. Amen.

The Ultimate Tums

God has not given us a spirit of fear and timidity,
but of power, love, and self-discipline.

2 Timothy 1:7 NLT

Lots of people live on a constant diet of Tums. They live in fear of not measuring up or not getting their work finished. They worry about impending downsizing or providing for their families. Fear comes in all shapes and sizes. It slips into our lives with little doubts and then grows, sending roots into every area... but we don't have to live that way.

Some Christians think of God as a last resort—they turn to Him only when all else fails. Others view Him as a bandage that covers a gaping wound. He doesn't really help; He's more of a feel-good patch. But Jesus is so much more than that.

As a Christian, you don't have to live with fear. Jesus didn't come to be your last resort or your feel-good image. He is your deliverer. He won't simply cover the problem; He'll eliminate it. If you're struggling with fear, turn to Jesus. He's better than any medicine you'll ever take. —*GM*

. . . .

Lord, I am so grateful that You are a real and personal God.
Instead of just helping me deal with my fears, I know
You can help me overcome them. I'm giving them to You. Amen.

Committed Contentment

Therefore, since we have been justified through faith,
we have peace with God through our Lord Jesus Christ.

Romans 5:1

A lot of people try to fill the voids in their lives with temporary things—money, fame, power, relationships, and more.
They assume that if they just attain one more thing or one more
promotion, finally, they'll achieve happiness. That rarely happens.

Every person is created with a spirit, and until that spirit
comes alive through Jesus Christ, peace will be fleeting. It isn't
enough to believe in Jesus or attend church. True peace and contentment come through a committed relationship with Him.
For some, the thought of serving Jesus wholeheartedly is scary.
They worry that they'll have to live by a lot of rules or they'll be
deprived of fun and relationships. But becoming solidly committed to Jesus will bring more peace and contentment than they
ever thought possible.

If you're considering becoming 100 percent committed to
Jesus and committed to living your life for Him, don't wait. It's
the most rewarding decision you'll ever make. —*GM*

. . . .

Lord, I am ready to live completely committed to You.
I trust You to make my life whatever You want it to be. Amen.

Good Things

For the LORD God is our sun and our shield.
He gives us grace and glory. The LORD will withhold
no good thing from those who do what is right.

Psalm 84:11 NLT

Have you seen the movie *Shadowlands*? If not, I highly recommend it. Just make sure you have a box of tissues next to you when you do. It's the love story of C. S. Lewis and his wife. At the beginning, Lewis is shown passionately preaching hellfire and brimstone. By the end, Lewis, now a widower, has changed. He's shown gently explaining the vastness of God's love to his stepson. It's moving.

God loves His children; we know that. But that love is more than just a lofty thought. It's real. This verse says, "No good thing does he withhold from those whose walk is blameless." That's a powerful statement of God's love and favor. He's not a hard God, but He does want us to obey Him in every area of life, including our work lives. Of course, when we do, He gives us His best.

Don't wait. Commit to walking obediently before Him. Then observe the good things He brings into your life. —*GM*

. . . .

Lord, I commit to worship You, and I thank You in advance
for the good things that You bring into my life. Amen.

One Day at a Time

Therefore do not worry about tomorrow,
for tomorrow will worry about itself.
Each day has enough trouble of its own.
Matthew 6:34

When the company I worked for announced that we would soon undergo a computer system upgrade, my stomach began churning. I started wondering about the switchover. I wondered if I'd be able to learn the new programs. I wondered if the new system would really work like it was supposed to. I wondered if the company would replace me if I didn't learn the new software quickly enough. I wondered myself into a state of worry. Maybe you can relate.

The key to facing change free from fear is to stop the fear before it begins. When you have that very first moment of wondering, speak to the situation. Say, "I will not worry about this situation." Instead of allowing your mind to wonder, which leads to worry and fear, find out what the Word says about your situation and speak those words of faith.

Fear is developed by meditating on Satan's lies, while faith is developed by meditating on God's Word. Don't waste your energy worrying. Use that energy to develop your faith! —*MMA*

. . . .

Lord, when worries overtake me, help me focus
on You instead of the situations I imagine might happen.
Help me to trust You. Amen.

All Those Isms

Each of us is now a part of his resurrection body,
refreshed and sustained at one fountain—his Spirit—
where we all come to drink. The old labels we once
used to identify ourselves—labels like Jew or Greek,
slave or free——are no longer useful.

1 Corinthians 12:13 MSG

It's sad to say that there are still a whole lot of *isms* floating around the workplace—racism, sexism, ageism. Though they're subtly brewing under the surface, if you listen, you'll realize that they're still there. I've been in meetings where several women were in attendance but only one or two men, and comments and jokes were made to put down the men. It's a sad commentary on how we don't completely respect each other, and it's counterproductive.

If you want to be productive in the workplace and make the most of your relationships with others, appreciate them—not just their similarities but also their differences. Put aside the stereotypes and realize that God created all of us. We're all made in His image, and none of us has a higher position than anyone else in the family of God. *—GM*

. . . .

Lord, help me to appreciate others around me—
not just the similarities but also the differences. Amen.

It's His Battle

No weapon forged against you will prevail.
Isaiah 54:17

Do you have a supervisor who has about as much backbone as the marshmallow monster in the classic movie *Ghostbusters*? You know the type. He tells you and your comrades, "Oh yeah. We're not going to put up with this latest corporate ruling. It's not fair to you guys. Don't worry. I'll fight for you. I'll make corporate understand what this new ruling is doing to our department." But when push comes to shove, he slinks out of his boss's office saying, "Yes, sir. Yes, sir," all the way down the hall.

Sure, it's frustrating. But don't resent your spineless boss. Instead, pray for him. You can bet he probably feels worse about the situation than you do. Besides, you don't need your boss to fight your battles. God says that the battle is His to fight. He also says that "no weapon formed against you will prevail." Confess those verses over your work situation. Whenever corporate comes up with an idea that won't benefit you or your coworkers, pray that God will enlighten the decision makers. Pray for favor. Pray for God to deliver you from that job. Just pray. Griping never changed a single thing, but prayer—especially Word-based, faith-filled prayer—changes much! —*MMA*

. . . .

Lord, help my boss to walk in love, not fear.
And Lord, help me to trust You more. Amen.

When No One's Looking

Once you had no identity as a people;
now you are God's people. Once you received no mercy;
now you have received God's mercy.

1 Peter 2:10 NLT

Isn't it obvious when the boss is out on vacation? The atmosphere becomes a little more relaxed. Some people like to treat it like a mini vacation for themselves—kicking back, doing only what is necessary to squeak by, basically taking an eight-hour coffee break. It's sad, and it certainly shows a lack of integrity.

When our bosses are out of the office, we should be working just as hard as if they were there, not just because we are trying to please them, but because we are doing what needs to be done and because we take pride in our work.

Imagine if God took a break from us whenever we weren't deep in prayer. What if He was there when we were on our knees, but the moment we got up, He sat back and took a Starbucks break. It would never happen. Why? Because God is diligent and faithful in everything. He never goes on vacation, and He's never out of the office. He's working on our behalf even when we don't realize it. His angels are protecting us, and His Holy Spirit is directing us. Even when no one is looking, God is still on the job. —*GM*

. . . .

Heavenly Father, thank You for Your faithfulness
and for continuing to work in my life,
even when I don't see You move. Amen.

Making the B List

Your love, LORD, reaches to the heavens,
your faithfulness to the skies.

Psalm 36:5

Every once in a while, something unexpected comes across my desk that makes me chuckle for the rest of the day. One day, I received an email invitation to a coworker's farewell party. After perusing it, I noticed something that made me stop. It wasn't addressed to me or the other twenty-plus people beside my name. We were in the CC, or carbon copy, address section. The "To" section was reserved for about six company bigwigs. Though the slight was unintentional, I'm pretty sure it was the equivalent of being asked to use the service entrance as opposed to the front door at a party.

I wasn't offended by it. In fact, I couldn't stop laughing. Unfortunately, my halo hadn't been polished that day, and I called the email's sender. Through snickers, I asked if I had been *invited to* or simply *informed about* the party. Was I an A-lister or a B-lister for this party? Yes, I was being ornery.

Isn't it nice to know that you are always on God's A list, and never—not even when your halo is in desperate need of scrubbing—on His B List? Regardless of where you are on the organization's ladder, you will always be on God's A List. —*GM*

. . . .

Lord, thank You for choosing and loving me
just as I am. Amen.

Say What?

But I say to you who hear, Love your enemies,
do good to those who hate you.
Luke 6:27 ESV

I'll never forget that Sunday morning. I was so distraught. I wanted to quit my job because my boss was impossible. She took great joy in humiliating her staff, and I had been her latest victim. I was hurt and confused, so I went forward for prayer. The prayer minister smiled and nodded empathetically as I replayed the events from the prior work week. Then I asked through tears, "What should I do?" I was expecting him to say, "Quit! God has something better for you." But that's not what he said. Instead, he whispered, "Pray for her. In fact, you might even give her a small gift—just to let her know you're thinking of her."

Huh? I looked at him, dumbfounded. Praying for her and buying her gifts were not at all what I'd had in mind. In fact, I was hoping he would call down fire from heaven to consume her...or something along those lines. But against my fleshly will, I did exactly what he said. My boss didn't change, but my obedience set me free. Do you need freedom today? Pray for your enemies—even if you have to do it through gritted teeth. —*MMA*

. . . .

Father, I pray for those who have hurt me.
Bless them today. Amen.

Members of the Sisterhood

Be good friends who love deeply; practice playing second fiddle.
Romans 12:10 MSG

One afternoon as I watched Judge Judy—one of my former guilty pleasures—I heard her instruct a young woman about the "sisterhood." The woman had become involved with a married man. Then, following the end of the relationship, she had begun harassing the man's wife. In her typical style, Judge Judy told this woman to grow up, move on, leave married men alone, and respect the sisterhood. I cheered.

As women, we can be hardest on each other. Instead of building each other up, we often drag each other down. As sisters in the body of Christ, we should support and respect each other. I've often heard women criticize each other because of their choices. Does she work outside or inside the home? Does she eat carbs? What school does she send her children to? What's her education? Is she committed to her career? On and on we go.

Each woman has to make choices according to God's direction in her life. As members of the sisterhood, we must respect that God made each woman differently. When we do this, we'll help the sisterhood and the body of Christ thrive. —*GM*

. . . .

Lord, thank You for directing me in my life.
Help me appreciate the differences in other women
so that I can encourage and be a blessing to them. Amen.

What Light?

*Write this. Write what you see. Write it out
in big block letters so that it can be read on the run.*
Habakkuk 2:2 MSG

Have you ever felt so discouraged in your job you just wanted to crawl under your desk with your favorite box of chocolates and cry? I think we've all been there. My mother had a collection of platitudes she'd pull out on days like that. "Into each life a little rain must fall," she'd say. "This, too, shall pass, you know. There's a light at the end of the tunnel." All three statements are quite true, but when you're right smack-dab in the middle of a discouraging day, it's hard to see that promised light at the end of the long tunnel.

Well, I have some good news for you—Jesus is the Light! He is there for you right now. No matter how desperate your situation at work may seem, the Lord can deliver you from it. No matter how disheartened you feel, Jesus can restore your hope and your vision today. Look—see the Light?

Don't let discouragement rob you of your dreams, your hope. Don't let it stop you.

Grab some notebook paper and write your vision. Write it big so you can see it. Write the dreams that God has placed into your heart. Then, like the Word says, keep that vision before you. Stick it inside your planner or tuck it away in your desk drawer.

Shine some Jesus-light on it, then come out from under your desk and run with your vision today! —*MMA*

. . . .

*Thank You, Lord, for restoring my hope
and vision today. Amen.*

Keep Praying

Bless those who persecute you; bless and do not curse them.
Romans 12:14 ESV

Okay, so you've tried to find some middle ground, but your coworker continues to be impossible. There are some people who are just flat-out difficult. (You're getting a mental picture of that person right now, aren't you?) No matter what you try, she won't cooperate. If you say black, she says white. If you say up, she says down.

Well, here's the deal. I've learned that sometimes God allows those difficult coworkers into our lives to grow us up in Him. Trust me, this isn't the only difficult person you'll encounter in your work life. There will be others, so you might as well learn what God wants you to learn while dealing with this one so you can move on (or so that He can move that aggravating coworker to a different department). Just consider this trying season as a season of intense growth. (In case you don't remember from your childhood, growing pains always hurt.)

Keep your eyes focused on the bigger picture and don't allow the impossible coworker to distract you from your goals, dreams, and destiny. —*MMA*

. . . .

Lord, help me to learn the lessons You want me
to gain from this season of growth. Amen.

Insecurities

Don't be afraid; you are more valuable to God
than a whole flock of sparrows.
Matthew 10:31 NLT

I love the Game Show Network. You can learn so many interesting tidbits from watching shows such as *Jeopardy, Hollywood Squares,* and even *Family Feud.* Recently I learned that a person isn't born with shyness. It's a learned trait. Well, if that's true, we must not be born with insecurities, either. Those, too, must be learned as we develop into adults.

If you grew up in a home where you were constantly put down and criticized, you probably struggle with a lot of insecurity, and that insecurity can make you less effective in the workplace. It's time you change the negative recording that plays in your head—the one that says you're not good enough—and replace it with what the Word of God says about you. For instance, God says you're the head and not the tail; you're above and not beneath; you're a victor, not a victim.

As Christians, we don't have to stand for that bondage of insecurity anymore. When Jesus died on the cross for our sins, He also bore our sickness, disease, insecurities, and fear. He took care of it all that day at Calvary, so walk in the freedom that already belongs to you. Hold your head up high as you go into work today. You are valuable! —*MMA*

. . . .

Lord, I give You all of my insecurities.
Thank You for loving me exactly the way I am. Amen.

Never Settle

*God is working in you, giving you the desire
and the power to do what pleases him.*
Philippians 2:13 NLT

An Instagram post recently caught my attention. It said, "Don't downgrade your dreams to match your reality. Upgrade your belief to match your vision." In other words, don't settle!

So often we end up settling, choosing to live a mediocre life when we were called to live an extraordinary one. We set ourselves up for dissatisfaction when we constantly settle for less than we want and deserve. So, what are you settling for in your life? Have you given up on God's best? Is there something in your past that makes you think you don't deserve happiness, love, wholeness, and peace? Listen, if you've accepted Jesus as your Lord and Savior, your slate is totally wiped clean. No matter what you've done or what someone else has done to you, you are valuable to God, and He desires good things for you.

Years of settling can wear you down and steal your hope and joy. But I'm here to tell you, it's time you stop settling for less in every area of your life—both your home life and your professional one. It's time you stop thinking that you don't deserve to be happy.

If you've been settling for less than what God has promised you in His Word, it's not too late to start expecting His goodness in your life. Ask God to help you realize just how precious you are to Him. Once you know that truth, you'll never settle again! —*MMA*

. . . .

*Lord, don't let me settle for less than You intend in any area
of my life. Help me to walk in the plans You have for me. Amen.*

Even in the Tough Times

While Joseph was there in the prison, the LORD was with him;
he showed him kindness and granted him favor in the eyes
of the prison warden.... The LORD was with Joseph
and gave him success in whatever he did.

Genesis 39:20–21, 23

Even in the midst of chaos, God is in control. When jobs are lost, when promotions pass us by, when marriages fall apart, when children wander away from the Lord, when parents face debilitating illnesses, when siblings make bad life choices, when churches split, when friends betray—when all the ugly parts of life raise their heads, God is still in control. He has a plan.

I always remember Joseph when tough situations happen. Sold into slavery, falsely accused of sexual misconduct, imprisoned, and forgotten...Joseph faced many obstacles. Yet the Bible tells us that "the Lord was with Joseph" and Joseph was mindful of the Lord. He followed the Lord's ways and relied on Him. Eventually the Lord used Joseph to save Egypt and his own family (even the brothers who sold him) from famine. When he reconciled with his brothers, Joseph said, "Do not be distressed and do not be angry with yourselves for selling me here, because it was to save lives that God sent me ahead of you" (Genesis 45:5).

Joseph recognized that God was in control even when times looked bleak. What a great lesson. Follow Joseph's example and press in to the Lord. Pray, spend time in praise and worship, and study God's Word. Joseph's life is a great place to start (Genesis 37, 39–45). Trust that even in times of chaos, God has you! —*GM*

. . . .

Lord, thank You for having a plan for my life,
even in times of chaos. Amen.

Get Happy

You were taught, with regard to your former way of life,
to put off your old self...to be made new
in the attitude of your minds...created to be like God
in true righteousness and holiness.

Ephesians 4:22–24

My mother had little patience for a negative attitude. In fact, whenever I was tempted to throw a fit as a child, she would look at me sternly and ask—usually through clenched teeth— "Do you need an attitude adjustment?" That translated to "Do you need a spanking?"

For my mother, attitude was everything. I would get in just as much trouble for a bad attitude as I would for disobedience or plain old brattiness. I didn't like it at the time, but I'm thankful today for her guidance. She taught me at an early age that my attitude was within my control and that I could get happy if I put my mind to it. That lesson has served me well.

If you find yourself needing an attitude adjustment, make one. Guard against taking your bad moods out on others. God's Word says to "be made new in the attitude of your mind." Let your thoughts and moods display the life that you have in Christ Jesus. With Him, you truly know what it is to "get happy." —*GM*

* *

Lord, I pray that my attitude and thoughts
would reflect the new life I have in You. Amen.

But I Can Do So Much More!

If you do what the LORD wants,
he will make certain each step you take is sure.
Psalm 37:23 CEV

Do you remember the first career position you held? Just thinking about mine keeps me humble. After numerous interviews and months of temp work, I finally landed my first professional position as a marketing assistant, responsible for helping the marketing supervisor. Within weeks of my arrival, my new boss, who had never before had an assistant, gained added responsibilities and became a one-woman superstar. She did everything for herself. My days, on the other hand, dragged. My daily highlight became delivering the mail. Sadly, it was the one ten-minute task I had to do.

Thankfully, four months later I was promoted, and I found a silver lining. Because of the things I'd learned, such as the department's procedures and vision, I was prepared to do more. I learned that every step is a preparation for the next.

If you're in a position and you think, *I could do so much more*, don't despair. God hasn't forgotten you; the skills you're learning will be put to a good use. Until then, be patient and learn all you can. As you trust God, He will make your steps firm. —*GM*

. . . .

Lord, I'm thankful for my job because I know You use it
to meet my needs. As I prepare for promotion,
I trust You with every area of my life. Amen.

Shaving Off Years

*I'll set honest judges and wise counselors among you
just like it was back in the beginning.*
Isaiah 1:26 MSG

Do you have a mentor in your work? Not just a teacher, but someone from whom you've learned how to be productive and efficient? You can learn a lot from observing people who have vast experience. It's a great way to shave years off your learning curve, and it's not a new concept.

The Bible gives several examples of mentors. In the Old Testament, you can study about Abraham, Isaac, and Jacob. Each learned from the one before him. Or think of Moses and Aaron. Or Elijah and Elisha. Naomi and Ruth. And then, in the New Testament, there was the greatest mentor of all—Jesus.

If you're looking for a way to boost your wisdom and improve your productivity, pray for God to help you find a godly mentor. In fact, you may want to find several to help you in all the areas of your life—work, faith, and family. These are people that God can place in your life to help you develop a wise and mature approach to living. —*GM*

. . . .

*Lord, thank You for the people You've brought into my life.
Help me learn from them. Amen.*

Little White Lies

For out of the heart come evil thoughts—murder, adultery,
sexual immorality, theft, false testimony, slander.
Matthew 15:19

Little white lies. Do you ever tell them? You know—you're running late for work, so you fudge a bit and tell your boss there was a major wreck that had traffic stopped for fifteen minutes. Or you're out of vacation days, so you call in sick so you can have a day off. Or you know you left the office unlocked last night, but you swear you weren't the last one to leave.

While describing these untruths as "little white lies" certainly sounds better than calling them "big, whopping dirty lies," they're still lies. And what's more, they are sin. Notice in Matthew 15:19 that God puts lying (giving false testimony) in the same sinful category as murder, adultery, sexual immorality, theft, and slander. Whoa! Those are some big ones, eh?

Lying compromises our integrity, and it opens the door to the devil. Don't give Satan any entrance in your life. Ask God to help you be honest in every situation—even when you're backed against a wall. No, it's not always easy to tell the truth, but it's even more difficult to keep track of the lies you've told. So walk in integrity. God will help you. And that's no lie! —*MMA*

. . . .

Father, help me to live a life of integrity,
free from telling lies—white or otherwise. Amen.

The Squiggys in Our Lives

He has made everything beautiful in its time.
Ecclesiastes 3:11

Close to my home is a small park with winding trails and a small creek. It's a slice of the country right in the middle of the city, and I love to walk through it. Along the way, I count the animals I come across—raccoons, snakes, birds, frogs, and my personal favorite: turtles. There is one small turtle in particular that I look for each time. I've affectionately named him Squiggy.

Often, as I search for him, other park goers rush past me, oblivious to the beauty around us. It makes me wonder: How often have I rushed by God's handiwork because I was too hurried to appreciate it? As busy as we are in our lives, it's easy to miss God's beauty—spring wildflowers, giggling children, and yes, even small turtles.

Today, take time to appreciate the beauty around you—in nature and people. There will always be a project due or a meeting to attend, but a year from now, will you really remember it? Don't be so focused on your work that you lose sight of the Squiggys. In the end, the small beauties will probably be what you remember most. —*GM*

Lord, thank You for the beauty that You've placed around me. Help me to appreciate those beauties every day. Amen.

God Sees

Search me, God, and know my heart;
test me and know my anxious thoughts.

Psalm 139:23

Y ou can see them coming. As soon as the boss enters the room, they smile as big as ever and schmooze their way into better assignments. They have the boss's ear on a whole host of matters, from new policies to other coworkers. They're doing more than simply being efficient at their jobs; they're out for power.

As Christians, we know God sees our hearts. He knows when we're trying to work with excellence and when we're attempting to undercut others to get our own ways. While some might feel nervous about God seeing everything they think and feel, I think it's refreshing. We don't have to try to live up to some perfect image with Him. He sees that, even when we fall short, we're still trying. He sees what we mean, even if others assume the worst. God sees.

Instead of trying to shut God out of the corners of your heart, go ahead and let Him in. He loves you. There's no flattering God or schmoozing your way into His good graces; He sees it all, and He loves you just the same. —*GM*

. . . .

Lord, search my heart. I don't want to hide anything
from You because I know that You already know
my deepest thoughts and concerns. Amen.

Beautiful Coats

For wherever there is jealousy and selfish ambition,
there you will find disorder and evil of every kind.
James 3:16 NLT

Remember the story of Joseph and his coat of many colors? Remember how his brothers sold him into slavery and then told their father that he'd died? Usually when we hear this story, we focus on Joseph and his trials. But I want to talk about Joseph's brothers today. Have you ever wondered how those boys went from loving him—or at least putting up with him—to hating him enough to sell him into slavery?

Jealousy. But how did that jealousy get started? My guess is the brothers had been comparing how their father treated them to how he treated Joseph for a long time. When Joseph strolled up in his fancy new coat, someone looked around and complained, "Hey, none of us has a colorful coat! What's up with that? How come Joe has one and we don't?" And in that moment, those smoldering embers of comparison and resentment exploded into a raging jealousy. Even if they felt justified, their behavior was wrong.

Are you in comparison mode today? Is there a coworker who is wearing a "coat of many colors" around the office? Well, before you dwell in that land of comparison too long, ask God to remove the jealous feelings stored in your heart and replace them with His supernatural love. Stay wrapped in His love. You don't need that colorful coat! —*MMA*

. . . .

Lord, please take away any jealousy within me
and replace it with Your love. Amen.

Emotional Roller Coaster

*And the people, that is, the men of Israel,
encouraged themselves.*

Judges 20:22 NKJV

If you're having an emotional roller coaster kind of day, you need to jump off that wild ride and take a few minutes to encourage yourself in the Lord. Have you ever done that before? If not, this is a good day to start.

Don't listen to the devil's lies today. When he whispers in your ear, "You're going to lose your job. You're not working to your potential. You're a big, fat failure," simply reply: "I am a child of the Most High King! I am more than a conqueror! Everything I touch prospers and succeeds! No weapon formed against me is going to prosper!" It's important to take every thought captive, like the Word of God says. In order to counteract the negative thoughts the devil drops into your mind, you actually need to speak the Word. Shout it out!

When you feel that emotional roller coaster starting its climb, stop it in its tracks and say, "This is the day the Lord has made, and I will rejoice and be glad in it!" It's amazing how speaking the Word can totally transform your mood and your day. Fight the devil with your mouth. Gain control of your emotions. And truly, have a good day! —*MMA*

* *

Lord, help me get off this emotional roller coaster. Amen.

It's a Judgment Call

Do not judge, or you too will be judged.
Matthew 7:1

Don't you hate being around judgmental people? I do. Unfortunately, I've caught myself being that judgmental person at times. I assumed I knew the best way something should be done or thought that someone should've handled or said something differently than they did. I've asked the Lord to help me with this, because I know it's the opposite of what the Bible tells me to do.

There's nothing wrong with being a black-and-white type of person, but it's dangerous for us to set ourselves up as the standard for others. It divides people and breaks down trust, so that no one wants to be vulnerable. And this Scripture is pretty clear that to judge is a sure way to be judged.

If you struggle with being too judgmental, ask God to help you become more mindful of what you think and say. Start sifting those thoughts and words through this Scripture. When you catch yourself thinking or saying something judgmental, correct yourself. In time, you'll break yourself free of that destructive habit and enjoy closer, more trusting relationships with those around you. —*GM*

. . . .

Lord, help me to not be judgmental toward others
so that I can build trusting relationships with them. Amen.

Six-Month Trial Period

So we say with confidence, "The Lord is my helper;
I will not be afraid. What can mere mortals do to me?"
Hebrews 13:6

I once worked for a boss who was intelligent, resourceful...and difficult. The first six months that anyone worked for her were a challenge. During that time, new employees doubted that she even liked them. In meetings, she spoke to everyone but the new person, and she avoided their company in social situations. But then, just when the person was certain that she disliked him, the six-month period ended, and she embraced the new worker.

New workers—both men and women—commented on her behavior. Veterans tried to encourage them. "Hang in there," they'd say. "She's just getting used to you." Eventually, the new person would discover it was true.

Fearing what others think of you can be paralyzing. It can inhibit you or cause you to try desperately to win others' approvals. But as the writer of Hebrews said, "The Lord is my helper... what can mere mortals do to me?" As you develop your relationship with Jesus, your confidence will grow. You'll have peace knowing that your security rests with Him. —*GM*

. . . .

Lord, I trust You, love You, and serve You.
As I pursue a deeper relationship with You,
I pray that You'll give me the confidence to face anyone
and anything that comes my way. Amen.

Leaving Egypt

I am the LORD your God, who brought you out of Egypt,
out of the land of slavery.
Exodus 20:2

Sometimes it's easier for people to stay in tough circumstances because it's familiar," a friend said. "They're content because at least they know what to expect."

As she spoke, I remembered a time when it had become clear that I needed to leave my job. I had remained in the position only because I was too scared to make a change. The corporate climate had become toxic, but because it was familiar, it felt safe. I was afraid of the unknown.

The Israelites faced this, too. Even after their miraculous deliverance from Egypt, they considered returning to slavery because it was familiar. Can you imagine? For me, I had to gain the courage to make a change. If you're in that same place, I challenge you to make your change, too. It might require you to return to school or improve your work skills with new certifications. It might require you to move cities or change industries. Whatever it is, rest in the knowledge that God will be there to catch you if you fall. He might even be waiting for you to be willing to take a chance on Him. Make the decision—trust God and follow Him out of Egypt. —*GM*

. . . .

Lord, I trust You to take me out of the Egypt in my life.
Please help me to have the courage
and faith to follow You. Amen.

Highly Favored

The LORD God is a sun and shield; the LORD bestows favor
and honor; no good thing does he withhold
from those whose walk is blameless.

Psalm 84:11

Growing up, I didn't understand God's favor. I thought I had to earn it. I thought that if I could just be good enough, He might toss me a bone once in a while. Is your thinking as warped as mine used to be? Just in case, let me shed some light on this favor matter for you. According to Psalm 84:11, God does not withhold any good thing from us. He takes great pleasure in sending down His blessings to us. He adores us. The Word says we are the apple of His eye (Psalm 17:8). And because He is God, you can be His favorite child, and so can I!

Psalm 5:12 says, "Surely, LORD, you bless the righteous; you surround them with your favor as with a shield." In other words, we are wrapped in God's favor. It's all over us. Expect good things to come your way at work today. Expect promotions. Expect pay raises. Expect extra vacation days. And don't forget to thank the Lord for every good thing along the way. You are highly favored! —*MMA*

. . . .

Thank You, Lord, for Your favor.
You are so good to me. Amen.

Better than Before

*Be strong and courageous. Do not be afraid or terrified
because of them, for the LORD your God goes with you;
he will never leave you nor forsake you.*

Deuteronomy 31:6

Two of my closest friends have ministered to me in a big, big way. Watching God orchestrate their family's steps is humbling. On two different occasions, I have seen the bottom fall out of their professional lives, only to watch God quickly move them into better positions. Observing them gracefully navigate the changes is amazing. They've learned that God—not the company, not the 401K, not the bank account—is their source.

I think of them when things aren't perfect in my own life, when situations aren't working out like I want. Their lives have served as reminders that God is working on my behalf, and He will never leave me nor forsake me. I'm one of His kids.

And guess what? You're one of His kids, too.

No, everything won't always be easy. But God doesn't fall off His throne when life goes crazy. His Spirit still comforts, and His Son still intercedes for us. With all of them working for you, how can you fail? —*GM*

. . . .

*Dear Lord, I trust You—regardless of what the situations
around me say. I know that You won't leave me or forsake me.
You're big enough to handle my dilemmas. Amen.*

What Are You Sowing?

Remember this—a farmer who plants only a few seeds
will get a small crop. But the one who
plants generously will get a generous crop.
2 Corinthians 9:6 NLT

Have you heard the expression, "You reap what you sow"? That's scriptural, you know. If you are arriving late to work every day, taking long lunches, leaving early, passing your work on to someone else, and spending hours playing on the Internet during the workday, you're sowing some bad seed. And you're giving God very little to work with.

God desires to bless His children, but if we show a lack of integrity on the job, we tie His hands. "But, you don't understand," you say, "my company treats every employee badly. They don't pay me enough for what I do anyway, so I'm just going to take advantage of them." Well, maybe that's true, but you don't want to sow bad seed to get back at your company. You know why? Because you don't want to reap that kind of negative harvest.

No matter how badly your company might treat you, give it your all every day. Do your work unto the Lord. Truly earn your paycheck and give God something to work with. Pretty soon, you'll enjoy a harvest of promotions, raises, favor, vacation days, or maybe a new job with a different company because of your work ethic, skills, and reputation. Your blessing crop can't be far off! —*MMA*

. . . .

Lord, I do my work unto You. Amen.

Okay, I Admit It

Praise the LORD, my soul, and forget not all his benefits—
who forgives all your sins and heals all your diseases.

Psalm 103:2–3

Don't you hate making mistakes? Small mistakes are one thing; others can be life changing. None of us *want* to be wrong. We want to believe that we have the best ideas and know the best way to work and live, but unfortunately, we all make mistakes.

Even David, the man after God's own heart, made mistakes. In fact, he made a doozy. Most people know the story of David and Bathsheba. Bathsheba was someone else's wife, but David wanted her. After getting her pregnant, he tried to cover his mistake by sending her husband to the front lines of battle to be killed. As terrible as David's behavior was, when he repented and returned to God, God showed him mercy. David came back to God and served Him with his whole heart.

When we make mistakes, we need to come back to God, too. Instead of trying to justify our poor decisions, we should run back to the Lord, knowing that His mercy and grace are always waiting. —*GM*

. . . .

Father, I'm sorry for making that mistake.
Thank You for Your forgiveness. Amen.

Managing Life's Loudness

*All the ways of the LORD are loving and faithful toward
those who keep the demands of his covenant.*

Psalm 25:10

I have worked near some loud coworkers. I'm not talking about sporadically noisy people. I remember one coworker... her voice could've rivaled a baseball game announcer. In fact, I kept a pair of earplugs in my desk drawer for the times when I couldn't drown her out with my low-volume CD player. No matter how hard I tried to ignore her, she distracted me and made it hard to focus.

Likewise, in your relationship with God, there are lots of distractions that could keep you from focusing on Him. Just as you have to find ways to overcome the distractions of a loud coworker, you must find ways to overcome the distractions that would keep you from pursuing your relationship with God. You might set your alarm a few minutes early or sit in your car during lunch or leave work at an appropriate time in order to pray or attend church. Whatever you have to do, it will be worth it. Keeping life's loudness from distracting you from God will allow you to enjoy a more fulfilling relationship with Him. —GM

. . . .

*Lord, thank You for knowing me and always
making time for me. Help me to protect my relationship
with You from distractions. Amen.*

The Real World

*Don't panic. I'm with you. There's no need to fear
for I'm your God. I'll give you strength. I'll help you.
I'll hold you steady, keep a firm grip on you.*

Isaiah 41:10 MSG

Okay, so your house doesn't look like the latest remodel on HGTV. When you throw a party, you don't bake a cake; you buy one from the nearby superstore. Your house definitely won't pass the white glove test. And you've been known to buy a new package of socks simply to avoid doing the laundry. Yep, we live in the real world.

It's difficult to juggle work, a family, a home, church commitments, friends, and more. But hey, "difficult" is a piece of cake for God. If He was able to create the world and everything in it in less than a week, He can certainly help you keep your life straight. But you have to ask Him to get involved in every aspect of your day.

Before your feet even hit the floor, say out loud, "Father, this is the day that You have made. I will rejoice and be glad in it. Order my steps, Lord, all day long. Help me to do exactly what You want me to do today." Talk to God throughout the day and include Him in all of it! —*MMA*

. . . .

*Thank You, Lord, for ordering my steps
every single day. Amen.*

Getting Noticed

As it is, you boast in your arrogant schemes.
All such boasting is evil.
James 4:16

We all know Brenda Brag-a-lot. She seizes every opportunity to share all about her successes. There's at least one Brenda in every company. She's easy to spot because she's always talking, and those surrounding her have expressions on their faces that say, "We really don't care. Why don't you take a personal day or something!"

In this crazy competitive world, many feel the need to brag on themselves. They believe the old adage, "If you don't look out for Number One, who will?" Well, God will! You don't have to toot your own horn to move up in your company. Quiet confidence is much louder than anything you might say about yourself. God will cause you to outshine others, and you won't even have to open your mouth.

The Bible says that God has crowned you with glory and honor and favor. He will give you favor with your bosses and your coworkers. He will cause your efforts and accomplishments to get noticed by the powers that be. God will do that for you. All you have to do is ask, then thank Him for it every day! Don't become a Brenda Brag-a-lot. Let God do your bragging for you. He loves to dote on His children! —*MMA*

. . . .

Thank You, Lord, for giving me favor with my bosses
and coworkers. I praise You that my accomplishments
will not go unnoticed. Amen.

Surviving Technobabble

Think about what I am saying.
The Lord will help you understand all these things.
2 Timothy 2:7 NLT

More than a few times, I've found myself sitting across a conference table from a computer genius, listening to him discuss some information technology hang-up. As he droned on, I sat there thinking, *Why can't I just push a button and make the system do what I want it to do?* Of course, I never wanted to admit that I was lost, but seriously, does any nontechnical person really understand the information technology world with its symmetric multiprocessing configuration without a kernel recompilation? No!

Regardless of where it comes from, confusion is awful, and you know when you're in over your head. You need help. Mercifully, God hasn't left you sitting across the heavenly conference table listening to Him talk incomprehensibly about your seemingly unfixable situation. No, He's waiting to help you cut through the confusion with clarity. By studying His Word and praying, you can find the answers to any situation. With His help, even the technobabble won't be quite so baffling. —*GM*

. . . .

Lord, I need Your clarity in everything I do—
every project on my desk and every person
I come in contact with. I trust You for it. Amen.

Prayer Partner

If two of you on earth agree about anything you ask for,
it will be done for them by my Father in heaven.

Matthew 18:19

I looked up at the poster above the conference table. It read: "T-E-A-M: Together, Everyone Achieves More." Maybe you've seen a similar sign in your workplace. It's a catchy little saying that speaks great truth. It reminds me of Matthew 18:19, which says if we agree together in prayer, it will be done by our heavenly Father. That's like the ultimate in teamwork, isn't it?

If your team at work has trouble working together to accomplish a common goal, you may need to find another Christian team member and begin praying for your overall team. Two prayer warriors in a company can totally transform the atmosphere of an office.

When I worked for a daily newspaper, I had a prayer partner named Glendora. I always teased her, "Glendora, when I need prayer, I come to you. I think you have a direct line with the Father." She'd always get tickled when I'd say that, but truly, Glendora knew how to touch heaven. If there's no "Glendora" in your company, why not fill that void? Start praying diligently for your coworkers, your bosses, and those you serve. And while you're at it, pray for God to send you a prayer partner. —*MMA*

. . . .

Lord, please send me a prayer partner. Amen.

Round the Mountain, Again

*He went on a little farther and bowed with his face to the ground,
praying, "My Father! If it is possible, let this cup
of suffering be taken away from me.
Yet I want your will to be done, not mine."*
Matthew 26:39 NLT

Think of the biggest problem you have at work—a difficult boss, a coworker who's driving you crazy, a client who won't pay his bill, or whatever. Now think back. Have you dealt with this same dilemma before? It might be that God is trying to teach you something through this adversity in your life. My mom always called it going around the mountain again when you have to go through a problem again because you apparently didn't learn what you needed to on the first lap around.

There are some areas in my life where I've practically worn out my track shoes going around that mountain, but eventually I get it. I finally see what God was trying to show me through the negative situation, and I get to move on!

If you're going around the same aggravating mountain today, seek God's wisdom on the matter. Pray, "Lord, what are You trying to show me through this? Help me not to miss it, Lord." Then, praise Him, and trade in your worn track shoes for a new pair—maybe a stylish pair of heels! —*MMA*

. . . .

*Lord, help me to learn what You want me to know through
every adversity I must face. I trust You. Amen.*

Where Am I Going?

Where there is no vision, the people perish.
Proverbs 29:18 KJV

Do you know people who have taken early retirement and then totally lost their drive for life? I've seen it happen. They lose their vision. They lose their reason for getting up in the morning. But you don't have to be of retirement age to lose your vision. I've seen women of all ages lose their hope and drive. In fact, I've been there myself. There have been times in my career when I felt as though I were drifting on a sea of pointlessness. How about you?

No matter where you are in life—right out of college working your first job or approaching retirement—you need to have a goal, a dream, a vision. If you don't, you'll wind up drifting on that same sea of pointlessness or possibly heading down the river of "I hate my job."

Do you know God's plan for your life? If not, ask God to show you His vision. Seek His plan, and once you discover it, write it down and keep it before you. Thank Him for that vision every day. Keep the vision close to your heart. Remind yourself of God's plan every time you're asked to do menial tasks at work. Remember, you're on your way to something greater. —*MMA*

. . . .

*Lord, help me to never lose the vision
that You've given me. Amen.*

Behind the Scenes

For He Himself has said,
"I will never leave you nor forsake you."
Hebrews 13:5 NKJV

When I first ventured out of the nine-to-five routine to free-lance full-time from my home, I had three steady clients. One of those clients had indicated that he'd be using me monthly, paying at least five hundred dollars. So I wasn't worried about losing my regular paycheck.

Two weeks after I came home to write, that client closed his ministry, so he no longer needed my services. But I still had two other clients, both dotcom companies. I wrote ten to fifteen articles for each one every week at fifty dollars per article, so I was good...or so I thought. Unfortunately, all of that dotcom family went under at once, and I lost both clients in one day. Panic-stricken, I signed up to substitute teach for our local school system. The substitute teaching gig didn't pay very much, and I really disliked it. I was unhappy, worried, and discouraged. But just when I was about ready to give up, God came through with a new client who asked if I could do about five hundred dollars' worth of work every week. *Cha-ching!* See, God didn't leave me. He was working behind the scenes on my behalf the whole time. Don't let setbacks worry you. Trust God. His answer is always right on time. —*MMA*

. . . .

Thank You, Lord, for always being right on time
with the answers I need. Amen.

Yes or No

All you need to say is a simple "Yes" or "No."
James 5:12

Do you have trouble saying no? I do. That's why a woman at my church gave me a book called *Boundaries*, but I let someone borrow it before I ever had the chance to read it. Do you know why? Because when asked to loan it, I couldn't say no! Isn't that ridiculous?

We need to learn that saying no isn't a bad thing. Actually, it's a healthy thing. If you're like me, you've said yes to so many things that your time is not your own—not only in your personal life but also in the professional realm. I remember once I said yes to two book contracts that had my final copy due the same week. That's nuts! But guess what? I didn't want to make anyone mad, so I said, "Sure, I can do that"—and I practically killed myself getting those manuscripts done.

God is teaching me in this area. He's showing me that I don't have to be pressured into agreeing to things I'll later regret. And neither do you! Ask God to help you say yes only to the things He has planned for you. He will get involved in every aspect of your daily life, if you'll ask Him. So ask Him today. He will say yes, I promise! —*MMA*

. . . .

Lord, I say yes to You! Amen.

Tangled Relations

Surely, LORD, you bless the righteous;
you surround them with your favor as with a shield.
Psalm 5:12

What do you do when your assistant is dating your boss's son? That was the dilemma I found myself in. I had recently accepted a position with a new company and had heard nothing but favorable things about my assistant. It was true that she was dedicated, decisive, and determined. It should have been a great situation—and then I discovered that she was like a daughter to my boss. I quickly realized that, although I was the manager, my assistant was the one with the power. She had the ear of the boss, and they talked regularly. My boss communicated about our area through my assistant. My assistant communicated to the boss about our area. I was in a tough spot.

You may find yourself dealing with strange workplace dynamics, too—an employee who has a personal relationship with a company leader or a leader's family member who answers to you. In those situations, it's best to pray for favor and use wisdom. Pray for God to show you how best to operate, then listen carefully to the leading of the Holy Spirit for direction. Don't let fear or suspicion paralyze you, but use wisdom. Your boss may very well be hearing about your work and decisions. Then trust that you are doing your best and leave the outcome to the Lord. He's the One who's truly in control of your future. —*GM*

. . . .

Lord, I ask for Your favor to guard me like a shield
as I do my best in my job. You alone control my future. Amen.

Singing through the Trouble

About midnight Paul and Silas were praying
and singing hymns to God.
Acts 16:25

When in a crisis, the last thing you want to hear is something along the lines of: "When God closes a door, He opens a window," right? I understand—however, in difficult situations, God does work in remarkable ways.

You've probably experienced difficult situations, and you know that even through them, God was faithful. You've learned to trust that when the challenges come, He'll be there for you, or at least you recognize that the persecution is small in comparison to His greatness.

That's why the story of Paul and Silas is so encouraging. They'd been thrown into prison, but they still praised God. They recognized that their suffering was only temporary and that God was greater than anything they had to endure.

The next time you face a setback, don't let discouragement and fear overwhelm you. Trust God and follow Paul and Silas's lead by praying and singing praises to Him. As you do, He will show Himself faithful. —*GM*

. . . .

Lord, I trust You. You know my circumstances better than I do.
I commit to praising You regardless of the outcome,
because I know You will take care of me. Amen.

Lose the Mask

*Stand up for me against world opinion
and I'll stand up for you before my Father in heaven.*
Matthew 10:32 MSG

Every year when I worked for that daily newspaper in Indiana, several preschool classes would trick-or-treat through our building on Halloween, showing off their cutest-ever costumes. Some wore scary masks. Some wore costumes their Pinterest moms had made. Others wore face paint. But all of them were disguised and animated as they paraded through the office.

Later in the year, we hosted those same students for a morning field trip, showing them how the newspaper process worked. Without their masks and clever costumes, they weren't nearly as confident. Some even hid behind the teachers!

We do the same thing. We wear many masks—the professional woman, the confident leader, the quiet support staff, the sassy office cutup—and that's just at work. We need to stop pretending. We need to show the world who we really are and trust that we are enough. Once we show our true colors and stop spending energy holding up our masks, we give God room to use the real women He created, for His purpose. —*MMA*

. . . .

*Lord, help me to be brave enough to remove my mask
and reveal the real me. Amen.*

All His Favorites

God does not show favoritism.
Acts 10:34

Throughout this year, I've told you that God will do for you the same things He has done for me and others. It's true—He doesn't play favorites. He gives His best to each of us. This lack of favoritism is part of His character. God isn't up in heaven throwing dice to determine who He's going to show His favor to next. Once we accept Jesus as our Lord and Savior, we are made joint-heirs with Jesus and heirs of God (Romans 8:17). Just as God accepts anyone who calls on the name of Jesus, He accepts us. And as we've already seen in Psalm 84:11, He doesn't withhold any good thing from those whose walk is blameless. As we do our part, He does His.

If you have a hard time believing that God will give you His peace (Psalm 85:8), show you His mercy (Isaiah 55:7), bless you with wisdom, knowledge, and happiness (Ecclesiastes 2:26), order your steps (Psalm 37:23), and empower you with the Holy Spirit (John 14:26), begin studying the Scriptures in this paragraph. They are His promises to you.

As we come to the end of this book, I want you to know that the favor of God follows you wherever you go. It isn't just for everyone else; it's for you, too. You are His precious child. —*GM*

. . . .

Lord, thank You for loving me as much as You love everyone else.
Thank You that Your promises are real and that
as I obediently serve You, I'll enjoy all of them. Amen.

Walking in God's Favor

You will arise and have mercy on Zion;
for the time to favor her, yes, the set time, has come.
Psalm 102:13 NKJV

Every new day brings a perfect opportunity to walk purpose-fully in the favor of God. Start each day declaring God's favor over your life. Say, "This is the day that the Lord has made, and I will rejoice and be glad in it. The favor of God goes before me and surrounds me today!" Establish a habit of confessing God's favor over your life, and you'll be amazed at the doors that open before you and the way people receive you.

When I began deliberately starting my day by speaking those Scriptures over my life, I just couldn't get over the positive changes that took place. It was as if I'd opened a gift from God that I hadn't even known existed.

Maybe this whole "favor of God" concept is new to you, too. Maybe you don't think you deserve God's favor. Maybe you think favor is only for super Christians like the late Billy Graham. But guess what? It's also for you! Now that you know about this great gift from God, you can unwrap it and enjoy it!

Go ahead—get excited! It's the best present ever. —*MMA*

. . . .

Thank You, Lord, for the favor
I walk in today and every day. Amen.